Deuteronomy

INTERPRETATION

A Bible Commentary for Teaching and Preaching

INTERPRETATION

A BIBLE COMMENTARY FOR TEACHING AND PREACHING

James Luther Mays, *Editor*
Patrick D. Miller Jr., *Old Testament Editor*
Paul J. Achtemeier, *New Testament Editor*

PATRICK D. MILLER

Deuteronomy

INTERPRETATION

A Bible Commentary
for Teaching and Preaching

WESTMINSTER
JOHN KNOX PRESS
LOUISVILLE · KENTUCKY

2012 paperback edition
Originally published in hardback in the United States
by John Knox Press in 1990
Louisville, Kentucky

12 13 14 15 16 17 18 19 20 21—10 9 8 7 6 5 4 3 2 1

Unless otherwise identified, Scripture quotations are from the Revised Standard Version of the Bible, copyrighted 1946, 1952, © 1971, 1973 by the Division of Christian Education of the National Council of the Churches of Christ in the U.S.A., and are used by permission.

Scripture quotations marked NRSV are from the New Revised Standard Version of the Bible, copyright 1989, Division of Christian Education of the National Council of the Churches of Christ in the U.S.A., and are used by permission.

The quotations from Karl Barth, *Church Dogmatics* II/1 (Edinburgh: T. & T. Clark, 1957), are used by kind permission of Continuum International Publishing Group.

Library of Congress Cataloging-in-Publication Data

Miller, Patrick D.
   Deuteronomy / Patrick D. Miller, Jr.
      p. cm. — (Interpretation, a Bible commentary for teaching and preaching)
   ISBN-13: 978-0-8042-3105-3
  1. Bible. O.T. Deuteronomy—Commentaries. 2. Bible. O.T. Deuteronomy—Homiletical use. I. Title. II. Series.
   BS1275.3.M54   1990
   222'.1507—dc20   90-32986

ISBN: 978-0-664-23860-5 (paper edition)

♾ The paper used in this publication meets the minimum requirements of the American National Standard for Information Sciences—Permanence of Paper for Printed Library Materials, ANSI Z39.48-1992.

SERIES PREFACE

This series of commentaries offers an interpretation of the books of the Bible. It is designed to meet the need of students, teachers, ministers, and priests for a contemporary expository commentary. These volumes will not replace the historical critical commentary or homiletical aids to preaching. The purpose of this series is rather to provide a third kind of resource, a commentary which presents the integrated result of historical and theological work with the biblical text.

An interpretation in the full sense of the term involves a text, an interpreter, and someone for whom the interpretation is made. Here, the text is what stands written in the Bible in its full identity as literature from the time of "the prophets and apostles," the literature which is read to inform, inspire, and guide the life of faith. The interpreters are scholars who seek to create an interpretation which is both faithful to the text and useful to the church. The series is written for those who teach, preach, and study the Bible in the community of faith.

The comment generally takes the form of expository essays. It is planned and written in the light of the needs and questions which arise in the use of the Bible as Holy Scripture. The insights and results of contemporary scholarly research are used for the sake of the exposition. The commentators write as exegetes and theologians. The task which they undertake is both to deal with what the texts say and to discern their meaning for faith and life. The exposition is the unified work of one interpreter.

The text on which the comment is based is the Revised Standard Version of the Bible and, since its appearance, the New Revised Standard Version. The general availability of these translations makes the printing of a text in the commentary unnecessary. The commentators have also had other current versions in view as they worked and refer to their readings where it is helpful. The text is divided into sections appropriate to the particular book; comment deals with passages as a whole, rather than proceeding word by word, or verse by verse.

Writers have planned their volumes in light of the requirements set by the exposition of the book assigned to them. Biblical books differ in character, content, and arrangement. They also differ in the way they have been and are used in the liturgy, thought, and devotion of the church. The distinctiveness and use of particular books have been taken into account in decisions about the approach, emphasis, and use of space in the commentaries. The goal has been to allow writers to develop the format which provides for the best presentation of their interpretation.

The result, writers and editors hope, is a commentary which both explains and applies, an interpretation which deals with both the meaning and the significance of biblical texts. Each commentary reflects, of course, the writer's own approach and perception of the church and world. It could and should not be otherwise. Every interpretation of any kind is individual in that sense; it is one reading of the text. But all who work at the interpretation of Scripture in the church need the help and stimulation of a colleague's reading and understanding of the text. If these volumes serve and encourage interpretation in that way, their preparation and publication will realize their purpose.

The Editors

PREFACE

Few books of the Old Testament take one so directly to the heart of Israel's faith as does the Book of Deuteronomy. To spend time with it is to find oneself confronted with its claims and its view of reality. If it is formative for other Old Testament literature, it also exercises its impact upon those who study it—at least that is the experience of this interpreter, who is well aware that his choice of this book for intensive study has been influenced by prior theological commitments but also that the study itself has profoundly shaped and reshaped those commitments. One hopes that the end result will be sufficiently faithful to Deuteronomy's understanding of the God of Israel and of God's will and way in this world.

This commentary is avowedly theological, an exposition of the meaning of the literary units within the book that seeks to be faithful to the meanings found within the tradition of interpretation that has flowed forth from the time of the earliest Deuteronomic strata. It is not possible, of course, even to know, much less to take account of, all that church and synagogue have discerned from this book. Particular attention is given to the impact of the book in its own times, the reading of it in the Reformation period, and the possible ways it may instruct the contemporary communities of faith. As is true of all the commentaries in this series, the reader is not provided a great deal of detailed textual, literary, and historical material that may be available in other commentaries. Such data are presupposed in the interpretation set forth, but rehearsed only as much as is necessary for the sake of intelligible exposition.

A word should be said about the translations used in this commentary. The Revised Standard Version (RSV) is the base text for this commentary series. By the time this volume is published the New Revised Standard Version (NRSV) will have appeared. Having worked for several years with the committee that prepared the translation of Deuteronomy for this revision of the RSV, I have cited it where that translation seems preferable or worth considering. In a number of instances I have given my own translation of the text.

The writing of this commentary has taken place over a

number of years. Many parts of it have been set forth in one form or another in seminary and church classes, lectures, and various publications. The writer is indebted to the editors of *The Iliff Review, Interpretation,* and *The Princeton Theological Seminary Bulletin* for permission to use materials that appeared in those journals and to the General Editor of the series, James L. Mays, for the freedom to develop this exposition over a fairly long period of time before final publication. Finally, no commentator on Scripture ever writes apart from the prior labors and interpretive discernment of others. In this case, I would particularly acknowledge the direct and indirect help of three scholars, who are not only friends but the foremost contemporary interpreters of the Book of Deuteronomy. For all that they have contributed to my understanding of this book I express my gratitude to S. Dean McBride, Norbert Lohfink, and Georg Braulik. I would also like to express my appreciation to Arlene Jones for her helpful editing.

No book of the Bible manifests a greater concern for the transmission of the faith to the next generation. In that spirit and in recognition of what parents learn from their children, I dedicate this book to our sons, Jonathan Sudduth Miller and Patrick James Miller.

P.D.M.

CONTENTS

CONTENTS

CONTENTS

INDEX OF REFERENCES
TO DEUTERONOMY

This index shows all references in this volume to Deuteronomy. The left-hand column lists the divisions of the book used in the outline of the commentary for the primary discussions of the texts. It also includes the parts of Deuteronomy that are not listed in the Contents but are discussed in the commentary. The **boldface** page numbers immediately following each listing are the primary reference, showing the part of the commentary that deals specifically with that portion of Deuteronomy. The list of page numbers following the boldface entry shows all other references in the volume to that portion of the book or parts of it.

INTERPRETATION

Introduction

The aim of this introduction is to ask some of the typical questions having to do with the background of a literary work and to think about it as a whole, in order to show how answers to such questions, insofar as they are obtainable, may give a reader of Deuteronomy some clues to understanding the book and its purpose.

The Names of the Book: What Do They Mean?

The title of a book normally gives some indication of its subject matter. Sometimes the meaning of the title may be enigmatic or clear only upon reading the book. Deuteronomy has received several designations, all of which give the reader some indication of the book's character.

The Hebrew title of the book is taken, according to custom—as is the case with all five books of the Torah, or Pentateuch—from its opening words, *'elleh haddebarim*, "these are the words." In Jewish tradition the book is also sometimes called *seper debarim*, "the book of words." While the title is in part an accident of Hebrew word order, it is exceedingly appropriate as a characterization of the content and subject matter of Deuteronomy. It is more a book of words than any of the other Pentateuchal books or the following historical books. There is no action here, except that associated with the words spoken, until the final chapter, when Moses is buried. The book is entirely the words of Moses; but his words are often a reflection of the Lord's words, and the book is clearly interested in the relation of Moses' words to those of the Lord (see 1:3; 5:22–27, 31–33). The book is a collection of words of command and instruction, words of preaching and exhortation. The title of the book is also a reminder of the centrality of the "ten words" (4:13), or the Ten Commandments. The book is one of the primary biblical sources for understanding the notion of "the word of God." It has much to say about the words of this book: They are not to be added to or taken from (4:2). The word "is very near you" (30:14). Frequent reference is made to "these words," sometimes pointing to specific words, sometimes to the whole book (4:30; 5:22; 6:6; 12:28; 30:1). That is, the title names the whole book but also refers to very specific words.

A second title from Jewish tradition is *seper tokahot,* "the book of hortatory directives," which aptly describes the style and literary genre of Deuteronomy. From beginning to end, a hortatory and homiletical style characterizes the book. Motivation clauses and other devices designed to exhort the listener/reader to obey its instruction fill its pages.

The name most familiar to English readers is "Deuteronomy," "the second law," a title of the book taken from the Greek translation of a phrase in Deuteronomy 17:18. The translation is probably erroneous. The Hebrew phrase seems to mean "copy of the law." But the title, with some justification, has stuck. The book does have the character of law. It is presented as law and meant to function that way. Furthermore, it does appear in the biblical story as a second law, following that given at Horeb, or Sinai. Therefore, it is an important example of the way law and teaching develop theologically to meet requirements of new times while preserving continuity with the old.

In the New Testament this book is grouped with other books under the overall rubric "Moses and the prophets" (Luke 16:29; 24:27; John 1:45). Deuteronomy is thus viewed as part of a larger whole that comes from Moses: the Torah, or Pentateuch. Part of the task of understanding the book is to discern its role as the final word of the Torah. This way of referring to Deuteronomy also emphasizes the crucial role of Moses in the Pentateuch, and especially in Deuteronomy. Moses is in many ways the central unifying element in the Pentateuch, and the last book of the Pentateuch is focused on Moses' departure. It is composed entirely of his words or the words of the Lord' through Moses. He does not stop speaking until the last chapter. If any book properly represents Moses and the law of which the New Testament speaks, it is Deuteronomy.

How Did Deuteronomy Come to Be?

Deuteronomy was formed in all likelihood through a complex process that reached at least from the eighth century to the sixth century—from the time of the divided monarchy into the exile. The book's affinities with other material that originated in

2

the Northern Kingdom, such as Hosea and the Elohist stratum of the Pentateuch, suggest the possibility that some of its traditions and materials originated there (see Weinfeld, pp. 366–370). If so, they are likely to have come into Judah in the eighth century, coinciding with the book's first stages in the eighth and seventh centuries. The many connections between Deuteronomy and the reform of Josiah depicted in Second Kings suggest that the time of Josiah and the events that followed his reign may have been the period in which the book took its basic shape. That, at least, is the period in which chapters 4:44—28:68 most likely received their basic form.

It is a help in understanding the book to recognize its relation to three significant periods in the history of Israel. The first period is the one given by the book itself as its setting, the time immediately preceding the initial settlement of the land. Deuteronomy is presented as Moses' words to all Israel before they entered the land. The book, therefore, is put before the reader as coming from the beginnings of a people, that point when they were forming a new nation. It is presented as being given by the original leader and thus carrying the weight such an authority figure from the past would carry. It was meant to found a people and to guide their ongoing life. This intentionality, authority, and normative character are conveyed by the setting given to the book. Whatever may have been the now disguised processes of transmission, Deuteronomy is to be received as foundational, Mosaic, original, for all the people, and authoritative. The ostensible setting of the book, therefore, is to be taken with utmost seriousness.

Still, from the clues mentioned earlier, we are aware that these words addressed—and were in large part created to address—the Israel of a later era. That audience was the kingdom of Judah in the one hundred to two hundred years it existed on the land before the Babylonian destruction and captivity. The reported words of Moses in these chapters would have reminded the people afresh of the promise of the land that they now enjoyed as God's gift with all its benefits. At the same time it warned against tendencies to disobedience, idolatry, and faithlessness that were present in the wilderness days and threatened again the possibility of long life in a good land.

Even as the book was still coming into being, however, the situation changed dramatically. The people experienced the judgment and loss of land that had been threatened if they were

3

disobedient and failed to put their sole trust in the Lord. So these words also addressed in a lively way a community that had been sent back across the border into the "wilderness." They helped to interpret their recent history as failure to live by the instruction of God, told them afresh that the promise was still good, and explained what had to be done to realize and maintain its possibilities.

The words of this book, then, could speak to the people of God in sharply different circumstances: (1) when they had not yet received or enjoyed the abundant gifts and prosperity of the land but had known only the difficulties of life in the wilderness; (2) when they had lived long on the land, enjoying and becoming accustomed to all the benefits of land ownership; and (3) when all the good gifts of God—the land, its abundance, and the temple—had been lost completely. Thus the book is, by necessity, engaged in a significant hermeneutical endeavor, speaking to new situations in light of the past, new situations that may be very different from previous ones.

The reader of the book must keep this feature in mind. At times the text is to be heard and received as for a people on the boundary between wilderness and land or home. At other times the text addresses those who are well provided for, who have prospered, and whose affluence has left them at ease, those who have sought and found security and well-being in sources other than the Lord of Israel and who need to know that everything is at risk and why. And the text addresses also an audience of those who have lost it all and need to know why. They need to know if there are any new possibilities and how they may be realized. In that situation, Deuteronomy seeks to bring a generation back to the boundary and give them instruction for life.

If the book is closely related to the reform measures of Josiah and significantly influenced by them, the reader needs to recognize the impact on the content and tone of this book of a time of serious religious apostasy and efforts to correct it. Some accounting for the zeal of the book and its hortatory character may be found in that setting. Reform depends upon zeal for purification and rectitude and upon exhortation to motivate a change of heart. This period is remembered in the Deuteronomistic History as a time of struggle for the soul of Judah; there was a real danger that Judah would shift its allegiance from the Lord to the gods of the Canaanites or Assyrians. The prophets,

4

the accounts of various kings (especially Manasseh), and Josiah's vigorous reforming activity reflect this threat. The emphasis on the commandment against worshiping other gods and making idols, the frequent use of the language "with all your heart and with all your soul," and the references to the utter destruction of the Canaanites in the taking of the land all make sense and have their dynamic in such a context in late pre-exilic Judah.

Who Wrote Deuteronomy?

It is rare that one can say precisely who wrote a biblical book. That is certainly the case with the Book of Deuteronomy. A history of composition stretching over a hundred years or more, as has been suggested above, would obviously make the identity of a particular author moot. The question of who wrote the book, therefore, has to be reformulated to ask, rather, what circles or groups of persons might have been responsible for formulating, collecting, editing, and expanding the work before us.

To ask this question and to seek its answer is not simply to fill in a blank about authorship. Attention to the question involves one in a look at perspectives. It heightens one's sense of the aims, intentions, and ideologies in the book. It is a way of asking what concerns and movements feed these injunctions and produce these emphases. In some sense, therefore, the answer to the question is less important than what is uncovered on the way to it.

Three major proposals (there are others) have been set forth to account for the source or origin of this book. The different proposals have arisen because each reflects some dimension of the book. It is doubtful that we can ever say decisively if one group is the true source for the creation of Deuteronomy.

The book may have arisen from *prophetic circles*. E. W. Nicholson has identified some of the grounds for seeing a close relation between Deuteronomy and prophetic groups:

> They both stand upon the traditions of the old Israelite amphic-tyony—their concern for the observance of covenant law, their adherence to the ideology of the Holy War, their strong attachment to the principles of charismatic leadership and their critical attitude towards the monarchy. The attitude of Deuteronomy towards the institution of kingship indeed has been taken by many as one of the strongest links between it and the

> traditions of northern Israel. The law in Deuteronomy xvii. 14f. reflects the antagonistic attitude of the northern prophetic party. Here the sacral ideas which grew up around the figure of the king in Jerusalem are entirely absent (p. 69).

Affinities between Deuteronomy and Hosea have led some to suggest that "the author of Deuteronomy was the spiritual heir of this great northern prophet."

Whether the prophetic affinities of the book reflect the circles out of which it was created or are only a form of expression growing out of the widespread prophetic trend of the period, it is clear that the book has some of the prophetic spirit. This is discernible in several of its emphases: its zeal for obedience to the covenant law; its focus on the issue of apostasy; its insistent claim that the Lord is Israel's only God; its concerns for social justice; its criticism of kingship not guided by the Lord's instruction; its conviction of Israel's election by the Lord and what that says about the love of God; and certainly its interest in the prophetic role, as reflected in chapter 18 and in the portrayal of Moses as prophet.

A second proposal is that Deuteronomy originated in *Levitical priestly circles*. This position has been espoused by Gerhard von Rad, though others have been persuaded similarly. Von Rad has pointed out the place of the Levites in the book (e.g., 18:1–8; 27:9–26; 31:9–13, 24–29). Even more important, in his judgment, is the necessity to account for who would have preserved the old sacral and legal traditional material that seems to be present in the book (von Rad, *Studies*). Further, who would have had the authority to interpret this material, and who would have set it forth in the highly hortatory and interpretive style characteristic of the book? It must have been religious figures. A primary indication that they may have been Levitical priests is found in Nehemiah 8:7–8, where it is said that the Levites "helped the people to understand the law . . . they gave the sense, so that the people understood the reading." In other words, we see that at a later time the Levites did have a responsibility for interpreting the law to the people. Von Rad identifies a further indirect suggestion of Levitical origin; it provides "a tenable explanation of Deuteronomy's remarkable Janus-like character, its combination of what is priestly and cultic with a national and martial spirit" (*Studies*, pp. 66–67). That is seen especially in the war laws of Deuteronomy 20, but not only there. The Levites would have had access

6

to the sacral traditions, and they were also the bearers of the ark of the covenant, the holy war palladium. By inference, as in the case of the supposed prophetic origin, the Levites appear to be the most reasonable source of the book.

This proposal also uncovers important features for understanding the book. It rests upon older traditions and thus stands in a line of continuity, rather than being simply a new creation in the history of Israel's religion. The Mosaic character of the book is an explicit effort to claim that continuity (see commentary on chapter 1). The claim of a Levitical origin also points to the hermeneutical and homiletical character of the book. This prominent feature of the material must be accounted for in identifying its source. Deuteronomy is law that is taught and preached, not simply promulgated; it must be understood as an activity of teaching and preaching if its aim is to be understood. While in one sense Deuteronomy says, "Here is the law," in another sense the exhortation "Choose life" (30:19) better illustrates its style and message. Also, the reader should not read what is said about the wars of conquest and the utter destruction that is enjoined against the inhabitants of the land without recognizing that the martial spirit in the book is not simply a matter of reporting or recording the past. It represents a revival and recrudescence of such a spirit at a much later time that is read back into the past. In other words, all of Deuteronomy's words about war against the inhabitants may tell us more about the spirit of Josiah's time than about what went on in the original settlement of the land.

The third major claim is that Deuteronomy originated in *wisdom and scribal circles,* a point of view worked out in detail by Moshe Weinfeld. A number of features suggest that such circles participated significantly in the formation of the book. Familiarity with the treaty formulations of the ancient Near East, which Deuteronomy attests, suggests its origin in circles having access to such treaties, specifically court scribes. Wisdom generally is esteemed in the book. It is a trait expected of Israel's judges (Deut. 1:13 and 16:19), and it is a characteristic of Israel, as reflected in its laws and the keeping of them. The great emphasis on material reward and retribution, depending on how Israel lives in the land, is consistent with the way wisdom is set forth in other books of the Old Testament. Other emphases found in Deuteronomy—the fear of God, the offer of life through obedience, and humane conduct toward people and

7

the natural order—while not exclusively the property of wisdom, are very much at home in its traditions and literature.

Once again, it may not be possible finally to lodge the composition and concerns of Deuteronomy within the circles of the scribes and the wise. But the intentions and emphases of this presentation of the Torah convey the deep concern of the book for passing on the formative story and its implications for life. The teaching character of Deuteronomy in effect begins the process of transmitting and interpreting the story of God's way with the people. After Deuteronomy, that enterprise will remain a significant part of the life of the community of faith. Transmission of the ancient tradition is, of course, evident long before Deuteronomy. But a self-conscious sense of the responsibility to inform and teach the ones who come after, so that they may understand the whence and wherefore of their life together and what the Lord expects of them, is particularly the contribution of Deuteronomy and those books that came out of the circles of wisdom. If Deuteronomy does reflect the humaneness and social morality of the teachers of wisdom, such a point of origin has produced one of the most significant ethical foundations of the biblical tradition. Equally important is the way two fundamental streams are joined within that tradition, the history of salvation and wisdom. These are usually seen as essentially different dimensions of Israel's life. But in Deuteronomy the revelation of God's way and will, as discerned from the story of Israel's redemption, is not separable from, much less antithetical to, the recognition of human wisdom as necessary for life and a true source of direction for human existence under God (for further discussion of its Mosaic character, see commentary on 1:1–5).

What Is the Literary Setting of Deuteronomy?

No study of the Book of Deuteronomy can ignore its literary context. It clearly picks up the narrative where Numbers leaves off. Moses and Israel, having gone through the wilderness, arrive at the plains of Moab. Moses is still the key figure, as he is in the preceding books. That no longer is the case after Deuteronomy.

At the same time, Deuteronomy is distinctive. It does not fit easily in its context. The preceding books, even when largely legal or instructional, are carried by a narrative. Here the genre is different. Deuteronomy is essentially speech. Furthermore,

8

after Numbers, there is some sense in which Deuteronomy is superfluous; the last part of Numbers tells everything about the death of Moses except the fact itself.

One notes further that Deuteronomy repeats material from the Pentateuch. The first three chapters recapitulate what transpired in the preceding book. The giving of the law at Sinai is repeated, as is the account of Israel's stubbornness. Laws from Exodus are repeated, albeit in updated fashion. But while there are repetitions, there are also contradictions between Deuteronomy and the rest of the Pentateuch. The journey around Edom as described in Numbers 20 and in Deuteronomy 2 is quite different. The reason why Moses is not allowed to enter the land in Numbers 27:12–14 is also different from the primary perspective on that issue in Deuteronomy 1:37 (cf. commentary on chapter 34). Finally, of course, one recognizes quickly that the language and style of Deuteronomy are quite distinctive when compared with the other Pentateuchal books, but they are markedly similar to much of Joshua through Kings.

All of this points to the *boundary* character of the book, both in its literary setting and in its presumed historical setting. On the one hand the book is shaped or understood by what has preceded it. It summarizes and brings to an end the beginning period of Israel's history, the story of redemption and the formation of a people instructed by the Lord. The character of the book, as a kind of last will and testament of Moses, and its conclusion, with the death of Moses, signal the end of an era; future generations now have in this book the full story of how they came to be and what God wants of them. The foundations are laid. Nothing more is necessary. The torah of the Lord is complete.

At the same time, Deuteronomy is quite self-consciously instruction for the future, not simply record of the past. Here, more than in any other part of the Pentateuch, one perceives that this book is a standard for the future, the plumb line by which generations to come will be measured. From this perspective, therefore, one is aware of Deuteronomy as the beginning of the Deuteronomistic History contained in Joshua through II Kings. Prior to its inclusion in the canon as the conclusion of the Torah, it must have existed as the introduction to that normative history of Israel's life in the land. Its opening chapters and some of the concluding ones may have been the narrative beginning of the Deuteronomistic History. Into this

9

the Deuteronomic legislation was set, to be understood now as the guide for Israel's life and for assessing and judging how well the people carried out and lived by the instruction of God. The books that follow reflect its language and substance. Kings and people are judged by its criteria of faithfulness and obedience. The very term modern scholarship has given to the history found in Joshua through Kings testifies to its being not merely a reporting of history but an accounting of how well and how poorly rulers, leaders, and people kept the torah of Yahweh transmitted by Moses on the plains of Moab.

Thus the Book of Deuteronomy is to be understood backwards; its significance is its summarizing and closing of the foundational period. Deuteronomy signals that the period is over. That very fact, however, means that the book is also to be understood from the future. Its impact is not fully comprehended apart from reading the books that follow and sensing sharply that the word of the Lord in Deuteronomy is always set for future generations. The intentionality of the book prohibits its ever being viewed as over and done, an enterprise belonging only to the past. No other book of the Old Testament is so straightforward and self-conscious about its character as a guide for the future.

What Is Deuteronomy About?

There are various ways of answering the question of what Deuteronomy is about. The suggestion offered here is that knowing the shape of the book is particularly helpful. That shape, however, may be perceived and characterized in more than one way. Here it is proposed that an explicit *literary* structure to the book is expressed in the sermons or speeches of Moses; a *substructure* is discernible in the covenantal character of the book; and a *theological* structure is revealed in its theme of the exclusive worship of the Lord as found in the Ten Commandments, particularly in the First Commandment and its positive expression in the Shema (Deut. 6:4–5).

The explicit literary structure of the book, its self-presentation as a series of Mosaic speeches, is signaled by four editorial superscriptions (1:1–5; 4:44–49; 29:1; and 33:1) "describing the particular character and content of each major part" (McBride, "Polity," p. 231). The significance of these superscriptions was recognized long ago. However, the work of Norbert Lohfink (see Robinson) and Dean McBride ("Deuteronomium" and

10

"Polity") has particularly developed that significance. Deuteronomy begins with "These are the words that Moses spoke to all Israel beyond the Jordan" (1:1), introducing the first speech as a *memoir* (so McBride) of the beginning history of the covenant people. The long section from 4:44 to 28:68 follows, headed by the words "This is the law [or torah] which Moses set before the children of Israel" (4:44). The heart of the book, therefore, is correctly described as a speech of Moses instructing the people in the way they are to live. McBride has aptly suggested that this torah is a kind of polity, or constitution, for the whole life of the people, "conspicuous in its concern to empower a broad constituency of the community whose integrity and political independence it seeks to protect" ("Polity," p. 237).

Moses' third speech begins with "These are the words of the covenant which the LORD commanded Moses to make with the people of Israel in the land of Moab" (29:1). The significant word here is covenant. What follows in the next four chapters essentially formalizes the covenantal relationship embodied in Moses' words, with particular reference to Moses' departure and the accountability of the people to maintain the torah that has been set before them. So this third speech, which is partly narrative, includes the solemn oath of the people to keep the covenant (chapters 29–30), with provision for leadership after Moses is gone (chapter 31), and Moses' permanent witness in the face of expected disobedience of the covenant (chapter 32).

The final speech of Moses begins in 33:1: "This is the blessing with which Moses the man of God blessed the children of Israel before his death." It is indeed a final blessing as his last testament to the people. An appendix in chapter 34 then tells of Moses' death and presents in the final epitaph (34:10–12) a kind of colophon for the whole Pentateuch. It emphasizes, as though from a long distance, the enduring preeminence of the work of Moses (McBride, "Deuteronomium," p. 536).

Discerning this structure in the present form of the text reveals some important dimensions of the book. Perceiving it as a series of speeches from Moses just prior to the taking of the land makes us more sharply aware of both the preaching character of the book and of the role of Moses. Mosaic speech is a literary and theological device used by the Deuteronomist to speak centuries later in an authoritative manner to the people

11

of his own day (see commentary on 1:1–5). Deuteronomy is concerned with making clear what the constitutional law is. But it is equally zealous to call Israel to a renewed obedience. The vehicle for that is preaching, by one whose authority to interpret and exhort would be recognized and accepted by the audience. These speeches are proper preaching in any age—the proclamation of the redemptive grace of God as a basis for exhortation to obedience. Deuteronomy, through the mouth of Moses, reminds the people of God's grace in the past. On that basis it calls them to a thankful, obedient response, instructing them in the way and character of obedience. Deuteronomy/ Moses is clearly the preacher/teacher, the interpreter reinterpreting the past and the older tradition, partly to serve a theological perspective and partly in light of changed circumstances (see commentary on chapter 5). Deuteronomy is a book of the law, of torah. It so describes itself. But that is *preached* law, another way of saying that it is *torah*. "Torah" is the one term connected with legal matters whose origin and meaning have nothing to do with law in the usual sense of the term. Torah is instruction and teaching, and that is what Moses does here (Miller, "The Way of Torah"). Furthermore, law as torah is grounded in the reality of God's redemptive activity. So while this commentary uses the term "law(s)" frequently, it is used with this understanding in mind. Deuteronomy is not to be received as a legal reference text for checking on particular matters. It is divine instruction—laid on the heart, encouraged, motivated, and explained. Several features reflect the book's character as speech or preaching: (1) frequent reference to "this day" or "today", (2) the use of "we" in the credos and elsewhere, (3) frequent emphatic use of second-person pronouns ("you"), (4) repeated summons to hearing, (5) numerous vocatives, (6) appeal to memory as a way of actualizing the past in the present, (7) use of threat and promise to motivate hearers to respond, (8) appeal to heart and mind, and (9) use of illustration (cf. Deut. 19:5 and Exod. 21:12–14).

The substructure often noted in Deuteronomy is found in its character as a covenant document. Features of the covenant formulary are clearly present in the book as a whole and often in individual segments. A number of years ago Gerhard von Rad suggested that the book had an original cultic setting in life (now abandoned for the form of homiletic instruction), probably in a feast of covenant renewal (*Deuteronomy*, pp. 26–33;

"Form-Critical Problem," pp. 22–23). His outline of the book suggests the cultic ties:

Historical presentation of the events at Sinai and paraenetic material connected with these events	1—11
The reading of the law	12:1—26:15
Sealing of the covenant	26:16–19
Blessings and curses	27—34

More recently, other scholars have discerned a covenantal structure by looking at Deuteronomy in the light of the numerous ancient Near Eastern international treaties that have been discovered (Klaus Baltzer, Dennis McCarthy, Moshe Weinfeld). Weinfeld has identified the following elements of the treaty form transformed into the covenant formulary:

Preamble	1:1–6*a*; 5:6*a*
Historical prologue	1:6*b*—3:29; 5; 9:7—10:11
Basic stipulation of allegiance	4:1–23; 6:4—7:20; 10:12–22
Covenant clauses	12—26
Invocation of witnesses	4:26; 30:19; 31:28
Blessings and curses	28
Oath imprecation	29:9–28
Deposit of document	10:1–5; 31:24–26
Periodic reading	31:9–13
Duplicates and copies	17:18–19; 31:25–26

Weinfeld comments that "only Deuteronomy has preserved the classic structure of the political treaty" (p. 66). That is seen particularly in the extended section on curses and blessings, witnesses, deposit of the treaty, duplicates, periodic reading, and the oath imprecation. It is worth noting that only Deuteronomy speaks of "the covenant and the oath," terms which correspond to the Akkadian treaty designation. Baltzer and McCarthy have particularly discerned the covenant formulary within segments of Deuteronomy. For example, in the central discourse of chapters 5—28, McCarthy points to these components of the treaty-covenant: historical and paraenetic introduction (5—11), laws or stipulations (12—26), and blessings and curses (26:15—28:68). He sees covenantal evidence in the framework surrounding the main discourse: setting (1:1–5), historical prologue (1:6—3:17), laws or stipulations (4:1–2, 9, 15–20), and sanctions (4:24, 26, 40).

13

The details of these analyses may not be universally accepted, but discovery of the ancient treaties, especially the Neo-Assyrian treaties, has clarified the covenantal character of the Book of Deuteronomy. Sections as well as the whole of the book have been shaped by the covenantal formulary. This covenantal substructure, like the speeches of Moses, has implications for hearing and understanding Deuteronomy.

For one thing, it clarifies calling the book, in addition to "the book of the torah (law" [II Kings 22:8]), "the book of the covenant" (II Kings 23:2–3). It shows why the people gathered together when the book was found in the temple to hear it read and to make covenant. The book is about covenant. Its powerful impact upon the people at that time—and at any time—comes from the teaching of Moses about the will of God and their recognition of the familiar form of covenant in that teaching.

This covenantal substructure adds a political character to the book's hermeneutical and homiletical aspects. Both Luther and Calvin saw its political nature. It deals with questions of authority, the ordering of life in the religious and secular sphere, who it is that rules and how. Questions of allegiance and loyalty are to the fore.

Looking at Deuteronomy from this angle, one can recognize the theological foundation for Israel's life as God's election and covenant. Here is presented the most developed articulation of Israel's election by the Lord of any book in the Pentateuch (e.g., chapters 7 and 9). However, Deuteronomy vigorously challenges any understanding of Israel's relation to the Lord as arising out of their greatness or righteousness or virtue. One senses in these challenges that there was a time when misunderstandings were indeed present and perhaps prevalent. Deuteronomy brings them under attack with the weapons of covenant theology.

Finally, it is important to call attention to the book's theological orientation around the Shema (Deut. 6:4–5) and the Decalogue (chapter 5), particularly the prohibition of the worship of other gods or idols. Both Martin Luther and John Calvin saw the book as an interpretation of these basic stipulations of the covenantal relationship. For Luther, the first part of the Shema, "Hear, O Israel: the LORD our God is one LORD," was

14   a call to faith, and the second part, "and you shall love the LORD your God," a call to love. Both Luther and Calvin saw the detailed laws as an explication of this structure of faith and,

more specifically, of the Ten Commandments found in chapter 5. More recently, Stephen Kaufman and R. P. Merendino have suggested similar understandings of the specific laws. They have to do first with relation to God, as in the first group of commandments, and second with relation to others, as in the second group of commandments. Kaufman has argued very specifically for an arrangement of the laws of 12—26 along the order of the Decalogue.

Whether or not one can finally perceive a clear outline of the book in terms of either the Shema or the Decalogue, there is no doubt that the themes, emphases, and often the language itself do suggest that one proper way of understanding Deuteronomy is as an explication of the Great Commandment, as that is also embodied and explicated in the Shema and the Ten Commandments. That is especially evident in the first eleven chapters. Chapters 1 to 3 are a confession of faith about God and what God has done with and for the people. Chapter 4 then identifies the heart of the response of love that ensues. The essence of that response is seen to be the exclusive worship of God and the prohibition of idols of any sort. These same chapters relate to the Decalogue; chapters 1–3 are an elaboration of the prologue, while chapter 4 explicates the first two commandments. The Decalogue is in chapter 5 and the Shema is at the beginning of chapter 6. Language from the Decalogue and the Shema pervades chapters 6–11, in such expressions as "the LORD your God" and "other gods" (6:13, 14; 7:4; 8:19; 11:16, 28); "worship and serve" (8:19; 11:16); "brought out of the land of Egypt, out of the house of bondage" (6:23; 7:8, 19; 8:14; 9:26, 28, 29); "with all your heart and with all your soul" (4:29; 10:12; 11:13; 13:3; 26:16; 30:2, 6, 10). The language and themes of the Shema occur frequently throughout chapter 11. The Shema structure of faith and love, "Hear . . . and love," is found in various other places in Deuteronomy: for example, 10:17–18 (faith) and 19–20 (love) and 27:9 (faith) and 10 (love).

Focusing on the Great Commandment and the Decalogue identifies a center around which other things revolve. It enables a reduction of the whole to its most important point, spelling it out in specifics and implications. A theological structure is thereby given to the covenantal community, one that continues throughout its life. It operates on two axes: the relation of faith and love or obedience, as succinctly set forth in the Shema, and the relationship to God and others as embodied in the Ten

Commandments. Readers of the Book of Deuteronomy, therefore, are constantly being given clues to what matters most for those who live under and with this God.

Why Read Deuteronomy?

In some sense the best answer to questions about the value of reading Deuteronomy is probably found in the rest of the commentary. But for a reader who may not be highly familiar with Deuteronomy, or not already drawn to its reading and study for one reason or another, some anticipation or foretaste may be appropriate.

One way of responding to the question of why one would read Deuteronomy is to cite the witness of those who have already studied the book. Julius Wellhausen claimed that the "connecting link between old and new, between Israel and Judaism, is everywhere Deuteronomy" (p. 362). In a similar fashion, von Rad regarded Deuteronomy as "the middle point of the Old Testament" (*Studies,* p. 37), and others find in it the center of Old Testament theology. One interpreter has argued that "there is no book of more importance in the Old Testament and no Old Testament book more basic for understanding the New Testament than Deuteronomy" (E. Achtemeier, p. 9). Martin Luther may have identified the significance of this book best when he wrote (p. 9) that

> it teaches this people to live well according to the Ten Commandments in both spirit and body. Furthermore, it sets up the inner rule of conscience together with secular government, then the outward manner of ceremonies with wholly divine justice and wisdom, so that there is nothing in the whole range of life that is not arranged here most wisely and properly.

Without going into detail about matters that will be pursued in varying degrees throughout the commentary, one can note several features of this book that suggest something of its significance and place.

1. Its existence as the book of the law par excellence in the Bible, raising all the pertinent issues and questions about the place and meaning of the law in our life under God.

2. Its emphasis on preaching and teaching, both by what it says and how it says it.

3. Its manifestation of a self-conscious hermeneutical concern and effort to speak the ancient word to a later time.

16

4. The presence of the central tenets of faith for Judaism and Christianity in the Shema and the Decalogue.

5. Its deep concern for the nature and purity of the worship of the people of God.

6. The centrality of the gift of the land, with all the attendant theological and political ramifications of that issue.

7. The extensive use of Deuteronomy in the New Testament.

8. The prominence of moral and ethical matters, establishing it as foundational, alongside the prophets, in its concern for a just social order.

To read and study Deuteronomy is to open doors into these subjects, to be challenged and perplexed, to be given an understanding of the past and a guide toward the future, and to be called into covenant with God; indeed, to be faced with life-or-death decisions. All of that is why Deuteronomy should be read. From the beginning, its words have claimed that its readers' lives depend upon careful attention to them. So read on, carefully.

PART ONE

Moses' First Address: Journey to the Boundary

DEUTERONOMY 1—4

The first major section of Deuteronomy moves from beginning to end with a unity of thought and structure that allows it to be heard and interpreted on its own. Most of the primary themes and concerns of the book appear in these chapters. Chapters 1–4, therefore, serve as introduction. They introduce the subject matter and the theological perspective, and they lead the reader into the book. The long speech of Moses in chapters 5–28, composed of exhortation in chapters 5–11 and laws or statutes in chapters 12–28, is the heart of the book. But the stage is set in chapters 1–4. They tell how Israel came to its present place, on the border between wandering in the wilderness and settlement in the promised land. This section presents a historical retrospect reaching back to Horeb (the alternate name for Sinai used by Deuteronomy) and tells of the movement of the people under Moses' leadership through the wilderness and through the territories of Edom, Moab, and Ammon, as well as the lands of Sihon and Og, which they captured. It concludes with Moses charging and calling the people to obey the statutes and ordinances of God (ch. 4).

Two things should be noted as one looks at this unit. First, the "movement" of the section places the hearers of Moses' speech on the border, with their goal in sight but not yet reached. The text is explicit about this at several points (1:1–5; 3:23–29; 4:44–49). While the land east of the Jordan has been taken, "the good land beyond the Jordan" (3:25), the heart of the promised land, has not. Moses does not instruct them after the goal is reached, the land taken, the people settled in. The words of Deuteronomy instruct people who find themselves on the boundary—with possibilities, promises, and problems before them. The possibility of crossing the border and fulfilling the promises will be conditioned by how the people receive the divine instruction for life now being given them. The problems they will confront "beyond the Jordan" are going to be manageable only if "these words" are taken to heart. The past of slavery (Egypt) and fear (wilderness) can be transformed into freedom for life only as life is controlled by this law, this word of God that is given for their wisdom (4:6) and their good (4:40—"that it may go well with you").

This does not mean that the relationship between God and people begins here only or that only from now on will the folk of God enjoy the divine blessings. On the contrary, the relationship reaches into the past, to the people's beginnings in Abraham, and was established in a full way at Sinai. All along that way, especially in the hazards of the wilderness, God's care and providence have blessed them. But the long journey is nearly at an end. To move on into the fullness and abundance of life they have been offered, the people must be instructed about what makes that possible. It is for persons on that kind of boundary that these words were set forth. Deuteronomy is given to people who want to move from death to life (30:15–20), from slavery to freedom, from the wilderness fraught with problems to the homeland filled with promise.

The second point to note in this unit is that texts that may have had separate origins have been brought together into a literary and theological whole. Chapter 4 is commonly regarded as being a later composition and as having been added after chapters 1–3 were already in place as the introduction to the Deuteronomistic History (Joshua through Kings). That may be a correct analysis of their literary formation, but the result is a powerful theological statement in which rehearsal of the story of the Lord's provision and guidance, as well as reminder of the people's faithfulness, becomes the ground for a call to obedient response to the Lord in the light of God's gracious care.

The "so now" (NRSV) at the beginning of chapter 4 indicates that what follows is the appropriate implication or consequence of the preceding historical review. This is reinforced by the vocative and imperative, "Israel, give heed." The past is recalled because it has implications for life in the future. The boundary on which Israel is poised is not purely geographical. It is also the boundary between chapters 1–3 and chapter 4, the border between the experience of a past shaped by the grace of God but distorted by human fearfulness and a future not yet shaped but whose direction is clearly indicated by the past. It should be marked by obedience and trust. The move across the border is a move from grace to faith, from deliverance to obedience, from gospel to response, from theology to ethics.

A theological structure, therefore, is set forth that will be echoed in different forms, from the Shema of 6:4–5 to the offering of firstfruits and credo of chapter 26 (see Introduction). The device, of course, is not purely Deuteronomic or even Old Testament. Paul's use of "therefore" at Romans 12:1; Ephesians 4:1; and 5:1—or in such places as Philippians 2:12; Colossians 2:16; and 3:5—demonstrates this fact. The gospel of the love of God in Jesus Christ calls those who have received that good news "therefore" to an obedience that is truly the way to life.

Deuteronomy 1—3
On the Way with the Lord

This section recapitulates the story of Israel's journey from Horeb to the border of the promised land in three main parts. The first is primarily a story of failure, frustration, and stymied progress (ch. 1). The second part records progress toward the land, achieved by peaceful encounter with kinfolk and victory over hostile inhabitants, the Amorites (2:1—3:11). The final unit reports the first allotment of land by Moses, the tribal territories in Transjordan (3:12–29).

Here the reader can perceive a clear interaction between divine intention and control of history and human response to conform to or resist that purpose. Moses' frequent use of such statements as "the Lord said" and "the Lord commanded" reveals that this is not simply an account of Israel's wanderings. This is report of a journey led by God, shaped at every point by God's command and the response of Israel and others to it. It is a journey from wilderness to fruitful land, but it is not made alone. Both progress and provision are given by the word and power of God. Even apparently aimless wandering is under the direction of God (e.g., 2:1–3).

Divine Guidance and Human Fearfulness (1:1–46)

The initial units of chapter 1 introduce the book and the journey: Moses' role is identified, the people's destination is delineated, and persons to assist Moses in the leadership of the people are designated. At verse 19 the journey begins. The first episode (vv. 19–46) is given as a kind of paradigm of the human failure to trust in the Lord who created them. It is clearly a lesson Deuteronomy sets before later generations of the Lord's people.

Introduction to Deuteronomy (1:1–5)

These verses introduce the book as a whole. Two things stand out as one reads this section: the degree of geographical and temporal detail and the impression of repeated introductions (vv. 1, 3, and 5) with a clear focus on Moses. Both aspects merit attention.

Time and Place. The precise information about time and place serves two purposes. One is transitional and introductory. It connects the Book of Deuteronomy with the preceding books and with the narrative of the journey through the wilderness, and it anticipates in very concise fashion the salient features of the opening chapters. Here is an indication that Deuteronomy does not stand alone; it is meant to be read with and out of the preceding books, thus creating that body of literature known as the Torah, or Pentateuch (see Introduction).

The second purpose is to root this book in very specific ways in history. It does not stand before us as a general statement about human conduct but has grown out of the life and experience of a people in their journey with God. That experience impinges upon, affects, and shapes the words and the instruction that follow. Torah as the Lord's teaching is not immobilized and restricted by the temporal context but is related to it. One often discerns what is at stake by hearing that instruction in its context. In this case, we have good reason to think that the teaching of this book was deliberately set against the backdrop furnished by these references, impelling us all the more to take it seriously.

22

Most of the interpretive comment made on the geographical details is to try to locate the places. Such endeavor is of only penultimate usefulness. Usually it founders on our inability to locate a number of the places, especially in verse 1, with any precision or certainty. We do know that Horeb refers to the mountain in the Sinai peninsula where the law was given to the people and that the Arabah is the geographical rift south of the Dead Sea. We know also that the other places are in the southern region of Palestine or, more likely, in the territory of Moab across the Jordan and the region north of it where the kings Sihon and Og ruled. Two or three of the places can probably be identified more precisely. The exact location of others is uncertain.

What is important, however, is that these times and places identify in shorthand fashion the central contextual matters one needs to keep in mind while reading the book. Several of those need to be lifted up.

The starting point is identified as Horeb. The covenant established between God and this people and the giving of the law are indeed the starting point and the basic assumption of all that follows. Again and again the chapters that follow will seek in some fashion to transport the people back to Horeb (Sinai) to identify the instruction and demands before the people now—whether "now" refers to Israel in the wilderness preparing to take the land or to Judah of the late monarchy trying to hold its place in the land or to the people in exile hoping to return to the land (see Introduction)—with those set before them at Sinai.

At Kadesh-barnea (1:2) the redeemed people failed to trust in their redeeming God. There they found that the promise would not come to those who were afraid and did not trust in the power of their God to keep the promise made. That story is told in the latter part of this chapter to indicate that if there is a relation between law and land, as Deuteronomy surely seeks to declare, there is also a direct connection between trust and promise. In both cases, one cannot expect the latter without the former. Reference to the fortieth year anticipates the fate of the fearful generation that was not allowed to enter the land; forty years is the approximate length of a generation (cf. 2:14–15). That period is described in chapter 8 as a time when the Lord humbled Israel, testing them (v. 2) but also providing for them (v. 4).

In contrast to the fearful expectations of the people, the

23

story of the victory given Israel by the Lord over the powerful and hostile kings Sihon and Og (1:4) clearly demonstrates the power of God to fulfill the promises to protect and provide for the people who trust and obey.

Most other geographical references are subsumed under or spell out the general locale of the wilderness and the land of Moab. Both designations remind us of the boundary setting of this instruction. The people are still in some sense in the wilderness, with all the vicissitudes and threats it presents, but in sight of the promise, of home, of a rest from tiresome wandering. How do they get across the border? How do they move from the wilderness to a promised rest? The answer as Deuteronomy gives it is that they move across through the power and instruction of God.

Repeated Introductions. Verses 1, 3, and 5 seem at first glance to be unnecessary repetitions. Verse 1a serves as an introduction satisfactorily without requiring the other references to Moses in verses 3 and 5. All three, however, do relate to the way the book is set up, what it is intended to accomplish, and particularly the question of its source.

Verse 1 identifies the words of this book as the words and speeches of Moses. This sets the book as human speech, given by a particular individual in a particular time and place and subject to all the contingencies, contexting, and limitations characteristic of any human words and instruction. Verse 1 also indicates—as do the following verses—that these words are not those of just any individual; they come from the one who is known as founder and leader, one whose words and way were set by the Lord.

This latter point is stressed in verse 3. Moses is the voice, but the Lord is the source and author of the words. Regularly Moses will be speaking, and just as regularly it will be said that Moses speaks according to what the Lord commands him.

The third introduction, verse 5, explicitly identifies Moses as the mediator, teacher, and explicator of torah: that is, of this instruction, which is indeed the role he assumes in the book.

All these introductions may be related to the role of Moses vis-à-vis the law and to the core of the book in chapters 5 and 6. On the one hand Moses is the speaker of the book from beginning to end, while on the other hand he is mediator and simply transmits the words of the Lord (see ch. 5). Equally clearly, however, one sees at the beginning of chapter 6 and elsewhere that Moses is teacher and explainer of the law, Deu-

24

teronomy. The word translated as "explain" is uncommon, appearing only here, in Deuteronomy 27:8, and in Habakkuk 2:2. It seems to mean "to make clear," to expound or explicate in a way that all may clearly understand. This verse therefore underscores the fact that Deuteronomy is not merely law; it is law expounded, interpreted, and explained. Moses is not simply promulgator of law but also teacher and interpreter of God's instruction.

What about the question of authenticity? Did Moses really receive these words from God and then pass them on, while also interpreting and elaborating them? It is highly unlikely that we have here an accurate historical report of words and actions by Moses on the plains of Moab before the settlement. The creation of Deuteronomy appears to have been a complex, prolonged process, most of which probably took place at a much later time. What was in the minds of the now unknown persons who over a period of time "authored" Deuteronomy can only be speculation. But it is likely that the ascription and reception of this book as Mosaic was done in a most serious fashion. The traditions, conceptions, and even particular matters of instruction were seen as reaching back to the beginnings. Deuteronomy was meant to be—and was received as—instruction about God's way. That way was rooted in, grew out of, and was consonant with the covenant stipulations and divine activity that created Israel as a people. While traditions and statutes were updated, they were regarded as part and parcel of the primary formulation of relationship between God and Israel. One assumed that this instruction that grew out of the Mosaic instruction belonged with it. Fresh explication of the law of God in a new time does not mean that it is new law. Rather, it is a part of the whole and properly carries the authority of Moses. The introduction, therefore, says in effect to readers of any time: Read these words as being God's instruction taught and explained by Moses, and you will know what force and authority they are to have. Read these words as guidance for people moving from slavery and wilderness and wandering into a land of opportunity, blessing, and life under God's rule, and you will know where and how they are to be heard.

The Gift of the Land (1:6–8)

The command "Resume your journey" (v. 7, NRSV) begins the narrative that runs through the first three chapters. Because these chapters describe stages of a journey, the units (or stages) are marked off frequently by either the command to turn *(panah)* and journey *(nasa')*, or to pass over or through *('abar)*, or by the report that the people have done so. The first of these journey markers is here, but it is not simply one stage to which the people are set. Rather, this is the introductory command to go up into the land; and as it is given, the promised land is defined in general and ideal form, extending from the Negeb in the south to the Euphrates River in the north. This is an extravagant gift echoing the promise to the patriarchs (e.g., Gen. 15:18–21), as indeed the divine word clearly indicates (v. 8). The limits set forth here were probably never reached except for a while during the reign of David. The proper extent of Israel's promised land is somewhat ambiguous in the Bible, whether one looks at the land as promised or the land as occupied. We are led to hear with unmistakable clarity, though, that there is a spot for God's people, that spiritual home is not indifferent to matters of geographical place—or, perhaps more simply, that one cannot truly speak about home or rest (to use the Deuteronomic term) without speaking about place. The precise shape of the gift may not be permanently or rigidly fixed. The important thing is that a place is provided for the people and that it is an unrealistically extravagant gift, as are all of God's gifts.

When one looks at how land and home are to come to Israel, three things immediately stand out. The land is promised, given, and taken.

It is *promised*, which means that there is a history to this transaction. The homeland arises out of the sworn purposes of God. It is not an accident or a casual and unexpected event. It has been at the heart of God's intention to bring blessing to the families of the earth from the beginning (Gen. 12:1–3; cf. Wolff). Because the reality of the land was for much of the time only promise, its realization assumed a history of trust as well as of promise. Deuteronomy will reiterate that word time and time again, beginning with these chapters: There is no promised land without trusting folk. For those who trust in the promise and are willing to act upon it, even the mountain of God is only a stage on the journey to the promised rest.

The land promised is also by definition *given*. Israel is to receive and conceive of the land as a gift from God. No more than any other gift of salvation or experience of blessing is the land deserved or to be claimed by a people. Deuteronomy

26

continually reminds the people that no merit (ch. 9) or power (ch. 7) on their part ensures or provides the place for life. Whatever complex historical processes led to Israel's settlement in the land, they are there only because a gracious God has provided for their life.

Those complex processes, however, are reflected in the fact that the land given is also *taken*. This too is in the divine purpose and out of the divine command. As Robert Frost expressed it in his poem "The Gift Outright" about another land at a much later time, "The deed of gift was many deeds of war." So Israel is told to go in and take possession, to conquer the land. Divine gift and human act are parts of a whole. The human process of occupation was surely more complicated than the biblical story indicates on the surface, but the heightening of the acts of military conquest is a way of underscoring the divine-human interaction. The land is seen as quickly taken, and so the power and intention of God to give the land are affirmed. The deed of gift is realized and dramatized in the many deeds of war. This juxtaposition of divine gift and human act, especially reflected in the pairing of words having to do with "giving" (Heb. *natan*) and "possessing" (Heb. *yaraš*), will be found repeatedly in Deuteronomy (e.g., 2:31, 33; 3:3, 12, 18; 7:1–3; 9:1–3). It reflects the typically synergistic character of biblical expression that insists on the unity and interrelatedness of the initiating and accompanying activity of the sovereign God and the effective action of the human creatures in response. (For elaboration of all the above, see the Excursus on "The Deuteronomic Theology of the Land" that follows this chapter.)

The Need for Experienced Help in Leadership (1:9–18)

One regular concern in Deuteronomy is the matter of government. Indeed, Dean McBride, following Josephus in part, has made the cogent suggestion that torah in Deuteronomy is best understood as *polity*. The book, therefore, is intended to provide the polity by which Israel's life should be ordered and ruled ("Polity of the Covenant People"). This concern for government, basic to the book as a whole, as McBride suggests, is specifically reflected in Deuteronomy in two ways: (1) provisions for setting up levels and positions of leadership and governance, and (2) instructions about the responsibilities of leaders that contribute to a theology of leadership. Both dimensions are present in this passage, where a kind of chain of com-

27

mand under Moses is set up to share the burden and responsibility of governing the people.

The passage is bracketed by the expressions "At that time I said to you" (v. 9) and "I commanded you at that time" (v. 18). It echoes matters that appear earlier in Exodus 18:13–23 (Jethro suggests to Moses a system to relieve his judicial and administrative burden) and Numbers 11:14–17 (Moses asks God for relief from the burden of leading the people). The precise literary or historical relationship of these passages to each other is unclear, but reading Deuteronomy in comparison with the other two serves to call attention to significant aspects of its report. For one thing, the Deuteronomic account *roots the need for organization and leadership in the fulfillment of the blessing God promised long before to Abraham.* The promise of blessing and posterity as numerous as the stars in the heavens (vv. 10–11), given to Abraham and Sarah (Gen. 12:1–3; 15:5; 22:17), is now fulfilled in this numerous people and the good land before them. But fulfillment does not mean that all is perfect and there is nothing left to do, as if the story of God's way with Israel were a fairy tale that comes to an end once the primary goal is reached and the narrator reports "they lived happily ever after." On the contrary, it is precisely the intention of Deuteronomy to say that receipt of the salvation gift opens up marvelous possibilities, but things do not end there. The blessing brings with it demands and responsibilities, indeed in a way not true before the promise was accomplished. From here on, Deuteronomy stresses that blessing, gifts, and prosperity, by their very existence, place burdens, require leadership, and demand shared responsibilities and work. When the promise is realized is, in some sense, only the beginning. Life now becomes more complex, requiring leadership, wisdom, structure, order, and fairness to an even greater degree than before.

The burden that has fallen upon Moses as the one leader is also clearly stressed in this account. Three terms are used to convey that stress: "weight," used negatively in Isaiah 1:14 to refer to Israel's festivals as a heavy weight on the Lord; "burden," a general term for anything that is to be borne; and "strife," (Heb. *rîb*), which can refer both to lawsuits or disputes (cf. Deut. 25:1 and Exod. 18:15–16) and to the larger strife, contention, and accusation against Moses and God that continue to come from the people: that is, the stife occasioned by the people as a whole (cf. Num. 11). So it is both the problem

28

of too many cases and details and the problem of the people's needs and complaints that are encountered by the leader and what he seeks to alleviate in a democratic way (v.13). This procedure is typical of the process by which leaders assume their position in the Book of Deuteronomy, as one sees in the legal stipulations pertaining to judges (16:18–20) and kings (17:14–15).

The functions of the officials described here are not easy to determine or distinguish. There may be military functions central to the role of "commander" (especially in light of the breakdown into units of thousands, hundreds, fifties, and tens), administrative responsibilities assumed for the "officers," and judicial functions for the "judges." It is likely that there are only two officials here (commander-judges and officers) or possibly only one, described with three terms that may in fact reflect a combination of military, administrative, and judicial responsibilities. Certainly the context, as well as Exodus 18, indicates that the primary function is judicial and the primary assignment *the maintenance of justice and equity,* reminding us of the centrality of the proper maintenance of justice for the social fabric. From Psalm 82 to Amos 5, one hears clearly that just judges deciding cases fairly are the cornerstone of Israelite society. Here, when a structure for that society begins to be formed, that cornerstone is laid first. The appointed judges are given four basic instructions, whose continuing relevance for those who care about justice in the courts is clear.

1. A judge is to determine the right in any case; or, as also reflected in the Hebrew, to decide who is innocent and in the right and who is in the wrong and thus guilty. The primary aim of the court is to seek the right (v. 16).

2. No partiality shall be shown, a requirement that can be measured by whether or not the weak and the poor (that is, the "small") get as much and as fair a hearing as the rich and powerful (that is, the "great"). In a similar spirit, the U.S. Supreme Court ruled that Clarence Gideon had a right to legal counsel for a misdemeanor indictment, even though he could not afford such counsel (Lewis).

3. Justice shall not be compromised by fear. This is the other side of the word about impartiality. Not only shall the weak be treated as well and fairly as the strong, but judges should not let fear of power and wealth compromise their insistence on equity and the right. An intimidated judge can never deal justly; nor

29

is there any place to turn for redress when the court is intimidated. Martin Luther said of this instruction, "This is the highest and most difficult virtue of rulers, namely, justice and integrity of judgment. For it is easy to pronounce judgment on poor and common people; but to condemn the powerful, the wealthy, and the friendly, to disregard blood, honor, fear, favor, and gain and simply to consider the issue—this is a divine virtue" (p. 19).

The word about not being afraid is not an assurance but a command, a command that makes sense through the motivation it is given. The judge should fear no one, because the judgment really is God's. Whoever receives the verdict stands before God and is confronted by God, not the judge. This also implies that fearfulness leading to partiality places the judge before a greater threat than the powerful defendant or plaintiff. God brooks no partiality and will hold accountable anyone who so renders God's judgment. The dual function of the Hebrew word *mišpaṭ* in referring both to judgment and the concept of justice corroborates the interpretation of Jacques Ellul: "It is God's personal will which renders justice (Deuteronomy 1:17) and hence pronounces a judgment which is the full measure of this justice" (p. 46).

4. When matters are too difficult for a judge to handle, there is recourse to the higher authority of Moses. Already in Deuteronomy, the social structure recognizes the need for a supreme court to handle the really tough judicial issues, a device that serves further to guard the system against breakdown.

Finally, notice should be taken of the *qualifications for leadership*. Moses' words refer to them twice. They are especially appropriate for those who have to decide issues and cases and resolve conflicts. Verse 13 gives three necessary characteristics: wisdom, understanding or discernment, and reputation ("reputable," NRSV). "Wisdom" in this case probably has to do with intelligence and knowledge acquired by experience that is assimilated and brought to bear on cases and new situations. "Understanding" refers to the ability to discern, to distinguish between matters of right and wrong, good and bad. "Reputable" (being known) means just what the text suggests. Leaders expected to make judgments acceptable to the persons involved and the whole community should be respected and of good repute. For Israel on the boundary, as for any community at any time, such qualifications are basic for those who would govern and judge.

30

A Story of Human Fear (1:19–46)

Now, in response to the command of verse 7, the report of the journey from Horeb begins with journey-stage language, "we set out . . . and went." A geographical-stage note follows in verse 19, which places the events of this story in the southern region at Kadesh-barnea. The acts and words recounted in this section grow out of the command of Moses in verses 20–21. He reiterates the original command of God at Horeb (vv. 6–8). The juxtaposition of land as gift and land to be taken appears again. This time, however, it is followed by words of strong assurance: Do not fear or be dismayed. That added encouragement both anticipates what is to follow and identifies the primary problem with this people—fear. In various ways, both structurally and thematically, the story uncovers the problem and its implications.

Structurally, the narrative unfolds in a series of responses to Moses' command and assurance that show an increasing development or intensity. The *first response* of the people is succinct and sound and does not yet reveal the latent fear about to erupt. They suggest that spies be sent to determine the best way to go into the land. Moses responds affirmatively, the spies are sent, and they return with a report that is accurate, theological, and encouraging: The land God gives is good.

In rather abrupt and surprising fashion, the *second response* of the people as reported by Moses (vv. 26–28) reveals a basic fear that motivated the first response. This fear was not clear at that point in the narrative. Reasons are given for the fearfulness, but the buildup of the narrative to this point indicates rather sharply that fearfulness is the wrong response. God has given the land *plus* words of assurance *plus* a report of the goodness of the land—these do not add up to a negative and fearful reaction. But the people are fearful, immediately and dramatically contrasting the power and promise of God with the weakness and lack of trust of the people. The story builds as Moses characterizes several components of the response of the people: they are unwilling; they rebel against the Lord's command; they murmur in their tents; they impugn the Lord's motives.

Moses answers this negative and fearful reaction with a further word of assurance, similar to the end of verse 21 but in much more extensive fashion (vv. 29–30). His response again assures the people that they do not have to be afraid; he adds some clear reasons. In effect we have here the primary gospel genre of the Old Testament, the promise of salvation. This word was given to people in distress and fear to say that they need be afraid no longer. Such assurance is grounded in a reminder of the relationship between God and the troubled one(s) and a promise of God's involvement to help and to save them out of their distress. One hears such words echoing through the Scriptures from Abraham (Gen. 15:1–5) and Isaac (Gen. 26:24), to the prophet of good news to the exiles (Isa. 41:8–13, 14–16; 43:1–4, 5–7; 44:1–5), to the angel's message to frightened shepherds (Luke 2:8–14).

Two important images, the Lord as warrior and as parent, convey Moses' assurance to the fearful Israelites. The image of God as warrior is rooted in the origins of Israel's existence and the conflicts with various hostile forces. Because the Lord fought for Israel and gave them victory, the primary demand on them was that they trust in God's power to save. This did not mean that Israel never fought. It meant that a power beyond themselves was at work in the conflicts, enabling victory when there was confidence in that divine power. Without trust, Israel had better not fight; the power of God was not in their midst, as this story in its conclusion shows well. The particular phenomenology behind this reality is hard to uncover. Some stories speaking of panic and confusion among the enemy and attributing that to God (e.g., Josh. 10:10) and occasionally to divinely directed human stratagems (Judg. 7:19–23) are suggestive. But the accounts testify both to the power of God and to the interaction of divine and human involvement.

The combination of the saving, fighting activity of God with the caring, supporting relationship conveyed by the parental image is a fundamental paradigm of Scripture for portraying God vis-à-vis the human community, both individual and corporate. It is intended to declare that in the deepest of troubles and in the face of the largest of threats you do not have to be afraid, for God is there with you to watch over you and will be at work to deliver you from trouble and threat. In this instance, Moses underscores the exemplary character of this promise of salvation by identifying God's saving activity here with what the Lord did in the exodus and God's caring protection with the way God bore Israel through the wilderness. In other words, the primal events and experiences of the people demonstrated the dual grounds for assurance in the future. Moses says, in effect, As God redeemed you at the beginning and was with you along the way, so it will be in the future; therefore, you need not fear.

The image of God as the father carrying the young, inexperienced, frightened, and not very powerful child is an apt simile for Israel's experience; it is also a rich and powerful picture of God to be exploited in the teaching and preaching of this text. It is not unlike the eagle imagery used in Exodus 19:4–6 and Deuteronomy 32:10–12 to speak of God's way with Israel in the wilderness—protecting, providing for, and training the people. The combination of the mighty arm to deliver (warrior) and the tender protecting arm to care and support appears frequently in Scripture, as exemplified in the functions of the shepherd's rod (to ward off wild beasts) and staff (to keep sheep from wandering astray) that alleviate fear and anxiety (Ps. 23:4) or in the picture of God the ruler coming as warrior and shepherd carrying the lambs that is the content of the good news announced to Zion (Isa. 40:9–11). These images—warrior, parent, eagle, shepherd, and monarch—belong together. They combine the traits that best characterize God and thus provide a continuing ground for assurance and good news to the community of faith.

The appropriate response to such a word of assurance, notes Claus Westermann, is trust and joy (pp. 11–12). The very declaration of assurance is intended to evoke such a reaction. But that is not what comes from the people (1:32–33). Their *third response* is still unrelenting fearfulness, despite continued reassurance. They do not trust in the Lord whose way with them, as Moses notes, has been trustworthy. Note that in verses 19–33 there are four statements about the Lord. Those of the spies and Moses are positive statements about what God has done in behalf of Israel (vv. 25*b*, 30–31, and 33). The statement of the people is a very negative one about the Lord's attitude toward them (v. 27*b*).

Then—and not surprisingly—comes the Lord's angry response, a vow of judgment characterized by irony: The land is given to you; you are afraid to take it; therefore you will not receive it (vv. 34–40). Only Caleb and Joshua, who believed in the possibilities of God and the people and the land, shall be allowed to see promise fulfilled and possibility become reality.

The sharp disjunction between a trusting response, willing to risk danger in the confidence of God's assurance, and fearful-

33

ness, that sees only danger and does not believe in the Lord's presence and power, is underscored by a repeated use of emphatic contrast language. The emphasis is present in the Hebrew but does not come through in the English until one underlines the following pronouns: *he* . . . to *him* (v. 36); against (angry with, RSV) *me* . . . *you* also (v. 37); *he* shall enter; encourage *him,* for *he* shall cause Israel to inherit it (v. 38); [*they*] shall go in there, and to *them* I will give it, and *they* shall possess it (v. 39); but as for *you* (v. 40). (On the anger of God against Moses, see the comment on 3:23–29.)

In verses 41–46 all is inverted. There is confession of sin on the part of the people and now obedience. But, ironically, the obedience turns into presumption and disobedience. The people who inverted the meaning of the exodus into an act of God's hatred rather than God's love (v. 27) find that their effort to wage holy war against the Amorites is turned into a very unholy war. Their battle cannot be the Lord's war if the Lord is not in their midst. Victory will not come to warriors who do not trust in the Lord—and so defeat ensues. The command given in verse 40 now is not to go up and fight but to turn and journey "in the direction of the Red Sea." Thus while seeming at this point to obey the Lord, they are again disobeying. The divine command is no longer to fight but to leave. The people, however, decide not to leave but to fight. Three times, with increasing intensity (vv. 22, 26–28, and 32–33), the people have refused to go up into the land. Then when God announces punishment and Moses says turn and journey, implying that this unhappy episode is over and it is time to move on, the people *disobey again.* So obedience became disobedience and the weeping and penitential rites of a faithless generation were not heard by the faithful Lord (v. 45).

One question may arise in the mind of the reader of this story: *Who are the Anakim?* The answer to that question is important, though not in the sense of trying to locate this people historically or geographically. References to them elsewhere in the Bible (cf. Num. 13:33; Josh. 11:21–22; 14:15; 15:13–14) and in extrabiblical texts place them as a group in southern Palestine, especially in the area around Hebron. Deuteronomy seems uninterested in such details, although it does show interest in the Anakim; they are referred to here and also in 2:10 and 20 and 9:2. To answer the question about the Anakim one must look at all of these references.

34

In 2:10 and 20–23 we have, in the midst of the narrative, rather extended parentheses about peoples who formerly lived in these parts. While it would be easy to skip over these parentheses, they are not merely historical footnotes of purely antiquarian interest. The Anakim are the primary category. They are the ones who strike fear in the hearts of the people (1:28; cf. 9:2); they are the ones to whom other people such as the Emim, Rephaim, and Zamzummim are compared. All the references describe the Anakim as many and tall and mention their great fortified cities. In the context of these chapters, therefore, the Anakim are a *paradigmatic symbol*. They embody the problem that is too great, that strikes fear into the hearts of the people. They point to the power of the Lord as the one who is able to overcome such mighty heroes as the Anakim. One notes in 2:36 and 3:5 that after the generation of the fearful ones is gone, the Lord's might enables the people to handle these tall people and great cities. That is also suggested by the parenthetical reference to the nine-cubit bed of Og (3:11). He is either one of the Anakim or like them, but he has now been defeated. The final reference to the Anakim (9:2) reiterates their fearsome reputation and character and declares that the Lord will destroy and subdue them, enabling the people to drive them out.

A further motif conveying the contrast between fear and faith at the heart of this story is *the seeing motif*. The critical question of the unit is, What do you see? The contrasting answers—and perspectives—are found when one compares verses 19, 30, and 31 with verse 28. Moses points out to the people that they saw the great and terrible wilderness through which they safely passed (v. 19), that the Lord fought for them before their very eyes (v. 30), and that they saw the Lord care for them in the wilderness (v. 31). Yet in spite of what happened before their eyes, they did not trust the Lord. They saw the Anakim (v. 28). In other words, they "saw" the might of the enemy and did not "see" all the demonstrations of the power of God. Further, Moses says, they passed safely through the great and terrible wilderness, as they saw, but now they are fearful of the greater people and cities they see before them. This seeing language parallels the belief language and is, in fact, a kind of faith language; the story really is dealing with the contrast between eyes of faith and eyes of disbelief. That contrast is accentuated in verses 35 and 36. Because the people did

35

not really "see" the Lord's power—that is, trust that the Lord was with them and could give them victory over their enemies—they shall not "see" the good land (v. 35). Caleb, according to the account in Numbers, did trust that they could take the land with the Lord's help; he will "see" the land (v. 36).

Conclusion. This lengthy narrative opens the Book of Deuteronomy with a history lesson whose focus is primarily on the persistent fearfulness and disobedience of a people in the face of an experience of the gracious love of God. Over and over, Israel received the divine promise and assurances (vv. 8, 21, 25, 29–31), but they were fearful and refused to act. The problem and disobedience of the people in Deuteronomy 1 is not pride and self-assertion (as, e.g., in Gen. 3) but sloth, fearfulness, and anxiety. They fear the future and its difficulties even when the past has demonstrated they can trust in the promises of God. The themes of this chapter, the Anakim and their cities, the seeing motif, and the holy-war language, all underscore the focus of Moses' speech on trust in the power and promise of God. This manual of instruction for life in that new land can be of no use if one is unwilling to risk the future. Fearfulness and anxiety about future large and real problems will not get one across the border into the new land. The issue is not whether the Anakim are there, mighty and tall. They are indeed. If one doubts that, one has only to view King Og's fourteen-foot bed! The issue, however, is whether the people will "see" that God has brought them safely by the Amalekites to this point (Exod. 17) and can and will give them victory over the Anakim they see ahead.

In that sense, chapter 1 sets up what Deuteronomy is about. It will echo and anticipate disobedience and unwillingness to live by promise and instruction. Further, the chapter gives us clues about the purpose and context of Deuteronomy. It is a word of instruction about how to live in the land, addressed to a people whose history reflects persistent faithlessness and disobedience (cf. the commentary on 2:14b–16).

Peace and War on the Way (2:1—3:11)

Chapter 2 marks the next stage of the journey (v. 1) in Moses' account. It is a story of uneventful encounters and large battles with hostile enemies as the people move from Kadesh-barnea around and through territory of neighboring peoples to

36

reach the border. These contrasting experiences on the way are important to the theological perspective of this book on the Lord and on Israel's relation to other peoples, especially her neighbors.

Each section of this unit has essentially the same structure:

	Journey-Stage Marker	*Divine Command*	*Report of Accomplishment*
Edom/Esau	2:1	2:3–7	2:8a
Moab	2:8b	2:9–13a	2:13b
Ammon	2:18	2:18–20	
Sihon	2:24	2:24–31	2:32–37
Og	3:1	3:2	3:3–11

This shared structure points out the degree to which events in this section are seen as thoroughly controlled by the divine intention. All that happens rises out of the divine command. This is one of the basic assumptions of Deuteronomic theology, that the Lord is sovereign over history, declaring a word and directing its accomplishment.

The events summarized here in Moses' speech are narrated also in Numbers 20–21 and 33:37–49, but the Deuteronomic account differs in several ways. One difference is the structured and very formalized, repetitive way the events are reported. For example, in Deuteronomy 2, Edom is designated only by the personal name Esau, never by the geographical or national designation. The kinship factor is what counts in Deuteronomy's understanding. Further, the Deuteronomy account depicts Edom as afraid, in direct contrast to the Numbers depiction of this people as hostile and threatening. In Numbers the Israelites are stopped and go around Edom, whereas in Deuteronomy Israel passes through and is aided (2:4, 6). These differences press one to wonder what really happened. But that is not so easy to determine in these reports. They describe events from a distant time and are accounts more in service of theology than history. Deuteronomy 2 and 3 by their very structure assume a theological intention that carries over into the presentation of events. Several aspects of that intention may be noted.

First, the conviction of Deuteronomy about the divine control of events is reflected here and in each of these sections. Nations opposing Israel were defeated; those they did not defeat are seen as not opposing Israel (Noth, p. 30). The Lord's gift

37

of the land brooked no opposition; the Deuteronomic narrative does not allow for or indicate any successful autonomous threat or resistance to the divine intention. Even Sihon's opposition is not autonomous in the eyes of Deuteronomy. The Lord's sovereign control is evident even there. God hardened Sihon's spirit, a point not made in the Numbers account (cf. the encounter with Sihon, Num. 21). The complexities of the actual events, from the Deuteronomic point of view, give way to the clear and present reality that the Lord gave the Israelites the land; divine power and intention affected and effected all the events along their way to claiming it.

Second, the narrative goes further. It does not simply report that Edom allowed Israel to go through peacefully. Israel is in control here, and Edom/Esau is afraid (v. 4). The avoidance of conflict is by Israel's decision at the Lord's command (v. 5). The narrative gives two theological grounds for leaving Edom/Esau alone, reasons that apply as well to the Moabites and the Ammonites. These are the kinship relation ("your brothers," v. 4; cf. v. 8; NRSV, "kindred" and "kin") with Edom/Esau and the divine allotment of land to Esau or Edom. Both reasons have a connection with fundamental biblical claims. The first is the significance of the category of "brother" (or "sister," as the case may be, for the term here must be understood inclusively, thus the NRSV "kindred"). From the story of Cain and Abel through Psalm 133 into the injunctions of Jesus about being reconciled to your brother (Matt. 5:24) and care for "the least of these my brethren" (Matt. 25:40), there is a fundamental assumption throughout the Bible that relationships count for something and affect the way the persons in those relationships live and act and think. To exist as brother or sister is to have a claim on but also a responsibility for another. Brothers and sisters stand on the same plane and share rights and duties. To live with a brother means to seek peace and harmony (Ps. 133). Deuteronomy sets forth a number of laws that describe special obligations upon each Israelite in dealing with a brother (e.g., chs. 15 and 25). The category of "brother" is connected also in Scripture with the categories of "friend" and "neighbor," which serves continually to broaden the possible implications of the former term. The category, however narrow or broad, is one of moral value because it defines a relationship in which certain kinds of acts are appropriate, especially those that demonstrate care, beneficence, and a sense of responsibility.

The other ground for Israel's not harassing Edom, Moab, and Ammon is the fact that the Lord gave them their territories as a possession. The text is markedly similar to the way Deuteronomy speaks of God's gift of land to Israel. Here the nationalistic concerns and claims of Israel are expanded. The Lord's gifts of blessing, as exemplified in the provision of land and place, are not confined to a single people. Others are given a possession. The family story is broadened here to include the children of Lot. The neighbors of Israel are not simply their enemies; some of them at least are to be regarded as kinfolk, sharing the blessing of God. The notion of divine allotments beyond that given to Israel is echoed in Deuteronomy 32:8–9. This broadening of the Lord's gift of blessing to include other peoples is paralleled by the clear declaration in Amos 9:7 that exodus deliverance by the power of God is something other nations have also experienced. Placed now in a larger context, the gift of land may be seen as in some way typical of the Lord's activity and not simply as peculiar to the relationship of God and Israel.

A third aspect of theological intention occurs at verses 14*b*–16, a turning point of some significance in this whole narrative. They demonstrate that the critical issue in these chapters really is the question of Israel's trust and confidence in the Lord's promise and gift of the land. The key for the remainder of the book is Israel's faithfulness to that promise, as demonstrated by their manner of life. In chapter 2, however, the matter of trust in the promise of God is the issue. For it is only after the death of this generation that it is possible for Israel to move on into the land and be victorious over her enemies. These verses report the demise of all the fearful holy warriors of the generation that came out of Egypt. Holy war language is used here: the hand of the Lord, which brings panic and plague (cf. Miller and Roberts), and the verb translated "to destroy" (*hamam*), the term that refers to the Lord's discomfiting (Exod. 14:24) and creating panic among the enemy (Josh. 10:10), thus destroying them in battle (Judg. 4:15). In this case, however, the holy war is against the fearful holy warriors of Israel. God will not give an enemy into the hand of Israel until the fearful generation is gone. The fundamental requirement upon Israel's soldiers in battle was trust in the power of God. Without that confidence, victories will not come. One notes that in this Deuteronomic report of the wilderness years there are indeed no military victories to this

39

point. Now the Lord can lead the people against Sihon and Og with soldiers who trust God to guide them.

A fourth point is that if land is seen as God's good gift to other peoples than just Israel, why do all the peoples not receive God's good gift of land? Or, to put it another way, why are some peoples destroyed in the process of God's provision for others? There are probably no easy or ultimately satisfying answers to such a question. One must acknowledge the partially ideological character of this material as a human justification for human goals and acts (see Miller, "Faith and Ideology"). But to acknowledge this does not by definition invalidate the claims of the text. We, at least, can recognize some concern within Deuteronomy for justification of the violent destruction, and some reasons are given. Apart from the Lord's intention to provide a home and land for God's people, there are two criteria for the destruction of inhabitants of the land: (1) those who oppose God's purpose and promise to Israel—that is, Sihon and Og; and (2) those who seem to pose in a special way the problem of religious contamination and syncretism—that is, the Canaanites and Amorites.

Two instances of such violent destruction of Israel's enemies are in this unit. In dealing with them, it must be said from the beginning that there is no real way to make such reports palatable to the minds and hearts of contemporary readers and believers. There certainly is no way such reports instruct our lives in the matter of the conduct of war or in dealing with enemies. We have learned too much from the Scriptures about humane treatment of other persons, about special regard for the weak and powerless (e.g., women and children), and about another way of dealing with enemies: with the power of love rather than hatred, belligerence, or destruction. We cannot step back from what the Bible has taught us about these matters and what we know to be true. What we can do is try to understand what these reports teach so that they make some sense to us in the whole, even if they give no moral guidance for war.

These accounts of total destruction of the enemy are not merely general reports of defeat and destruction. Where the Revised Standard Version uses the language "utterly destroyed" or "devoted to destruction" (Josh. 6:17, 18), it is translating words that have to do with a particular sacral war practice, often called the ban: that is, placing captives—and often booty—under the ban of destruction as a sacral act of

40

devotion to the deity. It was not a common custom, but neither was it peculiar to Israel. In Israel, it became increasingly a part of the ideology of warfare *in retrospect* more than in actual practice. It is likely that the ban was actually imposed rarely, and certainly far less often than later accounts indicate. Its frequent appearance in Deuteronomic literature is probably a reflection of the martial spirit of Deuteronomy, which in turn grew out of the conflict with the religion of Israel's neighbors and the revival of the militia and the martial spirit in Judah in the seventh century B.C.E. C. H. W. Brekelmans, in an extended study of this phenomenon, has made a good case for the conclusion that historically the ban was imposed in only three cases of offensive wars—Numbers 21:1–4; Joshua 6—7; and I Samuel 15. In the early period the ban was a vow to God, made in very dangerous and difficult battles to make certain of God's help. While the vow was acceptable to God according to the narratives, it was, in origin, essentially a human act *in extremis.* Three things happened to the interpretation of the ban as the Deuteronomic traditions and the literature growing out of them looked back on that early history: (1) The practice of the ban was leveled through the conquest traditions in Deuteronomy and Joshua in order to make it a standard element of the conquest wars, whether or not that was actually the case; (2) the ban, which at its beginning appears to have been an act of *human* initiative, was turned into a *divine* command; and (3), especially important, the Deuteronomist seeks to show, either implicitly or explicitly, that the purpose of the ban was to remove all aspects of the Canaanite religion and culture so that the worship of the Lord, the God of Israel, might not be corrupted. In 7:1–6 the command to impose the ban, utterly destroying the seven nations who inhabit the land, is expanded. In the prohibitions against making covenants or intermarrying with any of these people, the purpose of the ban is most clearly seen. The reason for such strong measures is that these nations would turn the children from following the Lord, thereby arousing the anger and judgment of God (v. 4). The same understanding of the ban is present in 13:6–18, where statutes are set forth decreeing the execution of any person who would entice others to serve other gods and prescribing the ban for any Israelite city whose inhabitants have been drawn away into the worship of other gods.

41

The ban, therefore, in the Deuteronomic ideology is a con-

sequence of its basic claim as embodied in the first commandment and the Shema (6:4–5). For Israel, there can be no other
God, nor can commitment to their Lord be less than total. To
the contemporary reader accustomed to modern notions of religious toleration, which are indeed worthy and to be carefully
protected, such a consequence seems extreme. It did in its own
time also. But Deuteronomy is not a theological statement ab-
stracted or created apart from the context of historical existence. On the contrary, it was formulated out of a long history.
That history was filled with intrusions of the religious claims of
Canaanites and the other peoples of Palestine; it included as
well the experiences of Israel's less than full devotion to the
Lord who saved and blessed them. The Deuteronomistic History in Joshua through Second Kings is a story of constant or
recurring apostasy. The tension between the Israelites and their
neighbors was fundamentally a religious conflict, a struggle for
the soul of Israel. Would it belong to the Lord, the God of Israel,
or to Baal of Canaan? The latter often seems to have won out,
at least temporarily. So those persons responsible for creating
and shaping the traditions of Deuteronomy saw the need for a
clear separation from religious movements that qualified the
full commitment to the Lord and the moral purity and righteousness that was the Lord's way for Israel (cf. 20:16–18). Maintaining such allegiance required, in their sight, removal of all
temptation. Thus, in the light of later history, the Deuteronomists reinterpreted the place of the ban, the devotion to destruction of the enemies, giving it a more significant and
fundamental place and transforming the early conflicts of the
settlement in the land into a thoroughgoing religious battle
with the ban at the center as a divine command to avoid Canaanite contamination (see Miller, "Faith and Ideology").

Moses: A Suffering Servant (3:12–29)

These verses report the first allotment of land, in this case
to the Transjordanian territory that had been designated for the
tribes of Reuben, Gad, and Manasseh. The land was to be occupied when these tribes had helped their kinspeople take the
land across the Jordan (vv. 12–22).

In this section we also have one of Moses' prayers (vv. 23–
29). These prayers contribute to a profile of Moses as a type or
model figure that is anticipatory of later figures in the biblical

tradition. The primary components of this profile show Moses as a suffering servant, teacher (see discussion of 5:22–33), intercessor (see ch. 9), and prophet (see 18:9–22). The first component comes to the fore in these verses as well as in 1:37 and 4:21. While at one point in Deuteronomy, Moses' failure to enter the promised land is attributed to his breach of faith with God (32:51–52), the dominant view is that Moses was the Lord's faithful servant and that his death outside the promise was on account of God's anger with the people. Frequently in Deuteronomic literature, Moses is designated as servant of the Lord (e.g., 34:5). In the passages cited here he is clearly identified with the people in the punishment that is placed upon them. But the judgment on Moses is for *their* sin (1:34–37). Moses does not share their fearful perspective, but he shares their existence and so must suffer with them. In 3:26 as well as 21–22, the emphasis is even more on Moses' chastisement as representative of the people. For Moses is prohibited from entering the land on account of the sin of the people who are allowed to enter. We do not have here a full-blown notion of the salvation and forgiveness of the many brought by the punishment of the one, but we are on the way to that; and in the line of that innocent suffering one who is designated the Lord's servant and of whom it is said, as the people could have said of Moses:

> Surely *he* has borne our sicknesses
>   and carried our pains. . . .
> *He* was wounded for our transgressions,
>   bruised for our iniquities. . . .
> The Lord has laid on him the iniquity of us all.
>   (Isaiah 53:4–6; author's trans.)

Moses' failure to enter the land is not seen here as a meaningless accident or even simply a personal judgment upon him. This happening, like all happenings, is by the purpose and power of God. Of all people, Moses merited the promise. Not to receive it can be only because of the divine will. So, for the sake of the people, Moses bears the judgment. The one identifies with and gives his life for the many. The texts of Deuteronomy nowhere say that Moses' death outside the land is *in order that* the people might live in the land, but 4:21–22 especially puts these two realities close together. The sentence that ties all these passages together is "The Lord was angry with me on your account." That repeated "on your account" is an anticipation,

43

a beginning point in that stream of innocent servants who receive judgment rightly belonging to others. Those words are
meant to echo beyond these texts, reminding all who hear that
judgment becomes grace in the work of this God when the
Lord's own servant receives the judgment of God "on your
account." (For further perspective on Moses' death see commentary on ch. 34 and Miller, "Moses.")

EXCURSUS

The Deuteronomic Theology of the Land

Any theological treatment of Deuteronomy must ask about
its understanding of the land and its meaning for the faith and
life of Israel. Land in general is not the concern; it is rather the
land where Israel dwelt and which in the Deuteronomic era
was in danger of being taken away from God's people who had
lived for centuries on it.

The central affirmation about the land is that it is the gift
of God to Israel. All descriptions of it, of Israel's relation to it,
and of Israel's life in it grow out of this fundamental presupposition. Statements to that effect are frequent in all parts of Deuteronomy. There are, of course, other things that the Lord
gives—cities (20:16), gates or towns (16:5, 18; 17:2), peoples
(7:16), booty (20:14), rest and inheritance (12:9), blessing (12:15),
herds and flocks (12:21), sons and daughters (28:53), strength to
get wealth (8:18). The preeminent gift, however, is the land.
Most other benefits are related to it.

The goal and desire of the people of God is life in the land
God gives. Israel's existence as a people depends upon this land
and the grace of God. For Deuteronomy proclaims that Israel's
acquisition and possession of the land do not rest on prior claims
of sequence of generation or blood relationship, or on any just
deserts (9:4–6) because of their size or their conduct as a people.
Before Israel's entry the land belonged to many nations (7:11;
9:1; 11:23), and it came to Israel only by the desire of the Lord
to give it and by God's willing faithfulness to the promises (7:8).
Possession of the land and life in it are, therefore, the gift of
salvation; and the prime punishment Israel can suffer is its loss.
It offers untold benefits and opportunities but at the same time

places significant demands upon the individual and corporate life of the people. By exploring the various Deuteronomic expressions about the land, we may see how all this is so.

The Promise of Land to the Ancestors

There are eighteen explicit references in Deuteronomy to the Lord's promise of land to the patriarchs, and all but three speak also of God's giving it. The two themes of promise and gift are thus tied together in the Deuteronomic theology of the land. The promise to the ancestors here is understood entirely in terms of the land, which corresponds to and emphasizes the importance of this element in God's saving activity.

One notes the recipients of this gift as they are designated in the promise-to-the-ancestors formula. The land is given "to them" or "to you" or "to us." Deuteronomy can say that the Lord swore to give it to our ancestors or swore to our ancestors to give it to us. There is no real distinction. The promise to the ancestors was a promise to us. The gift to them was a gift to us. The recipients coalesce: the fathers or ancestors, those entering the land in conquest, and the present hearers. Those in this last group must hear the fact that even now they have no claims on the land but receive it and its benefits only as a gift by the grace of God; they may in fact lose it if they fail to fulfill their responsibilities to Yahweh, a good part of which have to do with their use of the land or their life on it (see below). The only human factor involved in the gift to Israel was the unrighteousness of the nations (9:5). The other factors were the love of God for Israel (7:8) and the divine desire "to establish the word which the LORD swore to your ancestors, to Abraham, to Isaac, and to Jacob" (9:5). In any event, it is clear that the present occupants cannot separate themselves from the past and the way in which the land came to them.

Israel's Possession of the Land

Alongside the oft-repeated affirmation that the land is God's gift, there is the frequent divine command to go in and occupy or possess it (e.g., 3:12). The occupation of the land, therefore, is not due to divine activity alone. Human efforts in military conflict bring about possession. Because the Lord has given the Israelites the land, they can go in, drive out the prior inhabitants, and possess it. The two notions of God's giving and Israel's taking are brought together in the expression "the land which

45

the Lord gives you to occupy/possess" (3:18; 5:31; 12:1; 15:4; 19:2,14; 25:19; cf. 1:39; 4:1; 17:14; 26:2). In a similar way 7:1–2 juxtaposes *God's bringing* of Israel into the land and *Israel's coming* into the land, *God's giving over* of the enemy and *Israel's defeat* of the enemy. The ideas of divine gift and human participation are not incompatible but are, rather, a part of the whole. Obviously the people knew they fought and took possession of the land from its occupants and would not hesitate to express what was celebrated throughout their history. Understanding the land as God's gift provided the people of Israel with an ideological rationale for taking it and dispossessing the inhabitants. In need of land, they took it in various ways and proclaimed it as God's gift in fulfillment of his promises. They saw all their military operations as guided by the Lord who led them out, sent fear upon the enemy, and gave Israel victory even against heavier odds. Taking possession of the land, therefore, was for Israel an act of faith and obedience.

Descriptions of the Land

The promised land is described primarily as *the good land* (1:25, 35; 3:25; 4:21, 22; 6:18; 8:7, 10; 9:6; 11:17), desirable and beneficent. In 1:25 the spies judge the land to be good because of the fruit and vegetation there, some of which they bring back to the people. The most detailed description is in 8:7–10, where the land is praised for all its desirable qualities. The opening and closing verses designate it as good, and the verses between list what may be found there: brooks, fountains, and springs flowing in the hills and valleys; wheat, barley, grapevines, fig trees, and pomegranates; olive oil and honey; bread without lack (in fact, nothing shall be lacking); iron and copper. The people shall eat and be full and bless the Lord in the good land. In 11:10–11 the promised land is contrasted with the land of Egypt. There shall be mountains and valleys, plenty of water from the rains. In 6:10–11 we read of "great and goodly cities," of houses full of every kind of good thing, of cisterns, vineyards, and olive trees. And again the point is made that the Israelites will eat and be full. This is all provided as the gift of God. Repeatedly and emphatically it is made clear that Israel did not build the cities and houses or plant the vineyards and olive trees. These are a part of the possession or inheritance that Israel receives.

46

The land is spoken of also as "flowing with milk and honey" (6:3; 11:9; 26:9, 15; 27:3; 31:20). The picture, of course, is of the ideal land filled in abundance with all the necessary provisions for life, a kind of paradise. The Israelite is thus called to bring the firstfruits to the sanctuary in specific, regular, and public acknowledgment that God has saved Israel in giving the people this good land for their use and enjoyment (26:1–11). In the present context it is impossible to separate the confession of faith in Deuteronomy 26:5–11 from this specific act of acknowledgment of God's gift and of Israel's responsibility.

Israel's Life in the Land

Deuteronomy makes many assertions about the quality of Israel's existence in the land and what it offers. Basically, it is a dwelling place, a home for the people (e.g., 17:14; 26:1). That was no insignificant fact in the context of these sermons, set at the conclusion of years of foreign slavery and wilderness wandering. Deuteronomy offers a reminder to later Israelites, long accustomed to living there, that the Lord had provided a dwelling place for their ancestors and that is why they may now call it home.

Related to this but going beyond it is the frequent assertion that God will give Israel rest in the land (3:20; 12:10; 25:19). As von Rad has put it, this is

> the altogether tangible peace granted to a nation plagued by enemies and weary of wandering. . . . The life of the chosen people in the "pleasant land," at rest from all enemies round about, the people owning their love for God and God blessing his people—this is the epitome of the state of the redeemed nation as Deuteronomy sees it ("There Remains Still a Rest," p. 95).

It is the ideal state of existence in covenant with God—at peace, free from war and conflict. There is an element of expectation here. The Israel of the Deuteronomist's time, still plagued by enemies and conflicts, looks forward to God's gift of rest in the land.

> This was indeed the basic premise of the deuteronomic theologians: Israel has indeed entered the promised land, but because they forgot Yahweh and clung to the cult of the baalim the promises have not yet been fulfilled. Nevertheless, Yahweh has not revoked his covenant. Thus before our eyes a miracle of faith is performed: the intervening period, wasted as it has been by sin, is expunged from the record, and Israel is carried back again to the hour of its first election (von Rad, "There Remains Still a Rest," pp. 95–96).

47

When we examine the ways Israel's life is described here, we recognize that the essential message is the offer of *life* in the land and all that entails. Here we come upon the basic theme, the kerygma of Deuteronomy to its readers and hearers: the word of a good life in a good land and the offer of that life as a genuine option to later generations (5:16; 6:18; cf. 28:11). The alternative, of course, is death and loss of the land. In other words, Israel receives the possibility of a special kind of life— good, undefiled life in community, life in the worship of Yahweh, life at its fullest and best.

In the land, Israel shall be blessed (15:4; 23:20; 28:8; 30:16). Although the land itself is not generally blessed, almost all references to blessing in Deuteronomy have to do with the land, the sphere where blessing is promised to the people (28:8). It will give fruit and not be barren, and the fruit of the ground and the work of the people's hands shall be blessed. Rain shall be plentiful, vegetation and animal life shall be abundant, and the people themselves shall multiply and prosper. Long life shall also be theirs on the land God gives. This traditional form of blessing is offered by God as a reward for righteousness.

So out of God's graciousness and love, Israel hears and receives the divine offer of a pleasant life in this place of abundance. But Deuteronomy repeatedly insists that this is all completely and totally contingent upon the character of Israel's response to its giving Lord, upon its love for God and obedience to God's commandments. Ultimately, therefore, it is not possible to speak of the gift of the land apart from obedience to God and God's law.

Land and Law

The land is not only the context in which blessing and life and prosperity take place. It is also the sphere in which Israel does what the Lord requires; the obedience of the people shall be visible there (4:5,14; 5:31; 6:12; 12:1). In 12:1, the whole law corpus is set in relation to the land: "These are the statutes and ordinances that you must diligently observe in the land that the LORD, the God of your ancestors, has given you to occupy, all the days that you live on the earth" (NRSV). Obedience is the sine qua non for continuing existence in the land, for Israel's life. Disobedience leads to war, catastrophe, loss of land, and death (4:26). The people have no life apart from the land, for their national existence depends on it. These were strong words to the hearers of Deuteronomy placed back again at the beginning of their history to receive once more the gift of life and land; but with it they assume the obligations to obedience, righteousness, and the love of the Lord.

The commandments of Deuteronomy, however, do not function simply as threat. They are indeed the condition for life in the land, as Deuteronomy repeatedly emphasizes (4:25–26; 6:18; 8:1; 11:8–12, 18–21). But there is another side to the function of the commandments in Deuteronomy. They are also the *norm* for life in the land, the *modus vivendi* as well as the condition (4:5–49; 12:1; 17:14; 19:1, 9; 21:1; 25:19; 26:1); neither aspect should be neglected. The warning to obey the divine commandments as a condition for continuing to possess the divine gift is clearly set forth. At the same time, the people learn the guidelines for how life under God and in community is maintained and happily enjoyed. Obedience to the commandments is not simply a necessity for worshiping God or avoiding divine retribution. It is necessary for harmonious and satisfactory life in the land, and according to Deuteronomy it is a quite possible achievement (30:11–14).

Many laws in the legal corpus of Deuteronomy are specifically associated with the land and Israel's existence on it: the year of release (15:1–6); judicial procedure (16:18–20); law of kingship (17:14–20); law against abominable practices (18:9–14); cities of refuge (19:1–3); not removing a landmark (19:14); expiation for an unknown murder (21:1–9); law against leaving a hanged man's body on a tree (21:22–23); divorce law (24:1–4); just weights and measures (25:13–16). Introductory or motive clauses relating to the land appear in all these laws. In some cases, disobedience of the law brings defilement or guilt upon the land itself (21:23; 24:4). In other cases, long life and blessing are motivations for obedience. The regulations for establishing the cities of refuge contain repeated reference to "the land which the Lord your God gives you" (19:1–3). The ethical basis is avoiding the guilt of shedding blood, but central to this is a sense of right treatment and behavior upon God's gift—the land. Responsible action in that context means special safeguards to protect the life of the innocent.

The land is frequently mentioned also in the homiletical elaboration of the law concerning the year of release, in each case with special reference to the care of the poor (15:1–18). The preacher recognizes that there will always be poor on the earth. The consequence of this fact is not, however, a passive acceptance of the situation but rather the command to open wide the hand to care for the needy. All members of the community must have access to the benefits and produce of the good land that comes as God's gift. If some do not benefit as much as others, special provisions in the order of society must be set to ensure their well-being. The Deuteronomist clearly recognizes that some will benefit more from God's gift than others, but insists that others in the community be provided for. The land is granted to all Israel by God and is to be used in that light.

In the paraenetic expansion of the legislation concerning judicial procedure (16:18–20), the land plays a significant role. Life and land are dependent on the firm adherence to righteousness and justice. Of course, unrighteousness leads also to death and the loss of land. The mode of living demanded of those who would receive and enjoy the divine gift is characterized by the effort to ensure that all who live in the land shall be treated justly.

In elaborating the Deuteronomic theology of the land, one must recognize the theological justification given for Israel's possessing a land inhabited by others—and thus also for its dispossession of the former inhabitants. Their wickedness and God's gracious gift in fulfillment of his promises form a rationale for Israel's possession of the land. Over against this, however, is the Deuteronomic self-criticism of Israel's life and obedience and the assertion that possession of the land is not automatic or eternal. The ideology that contributes to a theology of the gift of the land can also be used against the people and made the basis for their removal. Israel cannot justify its *original* possession of the land on the basis of its behavior; however, it must justify or preserve its *continuing* and *future* possession on that very basis, both in terms of the worship of God and of a proper use of God's salvation gift.

Toward a Theological Understanding of Land

The question of Israel's possession of land is clearly prominent in the Old Testament. There are at least two strains of theological understanding of the relationship of people and land. One of these is found in the Abrahamic figure set as a model of the wandering people of God, the obedient servant and agent of God, responding to God's call and leadership, willing to pull up stakes and go to the new place where God sends him. The emphasis here is on God's people as mobile, looking for God's new land. The image, therefore, is "nomadic."

Alongside this is the Deuteronomic picture of salvation as God's gift of a good land: the settled state of long life, enjoyment of the land, and happiness in the obedience and worship of the Lord. The image, therefore, is "sedentary," the emphasis less on the service of God in the world and more on the proper enjoyment of the gifts of God.

Clearly, these models or images overlap. The promise to Abraham was of a land where he and Sarah and their posterity might dwell. Abraham's goal is reached in Deuteronomy. And Deuteronomy, which builds upon the promise of land to the ancestors, recognizes and affirms the tenuousness of Israel's life there. But Abraham and Sarah and Lot moved in obedience; disobedience is the reason for the movement of later Israel. And once again the promised land is set as Israel's goal.

These emphases are related but are also in some tension. Both point to valid aspects of Christian existence. The New Testament has focused primarily on the former, the Abrahamic image. Certainly historical and social circumstances had much to do with that. The promised land has lost its geographical character, and the people of God are pilgrims and strangers on earth. The salvation gift of God in the New Testament is something other than life in a fixed physical environment. We are properly warned against an overattachment to the things of this world and given the offer of life that is eternal and transcendent. The Christ event redefines and fulfills the promises of God, growing out of but surpassing the promises of land and people. So for those who live by faith in Jesus Christ and the meaning and hope found in him, salvation and obedience cannot be viewed simply in terms of physical life in this world.

But the Christian understanding of a pilgrim existence on earth and a citizenship in heaven has not obviated the necessity for a theological and moral approach to our present existence on the "land"—or in the place where God has put us—and therefore to the use of land and property, particularly insofar as this affects both our present neighbor and our future posterity. The vastly altered circumstances do not preclude the fact that the Deuteronomic theology of the land held by the covenant community can inform the present and suggest implications for the contemporary scene.

The church hears in the words of this preacher a positive affirmation of the human desire for land and home, a place where one can live to one's full potential. The enjoyment of home, family, work, and the fruits of one's labors is a part of human existence, the desirable goal of human life. It is, to use the language of Paul Lehman, part of what God provides to make and to keep human life human. Despite the complexities of modern society, the role of land—physical, geographical—is no less important today, for the land functions both as home and as the source of wealth, the means of life. The proper enjoyment of life by all members of the human community depends upon this.

A theological understanding of life on the land, however, sets this in a specific context. Although we see the land as bought, worked for, fought for, inherited, we know ultimately that it always comes to us as God's gift. We cannot really stake a final claim to its possession by legal right, family heritage, or our physical and mental labors. It comes and will always come not only by human strivings but by the gracious gift of God, who is the true owner of the land and enables us to live on it and use it. The way in which the Deuteronomic theology of the land holds together human action and divine grant is instructive in this regard. The essential fact, however, is always the grant or gift.

In the most elemental sense, therefore, the Christian and the Christian community accept these gifts and approach them primarily in an attitude of thanksgiving. Pride of ownership and possession and accomplishment is secondary and derivative. Furthermore, human ownership and use of the land are communal as well as individual. While we may and do react at times with renewed assertions of possession and right of ownership, we recognize with Deuteronomy that our life and death on the land are with our neighbor; the inheritance of one is a part of the inheritance of all. Contemporary society not only reflects the fact of our common participation in the gifts of God but in fact increases our awareness of the nearness of the neighbor and the claims of the neighbor to a part of the divine gift (Miller, "The Gift of God").

Deuteronomy 4:1–49
Call to Obedience

With this chapter, a significant turning point occurs in the Book of Deuteronomy as it reflects the movement of the people (see the introductory remarks on Deut. 1–4). Israel is now on the boundary, as verses 44–49 indicate with some specificity. The long trek through the wilderness is over and the opposing kings east of the border have been defeated. While it is true that the territory already conquered becomes a part of the divine inheritance or allotment to the tribes, the Deuteronomist constantly views the land west of the Jordan as the promised land the people are going in to possess (e.g., 6:1). They are now on the boundary, not yet in the land.

Moses, having recounted how they have been led by God's grace and providence—and, yes, under divine judgment also—to the edge of the promised gift, now tells them the implications of this story of God's providing care to this point. That begins in chapter 4 but continues through the rest of the book. At the same time—and this is the other side of the coin—Moses' call to obedience is a laying out for the people of the conditions and requirements for making it across the border. Obedience to the instruction of God is both the implication of their past history with God and the necessity for their future life with God.

The main part of this chapter is Moses' speech in verses 1–40. It is followed by a brief appendix on the cities of refuge (vv. 41–43), a subject taken up in more detail in chapter 19 (see commentary on 16:18—19:21), and by verses 44–49, which are a transition in that they summarize the book to this point and also serve as the introduction to the second speech of Moses in chapters 5—28 (see Introduction).

Within the speech itself (vv. 1–40) one may discern a prologue (vv. 1–8) and an epilogue (vv. 32–40), bracketing the core of the chapter in verses 9–31. Their character as brackets is demonstrated by the way in which they mirror each other and share certain formal and thematic elements: (1) Verses 1–8 begin with an injunction to keep the commandments and motivational clauses for doing so (v. 1), while verses 32–40 end in the same way (v. 40); (2) both introduction and conclusion share a reflection on the incomparability of Israel among the nations vis-à-vis Israel's *law* (vv. 1–8) and their *God* (vv. 32–40); and (3) both also use the device of rhetorical questions, a not uncommon feature of incomparability statements.

Law, Wisdom, and the Nearness of God (4:1–8)

Within this section two literary units, closely bound together by their similar structure, express different but related themes. This structure is that which appears elsewhere as a way of setting forth legal statements (Braulik, "Weisheit, Gottesnahe, und Gesetz," pp. 167–168). It begins with an *interjection* (hear!—v. 1 [RSV, give heed]; see!—v. 5 [RSV, behold]) calling for the attention of the hearers. Then comes the *legal statement* itself (vv. 1 and 5), centering in an *act of promulgation*. This is followed by motivations of reward (v. 1) and, in verse 5, by the legal basis for the passing on of the law (that is, "as the LORD my God commanded me"; cf. v. 20). There is as well an indication of the point in time when the law takes effect and of the sphere of its validity (v. 5*b*). *Imperative calls to keep the law* are set forth in verses 2*a* and 6*a*, and each is followed by *reasons or motivations to encourage obedience* (vv. 3–4 and 6*b*–8).

Several points stand out when the component parts of the passage are compared.

1. The first word, linguistically, structurally, emotionally, and theologically, is a call to attention and adherence that is picked up a second time in each unit: "Israel, give heed . . . and do them" (v. 1); "See. . . . Keep them and do them (vv. 5–6).

2. The hortatory style indicated by the imperative is carried further by the presence of motivation clauses for stimulating or provoking obedience. This is both rhetorical style and theological perspective. Obedience to the instruction of the Lord (or the teaching of Moses) is grounded in and encouraged by promise and claim. Here is no blind obedience, no testing of Israel, but a call to obey the Lord because that makes sense, is desirable and good. The preaching character of the book indicated already by the hermeneutics of history in chapters 1—3 is made explicit by the hortatory style of this chapter.

54   3. The motivations differ in the two units and are the primary manifestation of the thematic concerns of the parallel units. Verses 1–4 deal with *the laws of the Lord as the source*

of life. This is reflected in the clause at the beginning of the section where the purpose of obedience is "that you may live" and receive the gifts of life in the good land (v. 1). It is also indicated negatively by reminders of the life-and-death alternatives implied by obedience and disobedience (vv. 3–4). Following after the Baal of Peor is an explicit disobedience of the first commandment (see below) and brings death. Holding fast to the Lord, which is obedience of that same commandment, is life.

Verses 5–8 deal with *the laws of the Lord as the culture and wisdom of the people of Israel.* Here one finds in the motivation clauses neither promise of reward nor warning of judgment. Rather, the appeal is to the positive aspects of keeping the law and to pride in the reputation of Israel as *wise, close to God,* and *righteous.* All three of these characteristics are tied to the laws.

Keeping the laws of the Lord is not only appropriate, it is a demonstration of human wisdom. The point is not that the laws themselves are wise. The quality of the laws that matters here is their rightness (see below). Obedience conforms to the command of God, and keeping these laws works; it makes human community stable and ordered. The notion that keeping just laws is the smart thing to do, the wise thing to do, is of course intrinsic to any legal system or good instruction of any sort. Experience has taught that doing as one is commanded makes sense and enables the community to function harmoniously for the good of all. These characteristics, "wise" and "understanding," are generally applied to rulers (e.g., Joseph [Gen. 41:39] and Solomon [I Kings 3:12; cf. Isa. 11:2 and 29:14]) and identify a ruling wisdom. Here, however, regal-like discernment is available to and demonstrated by the people themselves in their keeping of the instruction for life given by the Lord.

The statutes and ordinances from the Lord through Moses are themselves *righteous.* What is probably being identified here is the social righteousness of these laws, their concern for the weak, the poor, and the slave. In that the law is humane, even with regard to treatment of the natural order, in that it seeks justice and impartiality in all cases, and in that it makes concern for the powerless and the disadvantaged the primary criterion of a just society, Israel's law as set forth in Deuteronomy demonstrated indeed a higher righteousness. The prophetic critique encountered elsewhere is not against the moral quality of Israel's laws but against the foolishness (i.e., lack of wisdom) and moral culpability of the people when they do not follow righteous laws and thus fail to manifest right conduct.

The relation of verses 6 and 8 to each other is clear in what they state about the wisdom of keeping right laws. But verse 7 seems to insert another matter altogether into the middle of the discussion—the nearness of God. It makes no allusion to the law and seems to be unrelated to its context as far as subject matter is concerned. Formally, however, the precisely parallel structures of verses 7 and 8 invite one to see a close association of the two verses:

> *What great nation is there that has gods near*
> *to it like* the Lord our God . . . ?
> *What great nation is there that has statutes*
> *and ordinances righteous as* all this law . . . ?

The italicized parts of the two verses are precisely parallel syntactically. Assuming that the train of thought between verses 6 and 8 is not intended to be interrupted, the collocation of verses 7 and 8 suggests that the nearness of God and the righteous laws are closely related. Two other passages help confirm this. In Deuteronomy 30:11-14, the near/far language appears again and sounds as if one is speaking of the nearness of God who dwells in the heart. But there it is the *commandment* that is near, not God. What is happening is that the commandment, the law, is almost a surrogate for God. The righteous laws being written on the heart and being kept are in some sense a manifestation of the presence of God. God draws near in the law that God gives. A similar perspective is found in verses 11–12, where God appears to the people not in any form but as a voice giving the words, the commandments.

Such an understanding of the law gives a different cast to Deuteronomy 10:1–5 from the one usually found in interpretations of this passage. It is commonly noted that the ark, which had earlier been viewed as the throne of the invisible presence of God (e.g., Num. 10:35–36; I Sam. 4:4), in Deuteronomic theology has become simply a container for the tablets of the law. But such an understanding ignores the high view of the divinely given instruction in Deuteronomy. If the law in some way embodies the presence or nearness of God, then the ark continues to function in some fashion as the vehicle for God's presence in the midst of the people. This word about the God who is near to the people in the law would have had a special impact on exilic Israel, far from the symbols of divine presence, set as they are in the midst of other nations. God can be, and is, near—in a way that is true of no other gods—in this law. And Israel will demonstrate its wisdom above all others in the careful attention it gives to keeping this law of God.

The relationship of divine word or instruction and divine presence is reiterated in verses 29–30, where seeking God wholeheartedly and with the whole self in exile leads to finding. This is juxtaposed with the declaration that there Israel will return to God and obey the voice of God: God's commandment. The point is even sharper if the use in both verses of the verb *maṣa'*, "find," is recognized in the translation so that verse 30 would read, "When you are in tribulation, then all these words [that is, the Lord's words of instruction] will find you in the latter days and you will return to the LORD your God." The words of the Lord, the law or instruction of God, will find Israel, which is at least in part how and why Israel will find the Lord. Once again, finding God is related to keeping the law.

Here, therefore, is a genuinely theological understanding of the law. It does not regard the commandments and instruction of God as a secondary matter or as a part of the horizontal human relationship distinct from the reality of the experience of God and the divine-human encounter. The righteous commandments and the keeping of them is the way that God is somehow known and found in the midst of the community. When the prophet Amos calls on the people of Israel to seek the Lord and live, and then equates that with the maintenance of justice in the human community, the same connection between worship and ethics, between the presence of God and obedience, is affirmed and reinforced.

A Sermon on the Second Commandment (4:9–31)

The Ten Commandments, given in chapter 5, are actually introduced in these verses and the central purpose of the law at Horeb (Sinai) and Moab is set forth: to hear and learn to fear the Lord. The aim here is both to teach the law and also, by the words of the Lord, to teach the fear of God: that is, the worship of God. The law of God has more than one purpose, but it is not an end in itself. It richly opens the way to the true worship of God, not only for those who first receive it but for succeeding

57

generations. They learn that in obedience to the law they may achieve that chief aim of human life as it is stated in the first question of the Westminster Shorter Catechism—to glorify and enjoy God forever.

The heart of the matter is the "ten words" (v. 13 margin,), which are identified as the sum and substance of the covenant. These ten words are the basic stipulations that declare the response and responsibility of the people of God. Further, it is indicated here and becomes increasingly clear in succeeding chapters that there is a kind of foundational, primary word beneath all the other words. That foundational word is embodied in the prologue to the Decalogue, together with the first and second commandments. The prohibition against images is the focus of this section, but the prologue and first commandment, the prohibition of the worship of other gods, are here also. Indeed, this is one of the texts that demonstrates how closely these commandments are tied together. The prologue is echoed in "the LORD has brought you forth out of the iron furnace, out of Egypt" (v. 20); the first commandment enters clearly in the allusion to bowing down and worshiping the astral bodies, other gods (v. 19). The covenant stipulation in this section is identified essentially with the monotheistic law of Israel. The expression of this that is the text upon which Moses preaches his sermon is the second commandment, whose language is pervasive in these verses: "you make a graven image for yourselves in the form" (vv. 16, 23; cf. 5:8), "what is on the earth (v. 17; cf. 5:8), "what is in the heavens (v. 19; cf. 5:8), "what is in the waters under the earth" (v. 18; cf. 5:8), "bow down to them and worship them" (v. 19; cf. 5:9), and "a jealous God" (v. 24; cf. 5:9).

The ground for the reiterated exhortation to keep the second commandment is laid in verses 11–12 with reference to hearing words but seeing no form. The primacy of the divine word in God's revelation is affirmed. And, paradoxically, the passage suggests that Israel had—and has—access to the Lord through the divine word but at the same time did not. There was no form—only word or voice. No figure, image, deity—only fire, darkness, cloud, and dark cloud. One should note the heaping up of these terms in verse 11 to emphasize the veiled, hidden mystery. The Hebrew text actually does not contain the words "wrapped in" (NRSV, "shrouded in"). The words "shrouded in" or "wrapped in" try to express in good English what the Hebrew simply juxtaposes in stark fashion as if to state a vivid paradox that cannot be explained: on the one hand, bright burning fire; on the other hand, the thickest black darkness. Thus are held together, as one, hiddenness and revelation, mystery and accessibility, transcendence and immanence.

The key symbol in the chapter is the fire, referred to seven times (vv. 11, 12, 15, 24, 33, 36 [twice]). This powerful image appears frequently in the Old Testament (Miller, "Fire"). Its symbolism in this context appears to be dual: illuminating and consuming. It is bright light, revealing, a radiance like the *kabod*, or "glory" of God, and thus appropriate for indicating the presence of God. But it is also mysterious. Fire repels as much as it draws. One is unable to touch it and is destroyed in touching it. It can be seen clearly but not approached and touched (cf. II Sam. 6:6–7). This point is explicitly indicated in the other references. Verse 24 speaks of the Lord as a devouring fire. Verse 33 asks if any people ever heard the voice of God speaking from the midst of a fire and still lived, implying that fire representing the divine presence is threatening and dangerous. The force of the symbol in conveying both the transcendence and immanence of God is seen in verse 11, where the mountain is spoken of as burning with fire *to the heart of heaven,* and in verse 36:

> *Out of heaven* he let you hear
> his voice, that he might discipline you; and
> *on earth* he let you see
> his great fire, and you heard his words
> out of the midst of the fire.

The images of cloud and fire and the voice without form point us to the heart of the prohibition of images as Deuteronomy 4 interprets it. The theological basis for this commandment is to be found in the mystery, transcendence, ineffability, and wholly "otherness" of God, who does not reveal self in transparent ways or in ways that allow one to see (as one sees the astral bodies) or touch (as with humanly created objects) God. Twice the claim is made: "You saw no form." Such is the reality of God, and no human action can alter that. The commandment is to ensure Israel's continuing realization of that transcendence.

59

The shape of the second commandment in verses 16–18, which is the most elaborated form in the Scriptures, indicates that the Deuteronomist has in mind the exclusion of any possible object of worship. But the motivation given here points strongly to the image of the *Lord* as the primary focus of the prohibition. Not only is the worship of other gods or images of other gods prohibited; any iconic form of the worship of the Lord is unacceptable. The commandment in its usage here thus points the people away from two categories of objects. One of these categories includes those objects that by their desirability and tangibility, their potential claim on our lives (e.g., sun and stars), could replace or contend with the Lord of life and nature and history for our fullest loyalty and surrender. The other category includes those objects that by their tangibility, visibility, and attractiveness could serve to represent God for us. They thus obscure the true relationship that belongs between Creator and creature, dissolve the mystery, eliminate the transcendence, and reduce the God above God to an "available god," opening up all our instincts to seek control over that which truly controls us. The true danger of all symbols, metaphors, and images (tangible, visible) is that they may reduce the irreducible reality that stands behind them all. That is even possible for the word in some form, but the word has a different character— both power and elusiveness, identification with the speaker and distinctiveness from the speaker. The word speaks and tells. It comes from the mystery that is God, but it does not eliminate the mystery. Here also, of course, is laid part of the ground for that understanding of revelation through the word that reaches its culmination in the Word made flesh that dwelt among us.

It is no accident that the interpretation of Christian faith found in Protestant Reformed theology, with its emphasis on the sovereignty of God and in the writings of John Calvin in particular, made the protest against idolatry a central theme. As John Leith has summarized Calvin's argument in Book I, chapters 11 and 12, of the *Institutes of the Christian Religion:*

> Idolatry is the attempt to get control of God by objectifying his power and presence and fixing them in some "thing." Idolatry is the transference of something that belongs to God to some created reality. It is the indiscriminate transference to the creature of what belongs to God alone (p. 113).

60

For Calvin, such idolatry was found in the veneration of saints, relics, icons, and the like. But Calvin was well aware that the problem was broader and not fully overcome by the removal of images and icons from all the churches, desirable as that may have been. Worship and liturgy can also be a means to attempt to manipulate God, to objectify and localize the Lord of history. Calvin even sensed the serious potential for turning our theological endeavors into idol factories, seeking by our theological systems and constructions to objectify the transcendent, deceiving ourselves into thinking that theologically we can see God. In the face of the second commandment as interpreted in Deuteronomy, preachers, teachers, and theologians hear a warning about the theological efforts that consume our energies. We may be playing with idols or playing with fire.

There is a postscript to this discussion of idols and images. When Deuteronomy 4 forbids making and worshiping the likeness of anything, male or female, any beast of earth, any winged bird that flies, anything that creeps on the ground, we hear in part the language of the Priestly creation story in Genesis 1; this biblical story reminds us that the human creature is the one permissible image of God. There one finds no human artifice to try to domesticate God or penetrate the mystery. Rather, in the human persons around us we encounter *God's* artifice, the divinely created image of God's self that the Lord has set in the world as ruler and steward. If we would look for something that in some way "images" God in a way accessible to our experience, we will find we have to deal with one another. It should also be all the more clear why the central revelation of God should come to us in categories of *word* and *incarnation* (Miller, "Most Important Word").

Such a God as This! The Sermon Concluded (4:32–40)

The conclusion to Moses' exhortation to obedience (vv. 32–40) in chapter 4 serves as a kind of epilogue balancing the prologue in verses 1–8, especially in its affirmation of the incomparability of the Lord of Israel; this claim in some sense echoes the claims of Israel's incomparability in verses 1–8. These verses, however, are not simply a concluding bracket to match the prologue. They arise out of the sermon on the second commandment (vv. 25–31) and build upon it in an almost climactic way that holds together—as Deuteronomy so often does—the *grace* and the *demand* of God.

The situation is that of a people in exile, under judgment, though the intention of the text is not confined to an exilic experience. As is so often the case in Deuteronomy, the text addresses different aspects of the human situation. Whether one does not yet enjoy the rich blessing of God in concrete ways, or has that blessing firmly in hand, or has enjoyed and then lost it, the claims of the text are several.

1. The demand of God in the primary commandment is serious, with life-and-death implications, a point especially made in verses 25–31. The extended exhortation to obedience of the second commandment leads to a recognition that if this is the heart of the law, it is also the heart of the people's failure (vv. 25–30). From this point on, the sermon explicitly addresses a people who had been tested and found wanting. The fundamental demand to let nothing take the place of God in the mind and heart, the eye and hand, the allegiance and commitment had crumbled and the promise of judgment built into the second commandment had become a reality (Deut. 5:9). Making idols is not just a bad idea. Whatever form idolatry might take, it brings the judgment of God, for the Lord is a jealous God (v. 24). Here, as in so many places in Scripture, the biblical writers seek to explain history, especially history cast in judgment. As is also frequently the case in the prophetic view of history, there is a profound irony or poetic justice perceptible (Miller, *Sin and Judgment*). Israel's willing idolatry leads to a forced idolatry (v. 28). To choose lifeless forms in place of God is to be given into the hands of lifeless forms rather than the living God.

2. The future remains genuinely open: repentance is possible; return is expected. Time and again Deuteronomy declares that judgment is not the final word; the way is always open for Israel's repentance and renewal. Two things are to be noted about this return. The renewal happens out of Israel's searching and finding and also from the Lord's neither failing nor forgetting (vv. 29–31). Renewal of relationship does not happen here without the earnest initiative of the people to seek the Lord, an activity that includes not only prayer but righteous living. But neither is that turning of the heart purely a human accomplishment. The return that will take place, the finding of God that will surely happen, is because the Lord does not fail or destroy the people bound in covenant. Nor does God forget the covenant. Although it was *made* with earlier generations, *God* does not set it aside (v. 31). Human seeking and divine faithfulness create a new possibility beyond the pain of judgment.

62

3. The triumph of grace is a testimony to the incomparability of the Lord of Israel. Here is the essential and climactic point of verses 32–40. Undergirding the claim that Israel will return because God is gracious and compassionate is a catalog of God's acts, laid out at length. They all manifest the divine will to save, preserve alive, or redeem (vv. 33–39). God is a jealous God (v. 24), but God is also merciful (v. 31), and God's grace is triumphant; these acts of God also serve to make the case that there is no other God but the Lord (v. 35). Karl Barth has caught well the relationship between God's grace and God's incomparability in the following comments:

> It is in His love above all that God reveals Himself as the One who is incomparable and therefore unique; which means He reveals Himself as the true and essential God. . . . The God of the Old Testament is not, then, the God to whom uniqueness accrues or is ascribed as a kind of embellishment drawn from the stores of creaturely glory, which He may now wear as the images of the heathen gods wear their embellishments of gold and silver. On the contrary, He is the God who possesses uniqueness in the love that is actively at work on Israel, a uniqueness that is His own, a divine, a unique uniqueness, unique in comparison with all human uniqueness (II/1, pp. 450, 452–453).

God's communication in word and fire, the mighty deliverance from Egyptian slavery and oppression, the love of God for the fathers and mothers of the past, the election and salvation of the present generation, and the gift of a place to live—all these things serve to undergird the two primary theological convictions of the Book of Deuteronomy, summarized succinctly in the Shema (Deut. 6:4): The Lord is our God and will keep the covenant relationship going, and the Lord alone is God. None can compare with such a God as this! In these verses, therefore, proclamation of the grace of the Lord and apologetic argument of the case for the Lord are joined together and form the ground for the final injunction, which is a return to the initial word: So keep the divine rules and regulations.

PART TWO

Moses' Second Address: The Law Proclaimed

DEUTERONOMY 5—28

The second speech of Moses is made up of two parts. The first of these, chapters 5—11, is a presentation of the basic stipulations of the covenant, the Decalogue and the Shema, set out in the context of an extended exhortation on the primary words of the divine instruction, which are expressed particularly in the Shema and the first and second prohibitions of the Ten Commandments. The second part is the promulgation of the laws and the blessings and curses that serve to sanction their obedience (chs. 12–28). The introduction to this long speech is found, as we have noticed, in the closing verses of chapter 4 (44–49). The "testimonies" referred to there probably are found in the Ten Commandments, while the "statutes and ordinances" refer to the various pieces of legislation contained in chapters 12–26. McBride suggests that here is the heart of the polity that Deuteronomy sets forth, found in the "treaty stipulations" (RSV, "testimonies") and the "statutory rulings" (RSV, "statutes and the ordinances").

Deuteronomy 5—11
The Most Important Words

In some ways these chapters are the centerpiece of the book. Clearly, these are the most important words for those who would cross the border to live as God's people in the place and in the way that God has set for them (Miller, "The Most Important Word"). In these chapters, the community receives both the "ten words," or Ten Commandments, the basic requirements for the community's life (5:6–21), and that summary statement of the demand of God known as the Shema, which in both Jewish and Christian tradition has come to be identified as the Great Commandment, the concise embodiment of all the commands of God—indeed, of all that matters in the relationship between people and God (6:4–5). The rest of this section is explicit exposition of the Shema and the Ten Commandments, especially the prologue and the first and second commandments (5:6–10), which are in some ways equivalent to the Shema or a form of the primary commandment within the Ten Commandments (cf. below on 5:6–21). Careful reading of these chapters uncovers continuing reference to the concerns of the Shema and the first and second commandments, as well as explicit repetition of their words and phrases. In such exposition, definition and identification of Israel in relation to God and to the neighboring peoples continues.

The Law Given and the Law Taught (5:1–5, 22–33; 6:1–3)

These verses form a framework around the Ten Commandments and the Shema. They serve also to give some indication of the importance of the commandments; they set them off from what follows.

Like the sections immediately before and after this one (4:1 and 6:4), this section opens with the call to hear; at one and the same time it is a call to attention and an exhortation to obedience (see commentary on 6:4). The opening words in 5:1 are echoed in the concluding words of 6:3, and together they serve to bracket the whole, setting all these words in the context of exhortation. Verse 1 proper seems not to refer to the Ten Commandments, or Decalogue, but to the rest of the laws, for the following reasons: (1) The reference is to "the statutes and ordinances," which are to be found in chapters 12—26, rather than to "the words" or "the ten words," as the Ten Commandments are called (cf. 4:13); and (2) Moses speaks in the present and future (v.1), whereas the commandments were spoken by the

Lord in the past at Horeb and Moses was the mediator of the "word of the LORD" (v. 5).

Verse 1, therefore, is probably better understood as Moses' own introduction to the primary Deuteronomic law he is going to teach them (chs. 5—26) and they are going to learn, as distinct from the narrator's editorial introduction in 4:44–49. By recalling at the start the givens of the Ten Commandments at Horeb (Sinai), Moses begins the teaching of the statutes and ordinances by rooting them in the covenant and its stipulations, the Decalogue. It is a way of saying that all his further teaching, all the rest of the divine instruction for human life, grows out of and is an explication of the basic requirements and directions set forth in the commandments.

A second feature of the opening words of chapter 5 is its insistence in verse 3 on the contemporaneity of the covenant. This verse expresses a kind of hermeneutical formula for the book. The time gap and the generation gap are dissolved in the claim that the covenant at Sinai, the primal revelation that created the enduring relationship between the people and the Lord, was really made with the *present* generation. The covenant is not an event, a claim, a relationship of the past; it is of the present. The time between the primal moment and the present moment is telescoped, and the two are equated. The covenant at Horeb was *with us here.* Indeed, the text explicitly declares that one is not to view the covenant as having been made with previous generations (3*b*). "Our fathers" (NRSV, "our ancestors") may refer to the patriarchs or to the exodus generation. But the effect is the same. The actualization of the covenant and its demands is for the present. The emphasis on the covenant as a present claim rather than a past event is laid out especially in the second half of verse 3, the force of which is best conveyed by reproducing the Hebrew rather literally: The covenant was made not with our ancestors but "with us, we, these ones, here, today, all of us, living." The text uses seven words heaped one upon another to stress the contemporary claim of the covenant. The effect is clear. The hortatory character of the chapter and the book combines with the actualizing language of this verse to cut across all the generations and renew the covenant afresh with *all* hearers of these words.

The main point in this framework section is that distinction already referred to between "commandments" and "the statutes." The commandments are given by God directly to the

67

people, while the statutes, the rules and regulations, are given to Moses to *teach* the people. This distinction is rooted in two related realities: the nature of God and the relationship between God, Moses, and the people. The understanding of God that contributes to this distinction is the same as the one found in the extended sermon on the second commandment of chapter 4. The mystery that is God, experienced in the encounter with fire and voice, cannot be approached. After receiving the commandments, the people fear to stand before either fire or voice, for both will destroy them (vv. 25–26). It is as if the people consider themselves almost unbelievably—and uniquely—fortunate to have survived such an encounter once; they survived when the ten words were given, and they dare not risk it again. The judgment of the people that Moses should teach the divine word is approved by the Lord (vv. 28–33).

There is within the narrative a tension about the direct hearing of the Ten Commandments. On the one hand, the text says that "the LORD spoke to all your assembly" (v. 22) and indeed "face to face" (v. 4). On the other hand, the people were afraid to go up, and Moses stood between them and the Lord to declare the word to them (v. 5). So even the ten words are seen to have been mediated to some extent. But a step further away from direct revelation is taken when the arrangement is made for the Lord to communicate only with Moses, who in turn will teach the people all the Lord's instruction.

Several important conclusions may be drawn from this narrative, especially if one compares the account in Deuteronomy 5 and following with the account of the giving of the law at Sinai in Exodus 19–24. A distinction between the Ten Commandments and other statutes and ordinances is made there also, as indicated by the fact that the latter are separated from the commandments and are given by God *through Moses* to the people, who are afraid to hear God's further words directly lest they die.

1. The Ten Commandments are distinguished from all other statutes or rules and are given priority. In both Exodus and Deuteronomy, they are separated from all other laws and are the first thing given in the covenant establishment.

2. Received as direct revelation, in contrast to law taught by human mediator, the Ten Commandments are thereby given greater weight and authority.

3. The setting forth of the Ten Commandments in two places underscores their great importance in the biblical literature.

4. Careful comparison of the Ten Commandments in their two forms, as well as the similarities and differences between the statutes and ordinances of Exodus 21–23 and Deuteronomy 12–26, reveals little significant variation in the two versions of the Commandments (except for the sabbath commandment) but considerable changes in the statutes and ordinances between Exodus and Deuteronomy.

The implications are clear and not unimportant. Both church and synagogue have given priority to the Ten Commandments over all other rules and regulations in the Old Testament or the Hebrew Bible. They have also claimed for the Ten Commandments an enduring relevance and applicability in later times and places that is not the case with other statutes and ordinances. Both claims are confirmed by the presentation of all this instruction in Exodus and Deuteronomy. The Ten Commandments stand *first, unchanged, and separated* from other laws. They are a kind of constitutional law that lays out the basic guidelines for ordering and regulating the life of the community to ensure its peace and harmony under the rule of God. In new situations, the basic guidelines do not change. Their application in different times and contexts, however, will change. It will be necessary to spell them out in particular cases and to modify particular applications in changing circumstances. This is essentially what happens with the statutes and ordinances of Exodus 21–23 and Deuteronomy 12–26, which in various ways are related to the Ten Commandments (note the frequent attempts on the part of interpreters such as John Calvin to organize the many regulations of Deuteronomy 12–26 according to the Ten Commandments—see Introduction). Yet major differences are discernible between the formulations in Exodus 21–23 and Deuteronomy 12–26 because of such things as the change from an agricultural economy lying behind Exodus to a more monied economic system in Deuteronomy (cf. Exod. 23:10–11 with Deut. 15:1–11).

So in the way in which Deuteronomy sets up the various facets of the community's law, the divine and human are joined in the creation, transmission, and understanding of the law; and the Decalogue is marked off as the special and primary revelation of the will of God for the people. The rest of the law, while also important, is seen to be a teaching of God's will growing out of the primary ten words. (Miller, "Decalogue").

EXCURSUS

Moses the Teacher

One feature belonging to the Deuteronomic profile of Moses is his role as teacher. By joining the teacher with Moses as suffering servant (see commentary on 3:12–29), intercessor (see commentary on 9:25–29; 10:10–11), and prophet (see commentary on 18:9–22), we are presented with a model figure that is instructive for later generations. Several aspects of Moses' teaching activity may be noted.

The teaching responsibility of Moses is identified both with his promulgation of the divine law and his exhortation to obedience. Thus, the teaching function is carried out first in his declaring or telling the law. In his *communication of the word of God* is his teaching task. While Moses typically is understood as lawgiver, in Deuteronomy that act of transmitting the law is a teaching activity. The Lord *tells* or *speaks* the commandments, the statutes, and the ordinances to Moses; he in turn *teaches* them, spelling them out, explaining them as clearly as possible, interpreting what they mean for Israel. In 1:5, Moses is described as seeking to "expound" or "explain" this law. The unusual verb *be'er* used there occurs in 27:8, referring to Moses inscribing the law as clearly as possible on tablets of stone that they may be easily perceived. That same sort of making clear for the sake of understanding belongs to the teaching task as defined by Moses' activity. Distinct from a giving of the law that is mere promulgation, which could be done by a spokesman, teaching the law means it "is to be explained and applied by Moses to the particular situation of the Israelites" (Craigie, p. 92).

But teaching the word of the Lord is not just communicating information and explanation. It is a *teaching to do.* Regularly, result or purpose constructions follow references to Moses' teaching, as in 5:31: "the ordinances which you shall teach them that they may do them in the land which I give them to possess" (4:1, 5; 6:1; cf. 4:10; 31:12). That is why the book has such a hortatory character and the law in it is seen as preached law. The teaching Moses does is in no sense the neutral communication of material; it is an intense effort to elicit from his audience a response of obedience. He seeks at every turn to convey, to explain, and also to stir the heart to respond to the divine instruction, to follow the way that is set forth.

A third feature of Moses' teaching is a concern for the passing on of the tradition to the next generations; they will not have seen the fire or heard the voice or experienced the Lord's provision and discipline along the journey, nor will they have heard Moses' exposition of God's will. He insists that the teaching not end with his own activity but go on in persistent and intense fashion (4:9–10), in the family (6:7, 21–25) and in the sacral gatherings of the whole community (31:13), that each new generation may come to know and obey (Miller, "Moses").

The Basic Requirements of the Law: The Ten Commandments (5:6–21)

While virtually all religious groups discern in this chapter ten commandments, there are different judgments about how they should be numbered. The numbering traditional in the Reformed Churches is followed here:

Prologue (v. 6)
First: against polytheism (v. 7)
Second: against image worship (vv. 8–10)
Third: against misuse of God's name (v. 11)
Fourth: sabbath observance (vv. 12–15)
Fifth: honor of parents (v. 16)
Sixth: against murder (v. 17)
Seventh: against adultery (v. 18)
Eighth: against stealing (v. 19)
Ninth: against false witness (v. 20)
Tenth: against covetousness (v. 21)

Other enumerations have legitimate basis also, and it is at the beginning and at the end where the differences occur. Jewish tradition sees the prologue as the first of the commandments, and while it is not actually a commandment, the text itself speaks of ten *words*, not commandments (4:13, margin), and the

71

prologue is the first word. Consequently, this same tradition regards the commandments against polytheism and image worship as a single commandment, as do Roman Catholics and Lutherans. Here also there is some justification, in that elements of the command against images are connected to the prohibition of worship of other gods: for example, "bow down to *them* or serve *them*" (v. 9; emphasis added). finds its plural antecedent in the "other gods" of verse 7 rather than the singular "graven image" or idol of verse 8. At the end of the Ten Commandments, or Decalogue, Lutheran and Roman Catholic tradition has seen two commandments against coveting, one having to do with the neighbor's spouse and the other having to do with the neighbor's house and other property. While the subject matter seems to be the same, as the Reformed enumeration assumes, there are in fact *two* prohibitions in verse 21 that are identical in form to the preceding prohibitions. The alternative enumerations, therefore, also have claim to validation in the text.

Although our primary interest is in the individual commandments, we need to be aware of some things about the character of the Decalogue as a whole as well as aspects common to several commandments. The Decalogue clearly brings together all that is important for Israel's life—religious, familial, social. In terms of *structure*, in both Exodus and Deuteronomy it moves from the fundamental requirements of Israel's relation to God to the basic guidelines for life in community. Thus, like the Great Commandment, it deals with responsibility to God and neighbor, and in the same order. In its form and character it is covenantal and so begins with the identification of the two parties in the covenant, but especially the identification of the One who by delivering Israel from oppression claims its response. The fundamental stipulation of that response and the covenant is the exclusive worship of the Lord commanded in the first two commandments and carried further in the third and fourth.

The sabbath commandment in the Deuteronomic formulation is both the *bridge* from God to neighbor, in that it deals in some sense with relations to God and responsibilities in the human sphere, and the *center* of the Decalogue. The centrality of the sabbath commandment for Deuteronomy has been pointed out by Norbert Lohfink (see Mayes, pp. 164–65) and is demonstrated in several ways: (1) It is the only commandment where there are major differences from the Exodus version, and these differences are very Deuteronomic in character; (2) it looks back to the prologue, in its reference to the Lord's bringing Israel out from Egypt, and forward to the end in its allusion to ox and ass (which are not in the Exodus form); and (3) the Sabbath commandment in Deuteronomy is the central long block in a series of long and short blocks (vv. 6–10, long; v. 11, short; vv. 12–15, long; v. 16, short; and vv. 17–21, long; the final commandments being held together by conjunctions, unlike Exodus 20).

The fifth commandment is also transitional. It moves into the human sphere by dealing first with the closest community, the family, and with persons who, like God, are authority figures. The remaining commandments also manifest an order, moving from the taking of life to the taking of spouse and then property. From there the commandments move from act against the neighbor to word against the neighbor (false witness) and finally to internal attitudes (covetousness) that may come out in action, such as killing, adultery, and stealing.

As to form, most of the commandments are *prohibitions:* They forbid without stating the penalty for disobedience. This means that they are in some sense absolute. Disobedience is not ameliorated by the exacting of some penalty. They are stipulations of the covenant, and obedience is expected in the relationship. As prohibitions, they also serve to identify certain actions that are not permitted, leaving large areas free. As Gerhard von Rad has put it, the Decalogue "confines itself to a few basic negations; that is, it is content with, as it were, signposts on the margins of a wide sphere of life" (*Old Testament Theology* I, p. 194).

The commandments as a whole are given to Israel as a whole. That is clear from the story. In that sense they are community policy. But each commandment is couched in the second person *singular* and thus addresses and applies to each individual Israelite. The commandments cannot get lost in the mass as generally applicable to the community. They are in force for each individual and are as direct and obligatory upon each member of the covenant community as they appear to be when read and heard.

But while they are direct and to the point, several of them manifest their character as exhortation and preaching as well as command in that they contain amplifications beyond the simple

73

prohibition or positive command. These amplifications function to *motivate* and *encourage obedience*. They give positive and negative reasons for obedience, showing the danger of disobedience (vv. 9, 11*b*) and the blessing of obedience (vv. 10, 16*b*). Or they explain the purpose of the command, as in the sabbath commandment. In various ways, therefore, the form of the commandments speaks personally and directly to those who belong to the Lord's redeemed people, laying down the basic guidelines for life under God and in community and encouraging obedience by reminding each person that these are matters of life (e.g., 16*b*) and death (vv. 9, 10; cf. Miller, "Decalogue").

Prologue (5:6)

The initial statement of the Decalogue, "I am the LORD your God," is the foundation stone of the Ten Commandments and indeed of the whole body of Deuteronomic law. It is both a self-presentation formula of deity and a claim. From this first word arise two questions: Who is the Lord? What does it mean that the Lord claims to be "your God"? The answers to both questions are one and the same and are found in the relative clause that modifies the divine self-presentation: I am the Lord your God, the one who brought you out of the land of Egypt, out of the house of slavery. There is no clearer, more precise identification. The first part of the Book of Exodus is set primarily to show that this God reveals the divine name and nature as one who hears the cries, the groans, the sufferings of people who have been enslaved and treated oppressively (e.g., Exod. 2:23–25; 3:6–10). The single ground for identifying the Lord and explaining why that one claims to be "your God" is the clause "who brought you out of the land of Egypt, out of the house of bondage." From beginning to end, this clause speaks of the liberation of slaves, not only in the expression "house of bondage/slavery" or even in the reference to Egypt, which remains a primal symbol of the experience of slavery and oppression, but also in the expression "who led you out," meaning *exodus*. "Going out is technical or juridical language for release of slaves or land, as one sees from the Book of the Covenant (Exod. 21:1–11), the Holiness Code (Lev. 25:41), and the Deuteronomic law (Deut. 15:16), which speaks of 'going out' when slaves are released. A slave goes out or is set free according to the statutes or is 'brought out/led out' by another party by a price of redemption or by force" (Lohfink, *Great Themes from*

74

the Old Testament, p. 45). It is this last forceful bringing out that happens in the exodus and is the defining word about the Lord's relationship to the liberated people. As one scholar has properly said, the claim found in this prologue and repeated in various ways throughout the Bible "comes very close to a theology of revolution" (ibid.). To the extent that liberation theology roots itself in this story of the Lord setting Hebrew slaves free, it is on the right track, for that story is profoundly theological as it seeks to speak about the nature and purpose of God. But any constructive theology that builds upon this base will have to go with the story's insistence that the God whose name and nature are so described claims a response of covenantal obedience from people. Having once been freed, they are commanded to live in conformity with the policy, the stipulations, the commandments given by the Lord. Setting free the oppressed is the will of a compassionate God. Life in community and obedience is the consequent demand of that same God.

First Commandment: No Other Gods (5:7)

The first commandment flows directly out of the prologue and is the most important word of the Lord to this people. The one who has saved them now stakes a claim on their exclusive loyalty. There can be for this people no other final claim on their allegiance. All other gods are forever ruled out of their worship, their obedience, and their affection. All other lords are lesser lords and may hold no ultimate control over the lives of these people. This commandment is positively stated in the Shema of Deuteronomy 6:4–5, which is the primary Deuteronomic form of the Great Commandment. The theological and personal implications of the first commandment are taken up more extensively in the commentary on that passage.

Second Commandment: The Jealous God (5:8–10)

This commandment is linked integrally with the prohibition of the worship of any other god or the representation of any god as an object of worship. The primary elaboration of the meaning of this commandment is given in the commentary discussion of the sermon on the second commandment in Deuteronomy 4.

The long motivation clause that begins in verse 9 is not discussed in that context and merits attention here because it ties obedience to some serious claims about the Lord of Israel.

The first of these is the assertion that the Lord is a *jealous* God. Jealousy is not an especially appealing characteristic; indeed, it is often associated with the wrath or anger of God. Two things, however, need to be said about the imagery of the jealous God.

1. The jealousy of God is the way in which the claim of the first and second commandments is expressed in terms of the attributes or perfections of God. The Old Testament gives more weight to this attribute than do most systematic theologies, identifying the name of God as Jealous (Exod. 34:14) and regularly calling upon this characteristic of the divine nature as the ground for the first and second commandments (e.g., Deut. 4:24). The *absolute* attribute of the *holiness* of God as one who is apart from all others, transcendent and distinguished from all other reality, has its correlate in the *relative* attribute of *jealousy* (cf. Josh. 24:19).

2. Saying that the Lord is a jealous God makes a covenantal claim about God and expresses a positive word about the proper and inherent exclusiveness that belongs to the nature of the relationship between God and God's people, or to the nature of covenant. As a covenantal claim, the jealousy of God has a double force: jealousy for Israel's full and exclusive worship of the Lord (Exod. 20:5; Deut. 32:16, 21; Ps. 78:50) and jealousy or zeal for God's powerful commitment to and love for his people, as one sees, for example, in such contexts as Isaiah 9:7; 26:11 ("Let them see thy zeal for thy people"); 37:31–32; 59:17 (where the armor of God is righteousness, salvation, vindication, and zeal or jealousy—all to do battle for justice). The jealousy of God, therefore, is that dimension within the divine encounter with the Lord's people that brooks no other final loyalty and ensures no other recipient of such unbounding love and grace. It is God's way of saying, I will have nothing less than your full devotion, and you will have nothing less than all my love. It is the kind of attribute that belongs to a marriage relationship, where there is a proper covenantal jealousy.

Further reason to obey is given in the statement that God responds positively to obedience (those who love me) and negatively to disobedience (those who hate or spurn me). (The Hebrew verb "hate" is used to indicate divorce in Aramaic marriage contracts from Egypt.) But the significant difference in the extent or character of these two responses indicates that the Lord expects obedience to be the primary response and desires to deal graciously and lovingly with his people. There is a clear statute of limitations on judgment upon those who reject the Lord and disobey the commandment. Punishment will go no further than the third or fourth generation. Similar formulas occur in Exodus 34:7 and Numbers 14:18 as well as in other places in Deuteronomy where the extent of punishment across generations is taken up (e.g., 7:9–10 and 24:16). A comparison of these with the expression here shows that the phrase "of those who hate me," which is not in the older formulations about punishment to the third and fourth generation, is included in Deuteronomy to indicate that such punishment takes place because the children continue like the parents to spurn the Lord. That is, God will punish no further than four generations if they keep on hating him. Presumably, if the children repent, God will forgive, though that is not explicitly stated in the text. Deuteronomy 24:16 shows that punishment of children for sins of parents was expressly forbidden (cf. Jer. 31:29 and Ezek. 18).

Chapter 7:9–10 clarifies and elaborates this understanding of the divine punishment and its relation to God's mercy. Those who spurn or hate the Lord are first spoken of in the plural; the explication of the judgment speaks only of the *singular* one who rejects the Lord and the Lord's commandments. The text has in mind neither generations nor large numbers of people. It states what God will do in those cases of rejection and disobedience. Over against this is the clear expectation in 5:10 of *thousands* who will love the Lord by keeping the commandments. In 7:9–10, where there is no reference to disobedience and divine judgment even to three or four generations, the text explicitly states that the Lord is "the faithful God who keeps covenant and steadfast love with those who love him and keep his commandments *to a thousand generations*" (emphasis added). The implication of these expressions for understanding God's expectation and God's nature is clear. Neither disobedience nor judgment is assumed to be the trend. The scales are tipped; the divine character is weighted toward mercy. Love and mercy are the dominant characteristics of the covenant relationship.

The primacy of divine blessing for obedience over against divine punishment for disobedience is expressed in other places in the Old Testament: in the call of Abraham, where the purpose of God is to bring blessing to the many and the possibility of curse is exceptional and not a part of the divine purpose, and

77

in Psalm 30:6, which contrasts the momentary character of God's anger with the perseverance of God's favor. Popular understanding of the God of Scripture often pictures the Deity as a God of love and wrath, mercy and judgment, as if these were equal sides of God's character and purpose, one more prevalent in the Old Testament, the other seen more clearly in the New. The God of biblical faith, however, is bent toward mercy and blessing. Judgment takes place when the loving intentions of a compassionate God are thwarted or opposed, but the divine way and purpose are not any less loving or set for blessing (Miller, "Syntax and Theology").

Third Commandment: Reverencing the Name of God (5:11)

While any image of God is improper and thus forbidden, the *name* of God is available. It is one way the community of faith can apprehend God and invoke God's presence and power. Indeed, it is given to the community as the revelation of God. In Deuteronomic theology, the name of God in a very serious way represents the presence of the reality of God. But that which stands for God and in some fashion claims the power of God by its very invocation cannot be treated lightly. That is the point of this commandment, which prohibits the use or invoking of the name of the Lord in an unserious or empty way.

The Heidelberg Catechism has properly understood the force of this commandment in its requirement that "we must not profane or abuse the name of God by *cursing,* by *perjury,* or by *unnecessary oaths*" (Q. 99, emphasis added). These are indeed the primary targets toward which the commandment is directed. Profanity has become such a part of contemporary life that it seems almost too trivial a matter to be covered by one of the primary commandments. But change in this case is not necessarily progress, and the commandment challenges us with the claim that the casual use of God's name is no light matter. It is possible as a widespread practice only in a secularized society. Those, however, who worship God as the Lord of all of life know that expletives that in some way use the name of God either treat what is most sacred and ultimate in our lives as utterly trivial or claim the transcendent power of God for our own purposes and against others.

78 Misuse of God's name, however, is not confined to profanity or cursing. Any situation wherein the divine name is used without seriousness violates this command. As several biblical pas-

sages indicate, swearing by God's name is not wrong (cf. Lev. 19:11–12; Deut. 6:13 and 10:20). Indeed, it is specifically commanded. Misuse of the name happens if one swears by God's name and then lies. The commandment, therefore, has to do with *telling the truth.* To invoke the name of the Lord is a commitment to tell the truth. While the commandment may not originally have envisioned the setting of the court but any occasion where one raises oaths to God as the ground for one's integrity, the court is one of the primary contemporary contexts in which oaths are taken. Without the assurance of truth in the court, where the conflicts and problems of the community can be resolved peacefully and in orderly fashion, the community will fall apart and justice will disappear. The Heidelberg Catechism rightly affirms the validity of swearing oaths by the name of God "to maintain and promote fidelity and truth, to the glory of God and the welfare of our neighbor" (Q. 101). Concern for the integrity and honesty of a person's word is not merely a human or communal issue. It has to do with one's allegiance to God, and so this commandment rightly follows upon the first two and extends their sphere of influence.

Finally, the catechism's reference to unnecessary oaths reminds us that there are many ways in which either individuals or the community may invoke the name of God as a kind of rubber stamp for one's words to claim an authority or validity that otherwise would not be present. One thinks of both religious and political occasions where this is easily and quickly done. The name of God can be used, but not unnecessarily and not casually. The preacher or the politician who easily invokes the divine name to ensure consent to deeds or words treads upon this commandment; God will not treat lightly the treating lightly of the name of the Lord. So, to put it in the positive formulation of the Westminster Shorter Catechism, the third commandment "requires the holy and reverent use of God's name, titles, attributes, ordinances, word, and works" (Q. 54).

Fourth Commandment: Keeping the Sabbath (5:12–15)

As we have already observed, this is the commandment that differs most from the Exodus version of the Decalogue and is in various ways the center of the Deuteronomic Decalogue. It receives, therefore, a special weight and character in this context. Some of its implications are discussed in other places in this volume (e.g., Deuteronomy 15), but the primary concerns of

79

the sabbath commandment are clear from its elaboration in the Decalogue.

A comparison of the structure of the commandment in Exodus and Deuteronomy underscores the particularity of the Deuteronomic form even though they both share a common fundamental intention: to provide one day that is without work and is set aside to the Lord. The simple structure of the Exodus form (20:8–11) is as follows: Remember the creating work of God and the rest of God; from that memory you are to rest and sanctify a day. Remembering the Lord's work of creation that ended in a day of rest will lead you to keep a day of rest and to set it apart to the Lord. The Deuteronomic structure works differently. The creation dimension is omitted. In terms of the logic, it is not *remember* to keep but the reverse: *Keep* the Sabbath, and by so doing two purposes will be accomplished. You will remember the redemptive work of God on your behalf, and you will provide rest for the slaves under your control. So in the case of Exodus, the community is called to remember and to obey out of that memory; in the Deuteronomic form, the community obeys to keep alive the memory of redemption and to bring about the provision of rest from toil for all members of the community.

When one asks what the believing community is to do on the sabbath, three things are indicated: (1) On a regular basis, members of the community are to set aside their normal routines and work activities to gain rest and refreshment; further, they are to see that such rest is available to all, including those who might not normally have the freedom to relax from work; (2) in some manner the day should be set aside to God: that is, worship and divine service are aspects of the day of rest; and (3) on the day of rest the community is to recall the redeeming work of God.

Obviously, there are various ways of carrying out these aspects of the sabbath, and the nature of contemporary society may complicate its observance. But the fundamental components are there for our guidance. The Christian move from sabbath to Sunday does not fundamentally alter these basic ingredients. Rest, worship, and recollection of God's redemptive activity (Sunday is the day to remember the resurrection of Jesus) continue to be the ways the Christian community responds to the divine command.

The centrality of the sabbath in the Deuteronomic Deca-

80

logue and in the Bible generally presses us to go beyond asking what is to be done in order to ask what sabbath means and what are some of the larger theological implications of its observance.

First of all, *the sabbath is a gift of God* as much as it is a command (Exod. 16:28–29). The Lord's blessing of the sabbath is the provision of the sabbath as a gift for human existence. The sabbath belongs to the providential work of God in providing for the continuity of life. It is given to bless human existence. Karl Barth has caught this very well; he claims that on this day we are to celebrate, rejoice, and be free to the glory of God (*Church Dogmatics* III/4, p. 50). Jesus means the same when he says the sabbath was made for human beings. Therefore, while it is something to be done by us for our good and thus comes to us as command, it is also something to be received for our enjoyment and benefit and thus comes to us as gift.

As gift, the primary character of the sabbath is rest. It places in the cycle of life a provision for freedom from the tyranny and oppression of unrelenting human labors, driven-ness, and the increasing pressure of unceasing work. The sab-bath commandment does not command work for six days; it assumes that human existence requires this hard labor. In the Old Testament, hard toil is a necessary evil that participates in and grows out of the sinful propensities of humankind (Gen. 3). Work has its reward, but only under the shadow and protection of the sabbath (cf. Pss. 127 and 128 for negative and positive views of human toil).

As rest, the sabbath looks backward to the exodus redemp-tion. Exodus 5:1–9, with its account of the Egyptian king's re-sponse to the request of the Hebrew slaves for a three-day break to worship the Lord, provides the fundamental background for understanding the sabbath commandment in Deuteronomy. There the service of God that gives rest to slaves is rejected in behalf of a secular insistence on the exploitation of human life and human work. If exodus was God's redemptive activity to give sabbath to slaves, then sabbath now is human non-activity to remember the exodus redemption. In effect the command-ment says, In breaking free from your labors, you will be re-minded of God's breaking you free from your hard toil and bondage.

As rest, the sabbath also looks forward to the promised rest of God. That is clearly seen in Deuteronomy, which views the goal of the people's present endeavors to occupy the land as a finding of rest. Such looking forward, however, is also present in the eschatological vision of a rest for the people of God hinted at in the visions of the Day of the Lord and the mountain of the Lord, where all shall come together in *shalom* (cf. Isa. 66:23). It is articulated expressly in the claim of Hebrews 4, "there remains yet a rest for the people of God." Furthermore, the sabbath looks forward to the promised rest also in the Christian shift to celebrate the day of rest on the first day of the week as the day of Jesus' resurrection, which is an anticipatory celebration of the rest that lies with God.

Such eschatological meaning to the sabbath continues in the Jewish tradition, as indicated by the following rabbinic legend:

> At the time when God was giving the Torah to Israel, He said to them: My children! If you accept the Torah and observe my mitzvot [commandments], I will give you for all eternity a thing most precious that I have in my possession.
> —And what, asked Israel, is that precious thing which Thou wilt give us if we obey Thy Torah?
> —The world to come.
> —Show us in this world an example of the world to come.
> —The Sabbath is an example of the world to come (A. Heschel, *The Sabbath*, p. 73).

The sanctifying of the sabbath serves to guard the first and second commandments. It helps protect against the idolizing of work by setting it as the center of value and meaning. The sabbath as a rest that is open to God relativizes human work and pulls people away from their own goals and energies and endeavors so they remember the larger work of God. It reminds the believing community that human plans and labors, intelligence and strength, gifts and accomplishments are not the be-all and end-all of human existence. "The holy day does not invalidate human work, but it limits and relativizes it. It does not forbid work, but it forbids ultimate trust in our own work" (Winn).

Setting apart one day regularly to the Lord inhibits the human inclination to justify oneself by job or work. The sabbath is a concrete symbol that God's saving grace is what redeems human life rather than any or all work. The sabbath is a regular time to stop striving and reaching, to stop trying to justify oneself before God and everybody else; it is a time to remember having been set free and accepted in the ultimate sense and to know that the chief end of life is not found in any human work or accomplishment but only in glorifying and enjoying God. As such, the sabbath is an implicit but important pointer toward the reality of justification by faith (Winn).

The Sabbath is one of the marks of the people of God. More than anything except the first and second commandments, the sabbath was the reality that identified and distinguished Israel (Neh. 9:13–14; Isa. 56:1–8). A regular time of rest is not in itself a sign of the people of God, a mark of the congregation. *Sabbath* is the sign that includes the rest at its center. There really is a difference between experiencing a day off and experiencing a day off sanctified to the Lord. Neither Jewish nor Christian existence can be maintained as a vital reality without sabbath sanctification. Nor does one receive the visible mark or share the identity of those whose God is the Lord without participation in the sabbath rest and the Sunday celebration.

The gifts of the sabbath are for all. The sabbath is set to provide the reality of freedom, celebration, and rest for everyone, especially for those who might not easily find it. This is why Deuteronomy especially focuses the purpose of the sabbath on the provision of rest for the manservant and maidservant (vv. 14b–15c). Those who have been slaves and have been freed by the power and grace of God can never treat slaves in the same way they were treated. Once the exodus was complete, slavery had not yet been eliminated, but it was on its way out if God was the one who brought a people out of the land of Egypt, out of the house of bondage. It was even further on its way out when the Lord set the sabbath in the midst of the community.

Here is why the sabbath commandment is, in Deuteronomy, a primary impetus to social justice as well as why it is the Deuteronomic expression of that call for treating other human beings in the same caring way we would be treated, as articulated in the Great Commandment's "Love your neighbor *as yourself.*" The Deuteronomic parallel is in the formulation, "You shall not do any work . . . that your man servant and maid servant may rest *as yourself.*" Love of neighbor is exemplified in providing sabbath rest for all members of the community. The extension of this commandment into a kind of "sabbatical principle" providing for social justice and humane treatment in

83

various aspects of community life can be seen in Deuteronomy 15 and the commentary on that passage (Miller, "Human Sabbath").

Fifth Commandment: Honor Parents (5:16)

In other formulations this commandment is specifically understood to prohibit striking or cursing father and mother, with a sentence of death for the one who disobeys (Exod. 21:15, 17; Deut. 21:18–21). The fifth commandment, however, states the requirement and the consequence in positive terms, thereby broadening the character of the command and opening up a rich promise for those who keep it. Several things must be kept in mind in seeking to understand its force.

The command is addressed to persons of any age whose parents are living. It was not primarily directed to children, to tell them how to treat their parents, but to *adults;* this means that this commandment has in mind especially how mature adults are to treat their older or elderly parents. Of course, that does not mean the commandment is inapplicable to younger children; it applies there too. But the problem addressed by the commandment is not that of the young child who is under the power and control of the parents and can be expected to respect them. This commandment focuses on the mature person, no longer under control of parents and now probably stronger than they are in every way. It has in mind elderly parents, the weaker and needier members of the relationship, who may be regarded by grown children as unimportant, burdensome, or unable to control adult children (see Heidelberg Catechism, Q. 104).

The character of the children's treatment of the parents is seen in the key verbs of the negative and positive formulations: "no cursing" and "honoring." The word "curse" *(qillel)* in this instance means to treat lightly or contemptibly, to regard someone as of little account, as Hagar regards Sarah when Hagar becomes pregnant and Sarah is barren, for example. It is not a matter of profanities uttered but of any way children treat older parents with indignity. *Honoring* the parents is required at all times. The verb "honor" *(kabbed)* is the exact opposite of "curse." It means to treat weightily and to regard someone as being of great worth. Brevard S. Childs has aptly summarized its range of meaning for this context:

84

To honor is to "prize highly" (Prov. 4:8), "to show respect," to "glorify and exalt." Moreover, it has nuances of caring for and showing affection (Ps. 91:15). It is a term frequently used to describe the proper response to God and is akin to worship (Ps. 86:9). Moreover, the parallel command in Lev. 19:3 actually uses the term "fear, give reverence to" *(tîrā'û)* which is otherwise reserved for God (*The Book of Exodus*, pp. 418–419).

That this is the first commandment with a *promise* attached to it is significant enough for Paul to call attention to that fact in Ephesians 6:1–4. The promise of long life on the land God gives is a frequent motivation in Deuteronomy. It is usually cited as a result or outgrowth of obedience to *all* the laws and statutes (e.g., Deut. 4:40; 5:33) but may be tied to particular laws (e.g., Deut 22:7; 25:15). When placed as a promised outcome of honoring father and mother, it suggests that each generation honoring and caring for its older members creates and maintains a social climate that enhances the possibility of good and long life for each person in the society and for the society as a whole. To the extent that indifference to and neglect of the older generation becomes a societal pattern, the possibilities of a long and happy life are diminished for all. For those who are young become old and will themselves need care and respect to find "length of days."

The commandment enjoins an attitude toward parents that parallels one's attitude toward God (honor, fear, reverence). This fact demonstrates the appropriateness of having this commandment at the point of transition from those that have to do with relationship to God and those that have to do with relationship to other members of the community. It also suggests why there is a long tradition in both Jewish and Christian understanding that this commandment instructs not only in the proper attitude to actual fathers and mothers but in the right approach to authorities in general. The Westminster Larger Catechism states, "By 'father' and 'mother' in the Fifth Commandment, are meant not only natural parents, but all superiors in age and gifts; and especially such as by God's ordinance are over us in place of authority, whether in family, church, or commonwealth." Martin Luther, in his Large Catechism, states it explicitly: "Out of the authority of parents all other authority is derived and developed."

Such an understanding can indeed only be developed out

of the commandment and is not explicit. Karl Barth warns against the danger of overlooking the concrete character of the command with such a generalization (*Church Dogmatics* III/4, p. 242). Indeed, one must not slide quickly over the primary word of the commandment to take up a secondary, derived, or implicit word. But it is the case that the filial responsibility to honor and respect parents is in some sense the starting point of the human experience with persons who exercise a proper authority over others by reason of relationship, wisdom, and experience. These may be teachers, employers, or civil authorities. Recognizing the need for proper respect of parents can at least open up in the community of faith a conversation about what sorts of relationship merit similar attitudes of honoring and exalting other persons and what is the content and manifestation of such serious respect.

Finally, note should be taken of the fact that the Decalogue says nothing about how parents are to treat children. Paul, in his instruction about relations between children and parents and between slaves and masters in Ephesians 6:1–4, does claim the need for those in positions of authority, honor, or control to exercise a proper care for those over whom that authority extends; he calls upon parents not to provoke children to anger (and thus acts of disrespect) but to bring them up in the nurture and discipline of the Lord. Here the implicitly reciprocal character of the relationship, which is obvious if not stated in the commandments that follow, those having to do with neighbors, is extended also to the commandment that might lead to one-sided obligations (those of children) without a commensurate sense of responsibility on the part of those who could abuse others precisely because of their honored position (the parents).

Sixth Commandment: Protection of Life (5:17)

The rubric "protection of life" actually describes both where this commandment began, insofar as we can understand its original intention, and where and how it is understood to function as instruction for community life today. Between those two points, however, much growth and development of its meaning and force have taken place within Scripture and beyond it in the tradition of Christian faith. Furthermore, its impact has extended far beyond the bounds of the Jewish-Christian communities, as is true of other commandments also, but markedly so of the simple (!) injunction, "You shall not kill."

This divine instruction begins those succinct guidelines that deal directly with community life and are formulated as prohibitions to safeguard the basic rights of each individual. The first is appropriately aimed at protecting a person's life against the threat of its extinction by someone else. As is frequently pointed out, the verb normally translated "kill" is not the common and general Hebrew verb for killing *(harag);* it is the verb *rasah,* which often refers to what we customarily think of as murder, the willful, premeditated killing of an individual out of hatred, anger, desire, greed, or other reasons the community regards as illegitimate or illegal (the New English Bible and NRSV translate the prohibition as "You shall not commit murder"). The verb *rasah,* however, can also refer to unintentional homicide or simply accidental killing, as one sees in Numbers 35:25–28, where the word "manslayer" translates *rasah* (cf. Deut. 4:41–42; Josh. 20:3).

The commandment, therefore, is directed toward personal violence against the life of an individual, which is killing "with malice aforethought," but it is open to include other forms of killing that are inimical to community life and order and deprive an individual of God's gift of life. Both the *primary direction* of the commandment—against murder—and *its openness to exclude other forms of killing* out of the sense of the sanctity of life, of God's gift of creaturely existence, are important dimensions of the commandment's continuing instruction. The obviousness of the basic intent—to prohibit murder—does not make that intent any less important. It is surely no accident that the original and primal social sin is the high-handed murder of a brother out of anger and with full intention (Gen. 4:1–8). Malicious violence that takes the life of a human being is absolutely contrary to the will of God and is destructive not only of life but of community.

The clearly broader force of the commandment in prohibiting other forms of killing opens up its instructive impact to ask about other ways in which persons are harmed—indeed, killed—and how these relate to this commandment of God. There is an openness to the commandment in its early force that leads to a deepening and broadening of its application. This is seen explicitly in Jesus' extension of the prohibition to guard against anger and insults, with its positive corollary in active movement toward reconciliation (Matt. 5:21–26). Thus, manifestations of anger and hatred at a less extreme level than mur-

87

der are seen to flow out of the sixth commandment or to represent an intensification of its force. This is not foreign to the Old Testament, which also has injunctions against hating a brother or a neighbor (Lev. 19:17–18).

When heard in relation to the love command of Jesus, extending even to enemies, the prohibition against killing has led to an understanding of God's instruction about the sanctity of life as a guard against harming others. Beyond that, it is a positive injunction to protect and preserve life from harm by doing that which sustains life ("Nature and Value of Human Life," pp. 3–4). For this reason, a number of basic issues of social life (e.g., war, capital punishment, abortion, and suicide) have properly been drawn into the discussion of this prohibition and its meaning and force. Any threat to a human life, whatever the reason, stands under the shadow of this commandment. If its force is to guard against harming life—by inevitable extension of such guardings, as well as Jesus' positive words about loving neighbor even to the outermost periphery of that category, one's enemy—and to work for the protection of life, all acts of killing and neighborly harm come under radical question. There may be occasions when the responsibilities of avoiding harm and protecting from harm come into irreconcilable conflict and a choice has to be made for one that leads to the other. In such cases, the comprehensive norm of respect for life that is discernible in the sixth commandment as it has been broadened and deepened in the Judeo-Christian tradition still remains the guide for resolving the conflict. (For a somewhat different perspective, to which the above discussion is much indebted, see Yoder.)

Seventh Commandment: Against Adultery (5:18)

"The prohibition against adultery stakes out the claim of the two partners in marriage to a relationship between themselves that is not to be compromised or destroyed by the action of either partner" (Harrelson, p. 125). The clear and specific force of this commandment is to guard the sanctity of the marriage relationship, and it recognizes that the sexual relationship of wife and husband is the center of intimacy and commitment, which must be carefully guarded if the marriage is to be carefully guarded.

In the Old Testament, this commandment meant that the wife was prohibited from sexual intercourse with any other male and the husband from sexual intercourse with any other married woman. A man could have intercourse with a concubine or a prostitute without coming under the sanction of this commandment. That does not necessarily mean that a wife was viewed as the property of her husband. It does reflect both the patriarchal structure of Israelite society and probably also the desire to guard the question of the paternity of the offspring of a marriage. The issue of fornication did not come into play. Sexual intercourse between unmarried persons came under some regulation, but adultery was viewed as a more serious moral issue. Various biblical stories (e.g., Abimelech, Abraham, and Sarah in Gen. 20; Joseph and Potiphar's wife in Gen. 39; and David and Bathsheba in I Samuel 11 and 12) testify to the moral seriousness of adultery, which was viewed in Israel and elsewhere as "a great sin" (Gen. 20:9).

As with other commandments in the Decalogue, various extensions of this commandment in the Scriptures and beyond show us once again how a fairly narrowly focused prohibition has implications on a wider scale.

First, by inference at least, differences between its application to men and women disappear. Intimacy and sexual activity with another partner violate the wholeness and commitment of the marriage relationship regardless of who the other partner is. A male-oriented ethos can resist that and continue to distinguish between types of sexual activity for men and women, regarding male use of female prostitutes as a minor, tolerable evil, for example, but the force of the commandment with its simple "you shall not commit adultery" does not allow for an acceptable intimacy outside the marriage relationship. Both persons in the marriage come under the commandment in the same way. And anyone, male or female, who from outside breaks the covenant of marriage between a couple acts in a way contrary to the intent of this divine instruction.

There is a broadening of the impact of this commandment in the Old Testament, particularly in priestly legislation, through laws prohibiting all unnatural sexual unions and especially sexual relations with any near kin, whether within marriage or not (Phillips, pp, 121–129). Here there is clear intent to affirm and guard the sexual relation of a man and a woman in the marriage against its violation by sexual activity unrelated to the marriage commitment and covenant. It is natural that the community should see in this prohibition the centrality of

89

the marriage relationship for the sexual activity of human beings. While it does not answer all questions about sexual involvement, the commandment gives a basic direction, the relation between sexual intimacy and marriage that has persisted in the Judeo-Christian community even when its members have acted differently or been perplexed about particular cases or issues of sexual activity.

Again, there is an explicit move in Jesus' teaching toward a more radical and internal understanding of this commandment, one that may be difficult to obey but at least shows the seriousness and sanctity of the marriage relationship: "You have heard that it was said, "You shall not commit adultery." But I say to you that every one who looks at a woman lustfully has committed adultery with her in his head" (Matt. 5:27-28; author's trans.). Not only the act but the thought breaches the marriage vow. Awareness of the psychological difficulty of adhering to Jesus' word should not be allowed to lessen its moral force as a reminder of where sexual thought and action have their proper place. Nor should recognition of the fact that not every moral issue or case having to do with sexual activity is, in the light of Jesus' words, immediately transparent to ethical reflection keep one from perceiving a direction and force here that offers basic guidance about marriage and sex.

Walter Harrelson, who was quoted at the beginning of this brief discussion, gives a simple but straightforward summary of the claim of this commandment that bears repeating as a conclusion:

> As in the case of killing, it cannot be claimed that this commandment should become an absolutistic and unbreakable norm, issuing in a commitment never to have sexual relations with anyone other than the marriage partner. But unlike the sixth commandment, this seventh commandment does allow for scrupulous adherence without any necessary harm at all. It is difficult to find a situation comparable to that of the pacifist who will not, because he or she cannot, lift a finger to restrain the taker of other life. It therefore seems entirely in order for us to claim that this prohibition can be the guideline for every marriage, expressing the commitment of the partners in marriage to treasure and preserve a unity that has been called into being in marriage and in the sexual relations they have engaged in as marriage partners. And certainly it would seem evident that, if sexual relations do in fact relate persons to one another in ways deeper than might then and there be realized, the wise course is for married persons to have sexual

relations with no one other than their spouse, ever (Harrelson, pp. 130–131).

Eighth Commandment: Against Stealing (5:19)

At the earliest stages of its history, this prohibition may have been a guard against enslavement. The theft prohibited under absolute sanction was the stealing of persons, or kidnapping (though probably for slavery rather than ransom). Joseph, as a slave in Egypt, speaks of himself as having been "stolen out of the land of the Hebrews" (Gen. 40:15). In Exodus 21:16 and Deuteronomy 24:7, further laws are found referring to stealing a person for slavery or for selling, and the punishment is death, the type of punishment appropriate to the laws of the Decalogue. The property theft laws outside the Ten Commandments are treated essentially as torts, wherein the aim of the law is restitution of property rather than punishment.

This dimension of the commandment is not to be overlooked even though the prohibition came to be extended. As David Little has remarked:

> Still, the original emphasis on persons rather than things was profound. The essential wrongness of theft is revealed in the act of stealing persons. As such, theft equals enslavement—the complete domination of one human being by another ("without his knowledge or consent") ("Exodus 20:15," p. 404).

The form of the commandment now, however, has no object (whether or not it ever did). The verb "steal" is used with things or property as its object as much as persons, even in legal material (e.g., Exod. 22:1, 12). So the prohibition is more inclusive, prohibiting property theft as well as theft of human beings. For "substantial domination is possible by controlling another's property, as well as by controlling another's person" (Little, p. 404); witness David's appropriate rage at hearing Nathan's story of the rich person's taking the single lamb of a poor man to avoid using his own (II Sam. 12:1–6). This safeguard on property "protects for each person a sphere of moral self-supervision and self-determination against the threat of enslavement or exploitation" (Little, p. 404). It is not accidental or a sign of selfishness that the frequent reaction of persons to theft of property in their home is a strong sense of having been personally violated. The joy and danger of having personal property is that it represents to some extent an extension of self.

91

In Israel, however, such protection of property was not intended to develop and accumulate masses of wealth and squeeze out others from a place at the table of resources in the land. Property was provided for each in the allotment of land. Not even kings could legally take that away, as the story of Naboth's vineyard in I Kings 21 makes clear. Laws allowing gleaning of leftovers by the poor and prohibiting usury and extortion, and requiring the return of garments taken in pledge were aimed at protecting property while resisting the exploitative and accumulative possibilities that arise out of a system of private property, possibilities that themselves can turn into forms of stealing.

For this reason John Calvin and other interpreters have rightly seen the prohibition against theft as a broad one, spelled out in many particular statutes. The verb for "stealing" *(ganab)* refers to secret acts of theft, but, as Calvin indicated, the problem was a broader one:

> Since charity is the end of the Law, we must seek the definition of theft from thence. This, then, is the rule of charity, that every one's rights should be safely preserved and that none should do to another what he would not have done to himself. It follows, therefore, that not only are those thieves who secretly steal the property of others, but those also who seek for gain from the loss of others, accumulate wealth by unlawful practices, and are more devoted to their private advantage than to equity (Calvin, *Commentaries* III, pp. 110–111).

Therefore Calvin included, in the exposition or elaboration of this commandment, laws on usury, pledges, bribes, correct weights and measures, moving a neighbor's landmark, returning lost property, fraudulent use of another's property (e.g., Exod. 22:5) and negligence (e.g., Exod. 21:33–36), as well as laws that protect the weak and poor from oppression, provide release for slaves, and ensure access of the poor to the needs of life (e.g., Deut. 23:24–25).

The eighth commandment, therefore, is a fundamental instruction with broad-ranging applications protecting the lives of members of the community from oppression and exploitation. For each person it provides against property being taken out unlawfully and against property being taken in unlawfully or unfairly. (On this commandment, as on all of the last five, the Westminster Larger Catechism is an excellent guide to those matters required and those prohibited in the commandments.)

Ninth Commandment: Against False Witness (5:20)

As is recognized in virtually all of the serious treatments of this commandment, its setting is the courtroom. Literally the commandment says, You shall not testify against your neighbor as a lying witness (Childs). The commandment is set as a safeguard of the judicial process or, more precisely, as a protection of the individual Israelite from being wrongly treated in the law court.

The ninth commandment stands in close relation to the third, prohibiting empty use of the divine name. That is seen particularly in Deuteronomy's version of the Decalogue, where the word for "false" is the same Hebrew word translated "in vain" (NRSV, "wrongful use") in Exodus 20:7 and in Deuteronomy 5:11. You shall not give worthless testimony against your neighbor. Or, you shall not testify to no good purpose against your neighbor. The third commandment has to do with truth-telling vis-à-vis God; the ninth commandment has in mind the same concern vis-à-vis the well-being of one's Israelite sister or brother. Israel's understanding of the centrality of the law courts for the proper function of society and the security and protection of each member of that society is accented again here. If the courts work improperly and one is dealt with unfairly, all is lost and anything can happen. Exodus 23:1 speaks of the false witness as a "malicious witness" or a "witness in behalf of violence," because false testimony is likely to bring harm to the one so treated. The guilt or innocence of an individual in the court is primarily determined on the basis of witnesses (see Deut. 19:15–21), so truth-telling in the court is no light matter. If found out, the one who brings a false accusation against another person suffers the same penalty as would have been carried out on the falsely accused (Deut. 19:19).

The dangers against which this commandment stands as a shield are well illustrated in the Old Testament. The lament, or complaint, psalms often petition God for help against persons who have endangered the petitioner by false accusations (e.g., Pss. 4:2; 5:6, 9–10; 7:14; 10:7–9; 27:12). The story in I Kings 21 is a vivid example of the violent possibilities when the court is perverted by lying witnesses. Ahab and Jezebel have Naboth judicially murdered and confiscate his coveted vineyard simply by having two hoodlums falsely accuse him in court of having cursed God and the king. In the New Testament, Matthew

93

writes that those who sought to have Jesus put to death tried to find false witnesses to testify against him because that was the way they could defeat him.

The question naturally arises: Do we hear in this commandment a more general injunction against lying and in behalf of truth-telling? The answer to that question is clearly yes if what has been said above is set as the ground of understanding: to wit, that the courts are the critical context in which truth-telling must be maintained, and the protection of the neighbors is the reason. The Old Testament itself expands the force of this commandment by connecting the witness in the court with more general practices of lying, particularly slander. That is probably seen in the "false report" of Exodus 23:1a. Leviticus 19:11 clearly shows us why this commandment is placed between those having to do with stealing and coveting (cf. Lev. 19:16). Both lying and coveting (see below) are forms or aspects of stealing, whether it be life, property, or reputation. Hosea 4:2 also suggests this broader understanding, as does Proverbs 30:8–10. Negative judgments against the false witness are set alongside positive statements about the witness to the truth in Proverbs 14:5 and 25, and Psalm 15:2–3 sets truthful speaking and not slandering with the tongue among the criteria for entering the temple.

The reasons for truth-telling and resisting lies do not change from one generation to another. Protection of the neighbor has been identified here as the primary aim, but that rationale can be expanded, also, as Charles Swezey has well illustrated in delineating reasons not to lie:

> Freedom of choice depends upon a knowledge of the case at hand, which lies take away. Integrity depends upon speaking from one's own perspective, which lies remove. When lies are habitual and the words of everyday discourse unreliable, we plunge into doubt and suspicion. Life together is not possible without a minimal trust in the veracity of words. An unwritten law exists: Unless checks are placed on the proclivity to evade truthfulness, corporate existence flounders and is altogether nasty and brutish (Swezey, p. 407).

Augustine put the matter even more succinctly and comprehensively: "When regard for truth has been broken down or even slightly weakened, all things will remain doubtful" (quoted by Bok in *Lying,* her valuable treatment of this topic [p. xv]).

94

Tenth Commandment: Against Coveting (5:21)

The commandment against coveting appropriately brings the list of basic obligations for individuals in community to a close. It draws together the prohibitions of the second table of the Decalogue and begins to move them to an even deeper level, the level of private attitudes as well as public acts.

Two verbs in verse 21 speak of coveting. In the first clause, "covet" is a translation of Hebrew *hamad,* used also in Exodus 20:17, which means to desire something inordinately or desire something belonging to someone else so strongly that one is moved to reach out and take it. Achan confesses that when he saw the beautiful treasures in the booty from Jericho, "I coveted them and took them" (Josh. 7:21), a sin against which Deuteronomy 7:25 warns Israel. The wealthy and unjust oppressors in eighth-century Judah so desire the property of their neighbors that "They covet fields and seize them; and houses, and take them away" (Mic. 2:2), a direct and explicit violation of this commandment. The inner feeling of envious and greedy desire leads to an act commensurate with the desire, and the result may be the violation of any or all of the commandments against killing, adultery, stealing, and false witness. One has only to recall again the story in I Kings 21 of Ahab's coveting of Naboth's vineyard and the subsequent acts of false witness, judicial murder, and royal confiscation (theft) or the account of David's seeing the beautiful Bathsheba and so desiring her that he commits murder and adultery (II Sam. 11 and 12). With its extended list of wife, property, and "anything that is your neighbor's," the commandment emphatically prohibits greedy and rapacious seizure of anything belonging to someone else, whether openly, by stealth, or by various criminal devices such as those used by David and Ahab.

The second verb used in this commandment for coveting is *hit'awweh,* a verb that also refers to a very strong desire— indeed, a craving for something—for example, David's longing for water to quench his thirst (II Sam. 23:15), the people in the wilderness craving meat instead of only manna (Num. 11:4, 34), and the Israelites of Amos' time inordinately longing for the "day of the LORD" (Amos 5:18). The term does not always imply a bad desire, but generally it refers to a desire strong enough to become lust and covetousness. As with the verb *hamad, hit'awweh,* which does not occur in the Exodus form of this

95

commandment, can refer to an excessive desire leading to action, as in the woman taking and eating the desirable fruit of the garden in Genesis 3:6. But this very desirability tends to heighten the subjective side of the prohibition and to make it more explicit. The commandment is a guard against an internal attitude or feeling that tends to erupt into public and violent acts against one's neighbor. The Bible, as we have seen, is full of examples of such feeling and behavior.

As it moves into the sphere of attitudes and inner desires and their capacity to lead to harmful acts, the commandment opens up the realm of mind and heart as subjects for moral direction and ethical reflection. Not simply what one does but what one thinks and feels may have—and often does have—moral effects. It is certainly the case that character and virtue are affected by the workings of the mind and heart. Disposition and action are important. But even as character and virtue are hardly explicable at any length apart from life and acts in community in relationship to others, so the disposition of the heart is a neighbor issue also.

At this point, the commandment against coveting creates a bridge or inaugurates a trajectory leading directly to Jesus' internalization of the commandments in the Sermon on the Mount (Matt. 5:21–30). The observation that feelings of anger and lust cannot be controlled in the same way in which murder and adultery can be controlled is to an extent true, but as a sole response to Jesus' injunctions against those emotions this is inadequate. Already in the commandment against coveting the clear connection between internal feelings and external acts, between private attitudes and public deeds, is explicitly recognized. The point is clear. The inner attitudes and feelings have to do potentially with the well-being and security of one's neighbor, and they are subject to a degree of control for the good of the community. Jesus' teaching, therefore, like that of the rabbis and philosophers, is an extension of the instruction clearly set forth in the last commandment and illustrated negatively so often in the Scriptures and in human life.

The significance of this commandment in the New Testament as a basic instruction for the Christian life is indicated further by the fact that it is singled out by both Jesus and Paul in teaching. Jesus sets this commandment at the base of his warning against greed and thus as a pointer to the nature of the Christian life (Luke 12:13–15). "He refuses to identify authentic

Christian existence with the possession of material wealth, even inherited—especially when abundant. It is much more important to *be* than to *have*—to be one who listens to God's word and acts on it than to live in an unnecessary abundance of wealth" (Fitzmyer, p. 969). Paul refers to this commandment when he is arguing that the law has showed him his sin; he also brings this commandment into direct connection with the basic or primary commandment of Deuteronomy when he declares that covetousness is a form of idolatry (Eph. 5:5; Col. 3:5). That is, the love of things and possessions replaces the love of God; put another way, the love of things transcends the love of God, and thus both the first and second commandments are also violated when covetousness takes over the human heart.

The Heart of the Matter (6:4–25)

The Great Commandment (6:4–5)

With this chapter we come to the pivot around which everything else in Deuteronomy revolves—the Shema or Great Commandment, as it has also come to be known (6:4–5). The centrality of these words in Deuteronomy is illustrated in two ways. One of these is its location. It is the first word of Moses' instruction to the people after the Ten Commandments have come as direct word of God to them and they have requested Moses to stand between them and God, to receive the divine word, and then to teach. That teaching begins here with the command to hear (v. 4) and love (v. 5). The location of the Shema also points to its character as a bridge between the Commandments and the other instructions given in the statutes and ordinances (chs. 12–26). In turn, the statutes and ordinances explicate in specific and concrete ways the meaning of Deuteronomy 6:4–5 for the life of Israel. That is why Jesus can later say that all the law and the prophets hang on this commandment (Matt. 22:40). One may speak of these verses as a summary of the law or of the Ten Commandments. More specifically, they are a summary of what Israel heard commanded of them in the prologue and in the first and second commandments. The commandment against worshiping other gods is in every sense the *first* commandment, the *first* word, and the Shema is a positive restatement of that primary commandment. The Shema was the touchstone for Israel's faith and life, the plumb line by which their relationship to the Lord of history was constantly being measured. For this reason later Judaism set these words to be recited by every Jew each morning and evening. This was not a legalistic or merely pious gesture. It was a true apprehension that those who live under the rule of the Lord of Israel are to set their lives and shape their daily conduct and their interior direction by these most important and primary words. The struggle of faith was and is a constant effort to discover afresh in each situation the experience of the confession that is made in the Shema and the requirements of the demand imposed by it.

The centrality and primacy of the Shema are also indicated by its repetition in the following chapters. The language of the Shema as well as the prologue to the Ten Commandments and the first two commandments appears frequently (e.g., 6:12–15; 7:8–10, 16b, 19b; 8:11, 15, 19; 9:1; 10:12–13; 11:1, 13, 16, 18–22, 28b; 13:2–5, 6, 10, 13; 18:9; 26:16–17; 29:26; 30:2b, 6, 8, 10, 16–17). Moses' speech, in chapters 5–11 especially but also to some extent in later chapters, is in effect a kind of sermon on the primary commandment in its positive (6:4–5) and negative (5:6–10) formulations, explicating and elaborating it, shaping Israel's identity as a people defined by this confession, "Our God is the Lord, the Lord alone," and this demand, "you shall love the Lord your God with all your heart, and with all your soul, and with all your might."

What then is the force of this great commandment? Like the Decalogue it begins with a claim, not a demand. The initial function of the Shema is to identify the one who for this people will be the center of being and value and to begin to characterize the nature of the relationship between God and people. It also serves to create an identity for this people. In the opening words, "The Lord is our God," a claim is laid on them, a confession is made by them that will serve to shape their identity and their way in the world in the profoundest way possible. They are the ones who say that we find God for us in the Lord. They are the ones of whom the Lord claims to be God for them, your God. Throughout the Book of Deuteronomy, when the Lord is referred to, one hears also the words "our God" and "your God," over and over, so that the expression "the LORD your/our God" becomes a kind of shorthand for the identifying claim that is in the Shema and the prologue to the Ten Commandments.

The confession of the Lord's people in Deuteronomy 6:4,

however, is not only "our God is the LORD." It goes a step further with the Hebrew expression *yhwh 'ehad,* which is ambiguous and capable of being understood either as "the LORD is one" or "the LORD alone." Either translation can be supported with arguments: the former primarily of a semantic character, in that *'ehad* commonly has to do with unity, oneness, or inclusiveness rather than uniqueness (see *lebad*); the latter primarily of a contextual and historical character in that Deuteronomy is concerned with the sole worship of the Lord, not multiple manifestations of Israel's God. In this interpreter's judgment, the ambiguity of meaning is accepted as irresolvable; the task for interpretation is to try to understand the meaning and implications of both translations.

It is sometimes said that the affirmation of the oneness of the Lord was not an issue for Israel, and therefore the unity of God cannot be what is confessed in the Shema. That is a less than satisfactory conclusion, however, on the basis of both extrabiblical and biblical evidence. With regard to the former, there are some clues, in popular religion at least, of a tendency to identify Yahweh, the Lord of Israel, with particular places or locales. This possibility is at least suggested by references to "Yahweh of Samaria" and "Yahweh of Teman" in Hebrew inscriptions from the eighth century found at Kuntillet Ajrud (in the Negeb). There is present also in these inscriptions evidence for an incipient reverence of the asherah as a Yahweh symbol before becoming a separate object of devotion (the phrase "Yahweh and his asherah" appears more than once in these inscriptions). This tendency could potentially bring about a splitting and multiplying of the divine manifestation and thus of the divine character and purpose.

J. G. Janzen has brought together a number of texts in this connection indicating that the integrity of the divine character and the unity of God's purpose was an issue, raising the question of God's oneness ("Yahweh Our God, Yahweh is One"). One of these is the conversation between Moses and the Lord after the manufacture of the golden calf in Exodus 32, recounted also in Deuteronomy 9. The Lord says to Moses,

> Go down; for your people, whom you brought up out of the land of Egypt, have corrupted themselves; . . . now therefore let me alone, that my wrath may burn hot against them and I may consume them; but of you I will make a great nation (Exod. 32:7, 10).

99

Here, in effect, the identification of the Lord as "the one who brought you out of the land of Egypt" (Deut. 5:6) seems to be canceled out so as to suggest that the divine integrity may be defined exclusively of the redemptive relation to the people (cf. Deut. 9:12). Moses' words of response, to this point, imply that the divine integrity may not be so defined—that in fact the exodus from Egypt remains the single ground for identifying Yahweh, such that to repudiate it opens up a rift, not only between Yahweh and people, but in Yahweh (Janzen, "On the Most Important Word in the Shema," p. 283).

The implication is reinforced, in the second place, by Moses' assertion that the finality of the divine wrath will allow Egypt to reconstrue Yahweh's original redemptive act as being not compassionate after all but evil in its intent (cf. Deut. 9:28). This in turn will imply either the fickleness or inconsistency of Yahweh (Janzen, "Yahweh Our God, Yahweh Is One"). Furthermore, the covenant with the ancestors, based on a divine oath and promise, appears in some sense to be abrogated as the seed of Abraham are threatened with destruction and the promise made to Abraham ("I will make of you a great nation"—Gen. 12:2a) is transferred to Moses ("but of you I will make a great nation"—Exod. 32:10).

The same thing happens in the incident concerning the report of the spies in Numbers 14:11–19. This time Moses' strategy is to represent Egypt as possibly concluding that the Lord who brought Israel out of Egypt is unable to bring them into the land as intended and so has killed them in the wilderness.

> A chasm opens up between the divine saving intent and the inability, in the face of the people's sin, to carry that intent through to completion. The chasm will be closed, and the divine integrity secured, only by a display of power (Num. xiv 17) consistent with the power displayed in the Exodus (Num. xiv 13)—a power of forgiveness enclosed in the promise of Exod. xxxiv 6–7 which Moses now invokes (Num. xiv 18–19). (Janzen, "On the Most Important Word in the Shema," pp. 284–285).

One can add to these passages such texts as Hosea 11:1–9, where the divided heart of God is resolved only in a decision of divine repentance and mercy (v. 9), or Jeremiah 32:38–41, where the one heart and one way (v. 39) given to the people is matched by the Lord's promise to plant the people in the land—"in faithfulness, with all my heart and all my soul," echoing in the

Lord's intention the same undivided commitment that is expected of the people in verse 39 and in the Shema.

To confess, therefore, that the Lord is "one" is to claim that the One who receives ultimate allegiance and is the ground of being and value is faithful, consistent, not divided within mind, heart, or self in any way. The reality of God in one time or place is wholly conformable with all other moments and experiences. The presence and involvement of God in the world and in shaping history and human destiny is not in one guise now and in another guise elsewhere. In purpose and being, God is one and the same though open and hidden to the future, becoming as well as being.

The alternate translation of the confession, "our God is the LORD, the LORD alone," anticipates the command of verse 5 and clearly speaks to the other issue of Israelite faith, the one toward which the first two commandments are directed, which is less the question whether the Lord and the Lord's purposes are divided than it is whether Israel's loyalties are divided. The Shema is a radical confession that Israel's loyalty is one, that it finds no other God than the Lord, and the Shema and the first commandments set forth commands and prohibitions to safeguard this claim as the reality determining Israel's life and creating her identity: "The LORD alone." "You shall have no other gods before/besides me." Israel frequently—according to the biblical record—found other gods more attractive, whether it was because they seemed to offer the promise of a more productive, richer land and life or belonged to national powers with which Israel sought to align itself or whether it was because human loyalties are truly fickle and easily seduced, even by would-be lovers who in fact offer very little by way of reward for shifting loyalties. One notes that in Mark 12:32 both meanings—the Lord is one and besides the Lord there is no other—are held together in the Great Commandment pericope, giving a canonical support for the claim that both meanings may be understood as legitimate interpretations of the text.

It is out of this command as formulated and repeated in Deuteronomy that the biblical injunction to love God has its roots. The use of the term "love" to define the relationship to God is essentially a distinctive contribution of Deuteronomic theology. Its use in Deuteronomy and in extrabiblical materials suggests strongly that what is meant here is the love of one partner in the covenant for the other, and especially the subor-

101

dinate to the superior (subjects to the king). In this context also, love does not connote primarily affective dimensions, nor is it vague or abstract in its context. It does assume a personal, intimate, trusting relation. While it is responsive or reciprocal in that it is rooted in the prior love of the One who loved the fathers and mothers of Israel (Deut. 4:37) and led their children out of oppressive slavery, it is not dependent entirely on a feeling of gratitude for its creation. As the Shema indicates, this love can be commanded. Its various associations and contexts in Deuteronomy tell us something of the character of the love that identifies the people who say "Our God is the LORD." It is closely related to fear and reverence. It is expressed in loyalty and service. Its primary manifestation is in obedience to the demands of the law, which are spelled out quite specifically in Deuteronomy. To love God is to be loyal to the Lord, to keep the Lord's commandments (10:12–13; 11:1, 22), to walk in the way of the Lord (19:9; 30:16), to do or heed the commandments, statutes, and ordinances. It was never left unclear how Israel was to manifest love toward the Lord. In worship and in obedience to the requirements of the covenant, the love of the Lord was to be demonstrated.

And as the final words of the Shema make clear, the love called for is a *total* commitment. Time and again Deuteronomy underscores its injunctions with a call for loving, obeying, keeping "with all your heart and with all your soul." Only here does Deuteronomy heap up three expressions to try to convey the totality of being and commitment appropriate to the love of the one Lord. The three parts of this expression have been interpreted in different ways.

1. Early Christian exegesis saw here complementary aspects of the human personality—mind, soul, and spirit, which together make up the person.

2. Jewish exegesis has seen here "distinct but complementary ways of manifesting love toward God" (McBride, "The Yoke of the Kingdom," p. 303):

heart—with an undivided loyalty, both good and evil impulses;
soul/life—commitment even to the point of death or martyrdom;
might—substance, wealth, property given in the service of God.

102

The impact of this understanding carries over in part in John Calvin's interpretation as he writes in one of his sermons:

> Thou shalt love God with all thy soul, is as much as to say thou shalt not spare thy life for the love of thy God. . . . Thou shalt love thy God with all thy mind or heart, betokeneth with them but as it were a comparison, so as a man should prefer God above all other things . . . and finally, thou shalt love God with all thy strength, imparted among them, that thou must love him with all thy substance and with all thy goods, as if the case required that thou shouldest be impoverished (Calvin, *Sermons,* p. 272).

3. It is most likely that the three phrases expressed a totality in a climactic fashion: heart-will, the whole self, to excess or muchness. The intention, as McBride has put it, is to express "the superlative degree of total commitments" (p. 304).

The most important word, therefore, in its character as a demand that shapes our identity is, Love the Lord your God wholeheartedly, with your whole self, with all your capacity. The oneness of the Lord your God is matched by the oneness and totality of your devotion.

In thinking about what is at stake in this essentially monotheistic claim, one can perceive both a theological and an anthropological implication. The theological implication has to do with the freedom and power of God. That is, the monotheism that arises out of this Deuteronomic center claims that there is only one ultimate or absolute—the power that undergirds all reality is one and not multiple, faithful and not capricious, a whole and not divided, and therefore capable of purpose and power because this one is not controlled and limited by other forces. The only limitation on the freedom and power of God is the self-limiting step that is taken by God in the act of creation. Without this freedom and power in God uncontrolled by outside forces, one would have to raise serious questions about the possibility of the accomplishment of the divine purpose or even the clarity of speaking of a divine purpose. For it is difficult to assume an order and a purpose to the universe if there is not a center or ground of being, value, and meaning that is one, comprehensive, and consistent.

Alongside this theological implication there is an anthropological one, the impossibility of human sharing of a loyalty that is meant to be ultimate. Penultimate loyalties to those beings and things that do not ground human existence, do not call human life into being or shape its destiny, are quite possible and indeed necessary and desirable; but the loyalty to the Creator, the Lord and Giver of life, Savior and Judge, cannot be satisfactorily divided. This claim is not merely abstract and theoretical. It is indeed personal and human and ultimately pastoral. For the oneness of the reality that grounds existence, God, is what keeps life from being chaotic and divided beyond the limits of human management. In the face of the multiple pulls and dimensions of human life and experience, human existence is held together and in order by that one and absolute object of our allegiance and loyalty. We do not find conflicting claims on our ultimate allegiance, only on secondary interests and loyalties. It is possible to deal with these secondary claims if we have a sense that our ultimate and full allegiance is directed toward one alone. The demand of the Shema is, therefore, finally not just a demand. It is also what makes human life possible. All claims on human life are relativized and subsumed within the one total claim of God so that the demand is ultimately the gift of grace.

The Preeminence of the Great Commandment (6:6-19)

If these words of the Shema are the most important words of all, what should one do with them to give them primary place? Deuteronomy 6:6–9 addresses that question as Moses gives several directions for keeping this basic claim and obligation to the fore. First of all, they are to be kept within the heart (cf. 11:18; 30:14; 32:46). That is quite important, for it guards against the easy assumption that keeping the law of Deuteronomy—or of the Old Testament generally—is a matter of the letter rather than the spirit. The first instruction about what Israel is to do with "these words" is to implant them in the heart, keep them in mind, make them part of one's very being. Verses 8 and 9 may be easily understood as indications of an external appropriation, but the symbolic acts referred to there are only in the context of an internal appropriation that makes this instruction second nature. Second, the primary commandment is to be taught to the children (see below). Third, the words are to be kept as a sign on one's body, residence, and city (vv. 8–9; cf. 11:18b–20). In chapter 11 the placing of them on one's body is seen as a concomitant action to placing them on the heart; inward appropriation and external symbol are held closely together (11:18). It is difficult to know whether these

104

instructions were meant to be taken literally or figuratively, but that is of little relevance for understanding their force. At a relatively early stage in Jewish tradition they were understood literally, and many devout Jews throughout history have bound copies of the Shema to their arms or foreheads and placed them on the doorposts of their homes. Even a figurative understanding of this command sharply underscores the fact that "these words" are to control one's individual behavior, the conduct of home and family, and the character of life in one's community (the gates of v. 9).

The command to bind this Great Commandment to the body, coming as it does after instruction to talk about these words at home, away from home, when one gets up, and when one lies down, suggests the imagery of the words as a kind of companion in life. They remind and admonish the wearer at all times and perhaps in some sense serve to protect the individual. The notion of instructive words being carried as a protecting companion (cf. Exod. 13:9, 16) is especially articulated in Proverbs 6:20–22, a passage that has clear affinities to Deuteronomy 6:6–9 and 11:18–20 (Miller, "Apotropaic Imagery"):

> My son, keep your father's commandment,
> and forsake not your mother's teaching.
> Bind them upon your heart always;
> tie them about your neck.
> When you walk, they will lead you;
> when you lie down, they will watch over you;
> and when you awake, they will talk with you.
> Proverbs 6:20–22

Deuteronomy 6:10–19 represents an elaboration and exhortation of the primary commandment as one encounters it in the Shema of 6:4–5 (positive command) and the first part of the Decalogue (5:6–11). Indeed, both positive (6:12*b*–13) and negative (6:14–15) formulations of the prologue and the first three commandments appear here. But the subject matter of these verses is not confined to obligation. The obligation that exists flows out of the reality of blessing and grace, which is the point of verses 10–11. The rich blessing of God's provision is articulated in the description of the land—large and fine cities, houses full of "everything good," hewn cisterns, vineyards, and olive groves. God's grace is expressed in the repeated emphasis on the fact that all of this is not the result of Israel's arduous labors but is the gift of God. One is reminded of Ephesians

105

2:8–9: "For by grace you have been saved through faith; and this is not your own doing, it is the gift of God—not because of works, lest [anyone] should boast." This same theology is set forth in Deuteronomy, but in terms of a kind of *spatial* notion of grace. Israel lives in the sphere of gift and grace of God, a sphere set forth in the promise to the ancestors. Whatever God's salvific work, it comes as gift, not as the result of human efforts. Moses and Paul make that perfectly clear, Moses in finding grace in God's gift of space and the provision of life, Paul in finding it in God's pardon and mercy. God's mercy ultimately transcends all experience of life as we know it, but that does not vitiate Israel's experiencing the provision of life in space and time as the free and gracious gift of God. We do not earn either divine gift and so cannot boast, as Deuteronomy 6–9, anticipating the theological structure of Paul in Ephesians 2:8–9, declares at some length.

Coming to verses 17–18, one seems to encounter a reversal of what verses 10–16 declare. There (vv. 10–16) Israel is led to obey when the Lord has brought them into the land. Here the people must obey in order to be allowed to go into the land. Norbert Lohfink has properly suggested that this is neither a contradiction nor evidence of a different literary tradition; it is an indication of the cultic setting of these texts. As they were taken up in the sphere of public and communal worship, Israel found itself in some sense always in the land and recipients of the gift of the land. But it is also the case that the cultic sphere, as the place where these texts always had potentially a present or fresh liveliness, was the vehicle by which Israel was led back to the threshold of the land, back to the boundary. Through Deuteronomy, the people of Israel became aware that they possessed the land but still did not possess it; they were recipients of blessing yet awaited blessing; because of the gift already received they were called upon to live a life of commitment and obligation so that the gift might indeed be received and perdure. The grace of God is the presupposition of the divine demand and at the same time the promised reward of fulfilling that demand. Indeed, the gift of life is possible only when it comes out of obedience to God's commands. The gift of a good and long life in the land, the place of God's provision, is at one and the same time the prior reality, the final results, and the ultimate reward for Israel's faithful and constant attention to "these words" (Lohfink, *Höre, Israel,* p. 67).

106

That the Children May Know (6:20–25)

The concluding verses of this chapter address a matter that rises a number of times in Deuteronomy: teaching the children (4:9–10; 6:7; 11:1–7, 19; 29:22–23; 31:13). There are a lot of references in this book to children, the next generation (cf. 1:36, 39; 4:40; 5:9, 29; 6:2). Receiving the land (1:36, 39), prosperity and good (5:29), long life on the land, and fearing the Lord (6:2) are all matters that at one place or another are explicitly related to the children.

The reason for this emphasis on the children is clear. Deuteronomy is always aimed at the next generation. It takes the present (next) generation back to the past and brings the past afresh into the present. The children are now the ones before whom all the choices are laid, and some day their children will be there and the divine instruction will confront them (e.g., 30:2). Can they learn afresh what it means to love the Lord wholeheartedly?

So Deuteronomy as a book of instruction is concerned about instruction—its necessity, its processes, its aims, and its results. It is concerned about learning (4:10*b*) and teaching (4:9–10). What the people learn from Moses and the Lord is to be passed on to the children so that each new generation shall be prepared to stand before God and "fear the LORD your God." The fear of the Lord is clearly the aim of educating the next generation in Israel, as several passages indicate explicitly. "Fear of the LORD" catches up all that is meant by loving the Lord and not having or serving other gods, other objects of one's ultimate allegiance. Reverence, obedience, total commitment are the ingredients of the fear of the Lord. In 6:13 the positive form of the first commandment is "You shall fear the LORD your God." To this end, all education among the people of God is set.

How does that education take place and what is its substance? The Book of Deuteronomy has a number of things to say about that in this chapter and elsewhere. One of the repeated points is that the divine instruction in this book (11:18–19), and especially its embodiment in the Great Commandment (6:7), is to be the subject of constant attention and discussion. The picture is that of a family continually in lively conversation about the meaning of their experience with God and God's expectations of them. Parental teaching of the children by conversation about "the words," study of God's instruction, and reflection on

107

it (cf. Ps. 1:2 and Josh. 1:8) is to go on in the family and the community. Whether at or away from home, "these words" are to be uppermost in mind and heart; parents should teach their children in such a way that their last thoughts before falling asleep and their first words upon getting up are about the Lord's command. The text is clear that "these words" are not simply to be recited or repeated. They are to be talked about— that is, discussed, studied, and learned. The practical implications for life are to be thought out and discussed with the children as much as they are in the Book of Deuteronomy itself.

A second feature of the educational process in Deuteronomy is response to the children's questions as a means of explicating the relationship to God. The children's questions are always there: "What is that?" "Why?" "Why do I?" In Israel such questions were the impetus for teaching the next generation the meaning of its rules and regulations, its social and religious practices, its signs and symbols (e.g., Exod. 12:26–27; Josh. 4:6–7). The response is often a story, an account of something that God did for the people. That is the case in 6:20–25. The nature of the response here suggests—as does the translation of the child's question—that the query is not simply to learn what the rules and regulations are but to find out why they are kept. What does all this mean? As Norbert Lohfink has observed, "This is obviously the question of a young man who sees the world of his ancestors constrained within a net of forms of authority, both gross and subtle, and yet they appeal to the name of God, and the young man wonders why such forms exist" (*Great Themes*, pp. 47–48).

The logic of the answer is tied to the opening words. Israel's prior existence as the slaves of Pharaoh is emphasized by the word order: "Slaves were we to Pharaoh in Egypt when the Lord brought us out of Egypt with a mighty hand" (v. 21; author's trans.). The change of master is the key thing. Whoever frees a slave is lord of the slave as far as the law and society are concerned:

> It is precisely this legal logic that the father is supposed to present to his son, if the son does not understand why there are so many laws and precepts in Israel and why they are still traced back to Israel's God. The father would explain: Without him, we would have remained under the laws of Pharaoh, and been exploited by him; for [sic] such an existence as that he has

freed us, and so we are legally under his rule (Lohfink, *Great Themes* p. 48).

What is crucial, however, is that the rule of God and the law/teaching that brings it about are not oppression, slavery, or exploitation, as was Pharaoh's rule; the rule of God is the gift of a good life to be received and apprehended in obedience to the new ruler.

The words of the parent explain, therefore, but they do more than that. They recapitulate the story of God's way with Israel as the basis for the people's present life and conduct. In so doing, they serve to create a memory for the new generation, who were not there and do not know. That is the point of the educational process, according to 4:9–10 and 31:13. In fact, Deuteronomy itself can be seen as creating such a memory for the new generation it addresses by painting pictures (8:7–10; 29:22–23) and telling stories (6:20–25), so the children may receive as real what they did not experience.

A good example of the creation of memory is found in 11:1–7, a passage that poses some textual and translation difficulties at the beginning. Some words apparently have fallen out of the text after "consider this day" (v. 2). There is no "I am . . . speaking" in the Hebrew text (so RSV). A plausible reconstruction of the text would lead to a translation along the following lines (see Lohfink, *Das Hauptgebot,* p. 221):

> Know this day that the Lord your God is the one disciplining you; for it is not your children, who have not known and have not seen the discipline of the Lord your God, his greatness, his mighty hand and his outstretched arm . . . but it is your eyes that have seen all that great work of the Lord which he did.

There are other hypotheses that may be proposed to solve the problem of the beginning of verse 2. The important thing is that verses 2b–6 explicate the "discipline [or instruction] of the Lord" in verse 2. So everything down to verse 7 is what the people saw but the children did not know or see. That then leaves the question: Why does Deuteronomy have this long account of what the children have not known or seen?

One answer that makes sense is that such a presentation gives emphasis to verse 7: *You* are the ones who have seen the great work of the Lord. This is to suggest that the instruction was really about and for Israel's "youth," a way of speaking that is not appropriate later when the child is grown up (see 8:5). So the later generations could not have known or seen all this directly, but *"you* have."

At this point, therefore, the text addresses the hearers, the assembled people of God, and roots the call to obedience in the direct experience of the Lord's work—note the repetition in the passage "what he did"—in nature and history. Those who have known the powerful work of God wrought in their lives and expressed through the forces of nature have been disciplined or instructed. Because they have seen and come to know the powerful work of God, they should acknowledge the Lord's rule and keep the Lord's commandments.

The concluding verse of this unit (v. 7) thus picks up a note frequently sounded in Deuteronomy: You have seen with your own eyes. In that reiterated emphasis, the reader/listener hears a challenge to the cliché that believers walk by faith and not by sight. At least at some points Israel was called to walk by sight. There is no assumption here that the people have not directly encountered and seen the power and work of God. On the contrary, they have seen with their own eyes and that is the basis for "walking," for their conduct before God.

Now what about the children? Are they dismissed from involvement here? Are they compelled to walk by faith and not by sight? No, in fact the passage is an implicit address to the children in order to give them sight. All the divine acts in this text are the object of the children's not having seen, not of the present generation's seeing. The latter is confined to a summary word in verse 7. By the time verse 6 is finished, the children have been shown what they had not seen and thus share by report and in detail what the earlier generation saw firsthand. They are instructed through the telling of the Lord's instruction or discipline of young Israel long ago. It comes as no surprise, therefore, that Moses' final words in Deuteronomy are, "Lay to heart all the words . . . that you may command them to your children": Teach the children (32:46–47).

The Election of Israel (7:1–26)

The divine gift of the land to Israel is given a positive ground and a negative implication in this chapter, which is one of the primary Old Testament texts for understanding the meaning of Israel's election. Israel is to conquer the land and

110

destroy its peoples. The positive reason for the gift and conquest is because God has loved and chosen Israel. The reason
for the negative implication—that people must be utterly destroyed—is that Israel has been set apart to the Lord and must
keep itself pure and totally loyal to God—again the primary
commandment (see the discussion of 7:1–6).

The heart of this chapter is verses 1–11. Here Israel is told
strongly, in various ways, to have nothing to do with the peoples
of the land and their customs (vv. 1–5) because they are a people
set apart to the Lord (v. 6). That rationale, however, opens up
the possibility of all sorts of chauvinistic and arrogant misunderstandings; so verses 7–11 clarify the meaning of that election,
giving both the reasons for and the implications of Israel's special place. The structure and movement of the first part (7:1–6)
identifies its concerns:

> *Basic command:* Utterly destroy the nations (v. 2b).
>> (Circumstances: When the Lord brings you into
>> the land vv. 1–2a).
> *Elaboration of basic command:* No relationships either
>> covenantal or marital (vv. 2c–3).
>> *Reason for this prohibition:* The danger of being
>> drawn into idolatry (v. 4).
> *Further elaboration of basic command:* No foreign cult
>> (a series of positive commands in v. 5 matching the
>> prohibitions of vv. 2c–3).
>> *Reason for the basic command:* Israel is chosen to be
>> God's people (a positive reason in v. 6 matching
>> the negative reason of v. 4).

The fact of Israel's election is stated simply and straightforwardly: "The Lord chose you out of all the peoples on the
earth." The purpose of that choice is indicated by two other
expressions: "a people for his own possession" and "a people
holy to the LORD your God." All the peoples belong to the Lord
in some sense, but Israel is the Lord's special treasure *(segul-
lah).* This is a technical term from the economic sphere indicating very valuable property, or treasure like gold and silver. But
to be God's special possession is to be holy to the Lord, set apart
from others for the Lord's service (cf. "a kingdom of priests" in
the similar passage in Exod. 19:3–6). They are to exist in a sacral
relation to the God of all the nations, serving the Lord, dedicat-
ing themselves totally as a people to God, setting themselves

111

apart from other loyalties, and manifesting the Lord's just and righteous way in the world (Gen. 18:19). To be chosen by the Lord is to receive and enjoy the benefits so graciously given, the land and its richness. It is also to receive an office or vocation within the divine purpose.

There is danger in stopping with such a straightforward expression of Israel's special treasured place in God's eyes, specifically the danger that God's people may decide that qualities within Israel elicit this divine favor. Neither Israel's history nor its theology, however, confirms such a view, as verses 7–11 indicate quite bluntly. Moses' speech at this point undercuts the false notions some held as the basis for Israel's special place (v. 7) and sets forth the true reasons (v. 8). He then goes on to spell out some of the implications of God's redemption and election for Israel's faith and life (7:9–11).

Moses therefore first gives the lie to the notion that there was any special attribute or characteristic in Israel that would evoke the Lord's love and choice of them. Quite the contrary. This people did not have especially attractive features. They were certainly not the most numerous or the greatest. Indeed, they were the least or the fewest of all the peoples. While that might seem hyperbolic, if Israel were compared with Egypt, Babylon, Assyria, and Aram, the point is well taken. A key expression in the argument is the phrase "set his love upon" *(hašaq)* in verse 7. In Genesis 34:8 and Deuteronomy 21:11, this verb is used for the strong physical desire of a man for a beautiful woman. The text indicates, therefore, that the Lord has the kind of strong desire for Israel that can be expressed by a word normally functioning primarily in the physical, erotic sphere. So also 10:14–15 says that the one to whom all the most attractive features of the universe belong "set his heart in love" upon Israel above all peoples. But contrary to what one might expect with this verb, there is in fact nothing in Israel's physical appearance that should evoke such strong desire, making one want to attach oneself—so the basic meaning of the verb—to the object.

What, then, are the reasons for God's choice of Israel? There are two of them (v. 8). One reason is that "the Lord loves you." It is as simple as that. Here is the usual word for "love," *'aheb*, not the verb *hašaq* (v. 7). At this point, there is bold statement without elaboration or explanation. By placing this simple reason over against the possible one in verse 7, the

112

choice of Israel is rooted utterly in the *love* of God. Any notion of inherent character, beauty, or merit leading to the Lord's desire and choice of Israel is explicitly rejected. The love of God, however, is intensely manifest toward this people, which is why one may properly speak of grace when talking about this divine election.

One must also speak of promise, however. The second reason stated roots the election of Israel in a history and in the self-assumed obligations of the Lord of history. In the call of Abraham, the Lord made an oath to provide land and posterity. So the gift of land now arises out of the *integrity* of the Lord, who keeps oaths even as Israel is called by God to keep its oaths and live with integrity.

There are significant implications of all this for both *faith* (7:9–10) and *life* (7:11). The implication for Israel's *life* is the continuing one in Deuteronomy: Be careful to keep the rules, the stipulations of covenant, for this demonstrates your holiness to the Lord (see 14:2, 21). The meaning of this election and redemption for *Israel's understanding of its Lord* is also spelled out. For one thing, it shows quite clearly that the Lord of Israel is God. Redemption from slavery and Pharaoh's hand is the evidence of the Lord's claim to be God. Claim to divinity is found here in the power to break the chains of slavery and oppression (cf. Ps. 82). Second, Israel learns that the Lord is a faithful God, one who keeps covenant and steadfast love with those who reciprocate such loving and keeping. An important feature of the text is the parallel between the characteristics of God that lead to Israel's election ("the Lord *loves* you and is *keeping* the oath"—v. 8) and demonstrate God's faithfulness ("who *keeps* covenant and steadfast love"—v. 9) and the characteristics of Israel required by its Lord ("those who love him and *keep* his commandments—v. 9). Israel's response to God is a reflection of the Lord's way with them. The one who keeps covenant expects Israel to keep the covenant commandments; the one who loves Israel expects this people to love wholeheartedly in return.

As this text speaks about the faithfulness of God with the language and expressions of the second commandment in verses 9–10, it brings one up against the hard fact that this faithfulness means both the Lord's keeping covenant and steadfast love with those who keep covenant in return and a requiting of those who hate God—that is, who do not keep the

113

commandments. (In Deuteronomy love and hatred of God are both expressed by one's decisions and actions vis à vis the commandments.) God is reliable and faithful, not simply to Israel but to *the Lord's purpose with* Israel and to the relationship. The disobedience-hatred of any within Israel thwarts the intention of God to create a faithful community and a righteous way in the world. So in this relationship there is a negative (judgment) dimension as well as a positive dimension.

The positive expectation dominates, however. There is no picture here of equal amounts of love and hate toward God and consequently of God toward the people. The Lord's keeping covenant and steadfast love extends to a thousand generations. It is expansive and ongoing. Those who love the Lord and keep covenant are *plural,* many (v. 9), whereas the hater of the Lord (v. 10) is *singular,* the exception rather than the norm in God's expectation of Israel's response.

When Israel so responds, the opportunities for life are abundant beyond all expectations (7:12–16; see the discussion of 10:12–11:32). The powerful link between covenant and blessing cannot be dissolved. In it lay all the possibilities for either life or death (30:15–20).

Remembering the Lord's Provision (8:1–20)

A familiar general exhortation to be careful to keep the commandment that "you may find life and blessing in the land begins the chapter. Of course, ancient Israel is addressed, but the "you" language always addresses in some way the present audience. The expression "this day" serves the same end. The time difference disappears and the people are addressed as a community living on the land in the sphere of blessing ("that you may live and multiply") but at the same time as a people still standing before the Jordan (that you may "go in and possess the land"). Thus, like all of Deuteronomy, the chapter serves to interpret and to expound the basic commandment and to carry the listener-reader back to the boundary; in this case particularly it can help the contemporary congregation understand the meaning of the primary commandment and to live by it in a time and situation of prosperity. To do that they must go back to the boundary between the difficult past life of the wilderness and the rich promise of the future on the land. The meaning and obligations of life on the land are found in going back to that time when home and place were not yet enjoyed.

114

Three literary units comprise the chapter: verses 2–6, 7–17, and 18–20. These are intricately held together around the related themes of (1) the Lord's provision and discipline and (2) Israel's remembering or not forgetting. What is said around these connected themes relates to the issues of the surrounding chapters, specifically the danger of arrogance on the part of the people of Israel because of what has happened to them and also the demand to love God totally and serve no other gods.

The opening section of the chapter (vv. 2–6) is similar in structure to chapter 7:7–11. Past history is recalled and implications for faith and life are derived from it. The experience in the wilderness between Egypt and Canaan is once again a lesson from the past. But the point of the present lesson is that the past was a lesson itself! The wilderness experience is given a focus different from that of chapters 1–3; it was a time of testing and discipline, of instruction and teaching, as a parent teaches a child with discipline. The nature of the test or experiment is explicitly stated: Will Israel keep the commandments (v. 2)?

The divine pedagogy proceeds by way of humbling the people, depriving them of all the ordinary human resources and placing them in a situation of extremity (cf. 11:1–7). In that crisis they learn their incapacity to survive on their own and the power and disposition of God to provide whatever they need. The imagery of parent and child as a way of speaking of God's relationship with Israel during the wilderness experience appears now a second time in the Book of Deuteronomy. Earlier, it was a way of characterizing God's protective and tender care during that difficult period (1:31). Here, in 8:5, the imagery points to the parent's instructive discipline. It calls to mind a different divine image that serves the same purpose in Hosea 2:14–15. There the Lord is depicted as a lover wooing the people back to the wilderness to discover, as they had done in that earlier situation, who alone is the source of all their life and all their good.

The lesson is expressed in verse 3, the most familiar verse of this chapter because of its use by Jesus in the temptation story (Matt. 4:4 and Luke 4:4). It is best translated as follows:

> He humbled you by letting you hunger, then feeding you the manna, with which neither you nor your ancestors were acquainted, in order to make you understand that human beings can live not only on bread but on anything that the Lord decrees.

115

Anything that the Lord decrees includes, in this context, both manna and commandment. The issue is not spiritual versus material food but trust in the Lord's provision and obedience versus reliance upon self. In the time of wilderness hunger, Israel was given nourishment and life by God's gift of manna. Time and again throughout the whole Book of Deuteronomy it is made clear that Israel finds its life also by keeping the commandments, the divine instruction (e.g., 4:1, 4; 5:16; 8:1, 19; 11:13–17; 30:15–20).

Jesus' citation of this verse on the occasion of his "testing" in the wilderness is fully consistent with the intended lesson of Deuteronomy. The issue is not whether one needs primarily spiritual or material food—or both—but that one relies on God for the provision of life and can be sustained by whatever God provides, and only by that. As Karl Barth says with reference to Jesus' response to the tempter,

> The reference is to the miracle effected by the Word of the Lord, which consisted in the fact that for forty years God led Israel through the desert, and that where there was no bread, and the people seemed likely to die of hunger, He nevertheless sustained them, namely by the manna which neither they nor their fathers knew. It was in exactly the same way (except that now there was no question even of manna) that God sustained the hungering Jesus in the desert (III/2, p. 67).

So Israel is meant to learn from the wilderness experience that its sustenance comes from God, who is to this people as a teaching parent. But the sermon of Moses indicates that the experiment in the wilderness was a test by which *God* also would learn something—whether Israel would keep the commandments (v. 2). The results of the experiment at that point are ambiguous. We are never told whether God received an answer or what that answer might be. That ambiguity or unanswered question is not unimportant for comprehending the purpose of Deuteronomy or the purpose of the narrative of Jesus' temptation. For it is precisely the case in Deuteronomy that the issue of the whole book is to answer: Has Israel learned the lessons of the past and will it now, in a (later) situation of prosperity and abundance, remember who is the provider and live by that one's word? The matter is still open-ended and even more acute, for the richness of life on the land with beautiful houses, lush gardens giving both the necessities and delicacies of life, and large mineral resources (v. 7–10) creates an even

116

larger possibility that prosperous people will forget the gift-giver and think, I did it all by myself (v. 17).

The movement from verse 10 to verse 12 provides the central axis of thought and thus the point of 8:7–17. Will the people, when they shall have eaten and are full, bless the Lord your God "for the good land he has given you"; that is, give thanks to the one who has provided it all (v. 10)? Or will they eat and be satisfied and prosperous with all the comforts of life and "forget the Lord your God by not keeping his command-ments" (vv. 11–12), "forget the Lord your God who brought you out of the land of Egypt, out of the house of bondage" (v. 14), and think, "My power and the might of my hand have gotten me this wealth" (v. 17)? Take heed lest the Lord find arrogance and the hubris of forgetfulness (vv. 14 and 17) rather than obe-dience (v. 2) "in your heart" (see vv. 2, 14, and 17). That is the clear and difficult word to a later generation of prosperity that has long experienced the blessing of God. Have you forgotten that the Lord is the one who gives you power to get wealth? If so, it is necessary to go back to the wilderness and the boundary to learn the lesson afresh.

The biblical account gives the impression that the people of God never learned the lesson very well. It is in the context of this reality that the account of Jesus' temptation is set specifi-cally in relation to Deuteronomy 6–8. Indeed, it has been ar-gued that the temptation narrative is a midrash on Deuteronomy 6–8, an application of these chapters to Jesus, themes and passages from these chapters providing the basis for the overall interpretation (Gerhardsson). The close ties be-tween the temptation text and Deuteronomy 6–8 are obvious: the testing theme, the wilderness setting, the theme of hunger, the forty years (Deuteronomy) and the forty days and nights (Matthew and Luke), and the quotations from Deuteronomy 6:16 and 8:3. Especially important is the parallel between Israel and Jesus carried in the notion of "son" (Deut. 1:31 and 8:5). In Deuteronomy the relationship between the Lord and Israel is compared to that of a father and son, a parent and child. The same is true of the relationship between Jesus and God. In contrast to Israel in the wilderness and in later times, this time the child (Jesus) is obedient to the parent (God). In Jesus, God receives an unambiguous answer to the question raised in Deu-teronomy 8:2 (Will you keep the commandments?). Here is the son/child who does keep God's instruction and does not tempt

God (6:16), who accepts the discipline and testing and knows that God, and not one's own power, is the provider. As such, Jesus is also the model for the way of the faithful community past and present. Those who would be open to the Mosaic instruction and exhortation in Deuteronomy can learn also from Matthew 4 and Luke 4 how faithful Israel should respond to the test and what sort of answer God seeks "in your heart" (v. 2).

A Sermon on Israel's Stubbornness (9:1–29)

These verses comprise a clear unity, with repeated expressions and continuing themes. In its discussion of what election does and does not mean, it echoes chapter 7; in its focus on the wilderness period as a lesson from the past, it echoes chapter 8. The point of the sermon is set forth in verses 1–6: Israel may claim no righteousness of its own, for the people are a stubborn people. The rest of chapter 9 shows this as one of the lessons to be learned from the wandering in the wilderness. In this manner the chapter compares in structure and content to chapter 7. The latter, however, is a positive word about the Lord as an interpretation of Israel's election; chapter 9 is a negative word about Israel and the nations as a comment on God's giving the land to Israel. Both chapters share several features: They attack the arrogance that can arise out of election and divine blessing, they declare Israel's nondeserving character, they root election in the Lord's keeping oath, they make a basic statement about election in verse 6 and elaborate it in the rest of the chapter, and they start with false reasons for election and then move to correct reasons. Chapter 9 then returns to the erroneous assumption about election (virtue in Israel) and demonstrates its falseness by making a case for the stubbornness (vv. 6, 13, 27), provocation (vv. 7, 8, 18, 22), and rebellion (vv. 7, 23, 24) of Israel during the time in the wilderness.

Verses 1–3 begin with the familiar declaration that the Lord is giving the land to Israel. Then it raises afresh and finally the original fear of the people: the inhabitants—the Anakim—are too powerful for anyone to overcome (cf. commentary on ch. 1). This time Moses declares—with emphasis—the greater and indeed invincible power of the inhabitants "whom you know" and "of whom you have heard" (vv. 1–2). The point of the might of the present inhabitants of Canaan is forcefully scored. The

118

wilderness generation of chapters 1—2 would seem to have been correct in their fearfulness. But that is immediately exposed as a false assumption. With the command "know therefore" (cf. 4:39; 7:9; 8:5; 9:6; 11:2); the function of these words seems to be "learn from this." Israel is to gain new knowledge about the Lord or to hear afresh from what has just been said a fundamental word about its God. Here in verse 3, Moses makes the basic claim similar to that in chapter 1; the Lord is powerful to destroy even the mighty Anakim. As Israel "crosses over" (v. 1; RSV, "pass"), the Lord will go over before them (v. 3). In chapter 1 the image of God's power was that of the divine warrior. Here the symbolism of the consuming fire of God, already developed in chapters 4–5, reappears. The emphasis on the power of the Anakim in verses 1–2 is matched by the emphasis in verse 3 on the power of the Lord, also reflected in the emphatic use of pronouns ("*he* will destroy them; [*he*] will subdue them before you.")

To be noted is the care with which the text expresses the unity of divine and human action in verse 3. The two kinds of action are simply conjoined: *He* will destroy them, and *he* will subdue them before you; and you will conquer (dispossess) them and destroy them. There is no explanation of how this symbiosis works, no indication of what part Israel plays over against the Lord's activity. The action of history is a shared enterprise in this instance. The victory is seen on both divine and human levels. What is clearly indicated is that Israel could not win the battle against such powerful and overwhelming forces on its own.

To claim the Lord's favor to the extent of a quick defeat of the much more powerful inhabitants of the land could lead to the assumption that Israel was especially deserving of that favor. Indeed, one may assume that in the years Israel occupied the land before the writing of Deuteronomy such an assumption was present if not indeed widespread. As it places the people of God once again on the boundary between promise and fulfillment, Deuteronomy seeks to shatter on the hard rocks of history any claim on Israel's part to have won the Lord's gift out of its own virtue. Verses 4–6 clearly deny such an assumption, and in fact the rest of the chapter illustrates the opposite picture of Israel's character.

To understand the nature of the argument in verses 4–6, one must realize that the quotation of the words or thoughts of

119

the people in verse 4 extends to the end of the verse. The change from first person at the beginning of the quote to second person at the end—"before you"—is not that unusual (cf. 1:8). The change may be due to the stereotypical character of the last clause of verse 4. Note, for example, the same expression at the end of verse 5. Verse 4*b* should be translated as follows: "It is because of my righteousness that the Lord has brought me in to possess this land, and it is because of the wickedness of these nations that the Lord is driving them out before you (i.e., me)."

The organizing rubric of these verses is found in the expressions "because of . . . righteousness" versus "because of . . . wickedness," and the logic of the argument is as follows:

PEOPLE: It is because of our righteousness and the nations' wickedness (v. 4*b*).

MOSES: No, it is not because of your righteousness but because of the nations' wickedness (v. 5). Furthermore, you are not only not righteous but stubborn (or, Your unrighteousness is demonstrated in your stubbornness; v. 6). Here are the facts of your behavior to prove it, beginning with Horeb (vv. 7–21) and continuing through the rest of the journey in the wilderness (vv. 22–24).

The words "righteousness" *(sedakah)* and "wickedness" *(riš'ah)* in this context are to be seen in terms of their juridical usage. The purpose of a court trial is to determine the innocent (righteous) and the guilty (wicked; cf. 25:1). In most instances when the question of innocence (righteousness) and guilt (wickedness) is posed, a judgment is made about both sides. In this case, the conflict between the Israelites and Canaanites is viewed in juridical terms as a trial by ordeal to determine who is in the right. God indicates by the victor who is in the right. Such a view of war was not uncommon in the ancient Near East. It is not surprising to find Israel interpreting the defeat of the Canaanites in these terms.

Moses, in anticipation of the victory over the Canaanites (though in fact it was Israel looking back on that event, many years later), warns the people against making the usual assumption that the victors are right or righteous and the losers are guilty or wicked. Part of the assumption is correct. The nations of the land are indeed guilty, and in Deuteronomy the displace-

120

ment of the Canaanites is understood as a divine judgment against them, a judgment that makes sense in the context of the Deuteronomic perception of their social and religious wickedness (see I Kings 16:29–34 and ch. 21). But over against Israel's assumption that the victors are therefore judged to be righteous comes the strong negative word that Israel is not righteous but, rather, stubborn, provoking, and rebellious, as demonstrated especially in the incident of the making of the golden calf at Horeb (Sinai). The implicit definition of righteousness by which Israel is measured and found wanting is the insistent theme of this book: The Lord of this people claims their full and exclusive devotion (5:7; 6:4–5). The failure of Israel to put its full trust in the Lord alone was demonstrated time and again in the wilderness, but it was also apparent in the later history with which the Deuteronomist would have been very familiar. This failure meant there was no possible justification for Israel to assume any righteousness on its part.

The issue of innocence and guilt, righteousness and wickedness, in these verses is not an issue of the relation of Israel to "these nations" but of each of them to God. Even the victor who is favored by God can claim no special merit; quite the contrary. The theological conclusion of these verses, therefore, is similar to the argument and claim of Paul in Romans 1–3 that all are under the power of sin, Jew no less than Gentile (3:9). Although he does not allude to this passage, Paul found basis for that conviction all through the Old Testament. He knew that the torah, the divine instruction, is to be kept (Rom. 3:31) and that the keeping of it is the responsibility of the people of God in their relationship with God. But the story will always show a failure to do so that vitiates any claims to righteousness.

Why, then, does the Lord decide for Israel in the conflict with the nations? Both Paul (Rom. 3:21–26) and Deuteronomy (7:6–11) see clearly that it is the grace and faithfulness of God that justifies. George Braulik ("Law as Gospel," p. 10) sums this up well:

> That which Israel's self-righteousness is not capable of attaining, however, is freely given to this guilt-laden people by its God in abundant mercy. It is allowed to enter into salvation's sphere, into the good land, given unto a sinful people but as a people yet unconditionally pardoned by Yahweh. . . . Yahweh's motivation is the promise he gave to the patriarchs (cf. Rom. 11:28).

121

The sinner who in relation to God can make no claim upon the land is "justified" or given the salvation gift (occupation of the promised land) by God.

One can see, therefore, an analogy between the argument of this chapter and the opening chapters of Romans. Deuteronomy makes less of a case for the wickedness of the "gentiles" (or "these nations") than Paul, though that wickedness is straightforwardly declared and in many other places. Here as in Romans, the case is made that all peoples are guilty before the Lord, or, at least, that even the ones whom the Lord loves have no justification out of their own merit but only through the love and faithfulness of God.

Moses as Intercessor (9:7–29; 10:10–11)

Another element in Deuteronomy's portrait of Moses is added with this passage. Along with the view of Moses as suffering servant (see commentary on 3:12–29), as teacher (see commentary on 5: 1–5, 22–33 and 6:1–3), and as prophet (see commentary on 18:9–22), the leader of Israel is also shown as intercessor, one who prays in behalf of those he leads. This function is not unrelated to others. The suffering servant in whose line the Deuteronomic Moses stands is one who intercedes for transgressors (Isa. 53:13), as is also the prophet on occasion (e.g., Amos 7:1–6).

The comparison with Amos is particularly appropriate, for this occasion of Moses' intercession for his people shares several features in common with the intercession of Amos.

Like Amos (and indeed like the suffering servant), Moses prays for divine mercy for the people, knowing fully their sin and disobedience. In both cases, the sin of the people is not a single, rash action against the will of God but a persistent pattern of disobedience—at Horeb (v. 8), Taberah, Massah, Kibroth-hattaavah, and Kadesh-barnea (vv. 22–24). The prophet knows the people's sin but dares to appeal to the mercy of God no matter how extensive the history of rebellion and stubbornness. It is almost characteristic of the intercessors of the Old Testament that their passionate intercession is most clearly present when the sin is greatest (cf. Abraham's pleas for Sodom and Gomorrah). It is as if they know that the mercy of God is equal to and is as intense as the judgment of God.

The intercessor, to motivate and urge a positive response to

122

the prayers in behalf of the people, appeals to various aspects of the Lord's character and concern. For Amos, the appeal is rooted in the prophet's knowledge of God's special concern for the weak and defenseless ("How can Jacob stand? He is so small"). Moses makes several appeals.

1. He appeals to the nature and quality of the relationship. Israel is God's chosen people, God's peculiar treasure or possession (9:26, 29). So Moses urges that God not destroy the relationship that has been created.

2. Moses appeals to the redemptive work of God, the saving act by which God redeemed Israel from slavery (9:26). It is as if Moses says, Do not bring to nought the work you have done in this people.

3. Moses then draws upon the election of Israel mentioned earlier in the chapter, the oath the Lord swore to Abraham, Isaac, and Jacob (see the parallel verse in Exod. 32:13). God's own faithfulness serves here as ground for Moses' plea for mercy.

4. Finally, Moses appeals to the reputation of the Lord's power in the world, which is really a call for the vindication of God's power before the people. It is an appeal to the integrity of God, the faithfulness of the one who is consistent in dealing with the people.

The result of Moses' intercession is the same as that of Amos—the rather startling word that the Lord listened to Moses' prayer and heeded it (cf. Exod. 32:14—"And the LORD repented of the evil which he thought to do to his people"). It is startling because it suggests that a change of mind is possible for God and indeed happens, a notion that cuts against our ideas both of divine consistency and of the nexus of cause and effect that seems to operate in all matters. Furthermore, the various efforts on Moses' part to motivate God to turn from judgment to mercy may seem inappropriate if we have learned that the essence of prayer is "Thy will be done."

But the Scriptures persistently testify that the heart of God is moved by the importuning prayers of chosen servants and that a dimension of the divine consistency is precisely the continuing inclination of God toward a merciful dealing with humankind, and especially with those who are God's people. What is clear from the motivating appeals of Moses is that the prayer is not for an arbitrary or inconsistent action on God's part. It is a prayer for the divine will and purpose as it has been

123

manifested over and over again—a faithful, redemptive, forgiving purpose grounded in perduring relationships and constantly being vindicated before the public audience of peoples and nations. The prayer, with all its appeals and as it pushes God, is precisely in tune with who God is and how God acts. It anticipates later prayers in behalf of a sinful humanity ("Father, forgive them"—Luke 23:24) and the hearkening response of God that will withhold appropriate judgment in favor of mercy, yea, even take the judgment for the sake of mercy ("Truly this was the Son of God!"—Matt. 27:54; see Miller, "Moses").

The Sermon Concludes (10:12—11:32)

Moses' great sermon on the most important words (5:6–10 and 6:4–5) comes to a close as he moves to set forth all the statutes and ordinances by which the people shall live (chs. 12—26). The basic themes of the preceding chapters are sounded again in summary fashion:

10:12–13, 20; 11:8, 13	The requirement of total commitment to the Lord (cf. 6:4–5, 13; 7:9)
10:14–15	The Lord's election of Israel in love (*ḥašaq* and *'ahabah;* cf. 7:1–11)
11:1–7	The Lord's discipline and provision in the wilderness (cf. 8:1–6, 15–16)
11:1–7, 18–21	The teaching of the next generation (cf. 6:4–9, 20–25)
11:6	Israel's rebellion in the wilderness (cf. 9:1—10:11)
11:8–17	The gift of a rich and abundant land (cf. 6:10–11; 8:7–10, 12–13)
11:16, 28b	The rejection of all other gods (cf. 6:14–15; 7:4–5, 16, 25–26; 8:19
11:24–25	Israel's capacity by the Lord's power to overcome all her enemies (cf. 7:17–26)

Two sections of this conclusion merit a special word and take up themes from preceding chapters not yet addressed in these pages. The first of these is 10:12–22. The character of chapters 10 and 11 as a summation to drive the main points home is signaled by the opening of this section (10:12–13) with its direct address to the people ("Israel"), indicating that the conclusion one should draw from all that has been said ("and now . . .") is here; the forthright rhetorical question reminiscent of Micah 6:8: "What does the Lord require of you?" signals the fact that this is what it all boils down to. Indeed, Deuteronomy 10:12–13 qualifies as much as its more famous co-text in Micah as a summary of the Lord's requirement. Certainly it is a full and precise summary of all the positive Deuteronomic formulations of the appropriate human response to the Lord: hearing the Lord your God, walking in the ways of the Lord, loving the Lord, serving the Lord your God, keeping the commandments of the Lord. And all these completely synonymous acts, which provide varying images and rich theological vocabulary to speak about our commitment to God, are to be done with all your heart and with all your soul: that is, they are to be carried out wholeheartedly, with your total being.

Then, in summary fashion again, the Lord's electing love of Israel is set forth and two implications for Israel's conduct are drawn. That is, the Lord loved your ancestors and chose you (vv. 14–15), so circumcise your heart (v. 16) and love the stranger (v. 19). These actions are motivated by reference both to Israel's experience and to the character of God. The call to circumcise the heart is grounded in that inexplicable and astonishing electing love and the nature of God as great and mighty and just. The call to love the stranger is grounded in God's love of the stranger or sojourner and Israel's own experience as strangers and sojourners in Egypt (vv. 18–19).

The injunction to "circumcise the foreskin of your heart" (v. 16) has not occurred previously in Deuteronomy, but the image is found elsewhere in the Old Testament (Lev. 26:41; Jer. 4:4; 9:26; Ezek. 44:9) and is one that Paul develops pointedly in Romans 2:25–29. The meaning is quite clear. While we do not know all that lay behind physical circumcision, it symbolized a vow of dedication, an initiation into the demonstration of the covenant relationship. In addition, circumcision probably represented in some sense a purification rite. All that is taken over in the notion of circumcising the heart. But here the act is not physical or symbolic; the mind and will, consciousness and freedom, are now to be purified and brought into relationship with God. There is an implicit recognition in this and the related texts that physical circumcision is important on both physical and symbolic levels but insufficient as a manifestation for one's inclusion in the covenant community apart from the transformation of the heart. The New Testament community stressed

125

this point so far that it eventually came to regard the physical-symbolic act as unnecessary. While Israel always maintained the practice of physical circumcision for its males, it never regarded the circumcision of the heart as unnecessary or unimportant. In that sense, Paul's argument in Romans 2:25–29 is simply a logical extension of the Old Testament law and the prophets: Circumcision is of value if you obey the law; but if you break the law, your circumcision becomes uncircumcision (i.e., uncircumcision of the heart). Paul Achtemeier's summary of Paul's theology in Romans (p. 51) is fully applicable to Deuteronomic theology at this point:

> True "chosenness," "true Jewishness," is not a matter of outward marks or appearances; it is a matter of inner reality, a reality perceived not by other people but by God, before whom such reality is honored and where the appearance, however honored by other human beings, is not.

A further development of the symbolism of circumcision, which also has its affinities with Paul and the New Testament, will be found when we come to chapter 30. The injunction "be no longer stubborn," which parallels the command to "circumcise the foreskin of your heart," is the chief clue to the fact that 10:12–22 is to be read not only as a general conclusion to chapters 5–11 but also as implication specifically of the story that has been told in 9:1–29 and 10:10–11. The point of that sermon-story, as we have noted, is that Israel can claim no righteousness of its own, for the people are stubborn. The solution to that very real problem, which had nearly destroyed the people (9:19), is now presented. One notes that, as Moses' sermon states it, the history of the people has been a continuing story of rebellion against the Lord, from the deliverance out of Egypt up to the arrival at the boundary of the promised land. Even after the Horeb apostasy, they continued to rebel (9:22–24). Nothing is indicated by way of change or repentance on the part of the people. Only Moses' intercession has stayed the Lord's destroying anger (9:19–20; 10:10). Continued rebellion, however, can surely not avoid disaster, and intercession cannot hold off the divine wrath forever (see Amos 7:1–8:3). So—circumcise your hearts and cease your stubborn rebellion. Rather than stiff necks (which is the actual language translated as "stubborn" in RSV) circumcised hearts are what God requires, mind and will purified and devoted totally to the Lord.

Love of the stranger is the corollary of circumcision of the heart. Little is said about that here, but hearer and reader are reminded by two things: (1) the life lived in relationship with God is characterized by a heart not only purified and bound to the Lord but also open to the other; and (2) the experience of being slaves and strangers marks forever the way those who have been released and given a home treat others whom they encounter as slaves and strangers. Love the Lord and love the stranger—that is indeed the greatest of the commandments.

Finally, Moses' long exhortation on the most important words, the basic commandment, comes to a close in 11:26–31. The second speech of Moses is not yet over. It continues in his setting forth the statutes and the ordinances in chapters 12–26. But a conclusion is reached at this point, as seen by the way in which these verses anticipate the actual conclusion of the second speech in chapters 27–28, as well as the conclusion to the third address of Moses (chs. 29–30), and by the echo of these verses at the end of chapter 11. In all three cases two things happen: The Lord sets blessing and curse before the people, and the people are called now to make a choice.

The word of blessing has been sounded again and again in chapters 5–11, most clearly in 7:12–16. The blessings, of course, are explicitly tied to the land. They are to be experienced and received in Israel's growth as a people on the land and in the fertility of flocks and herds as well as in the rich abundance from the land. Land in Deuteronomy is not promised only as past fact. It always carries with it promise as a future reality; it holds the promise of material goods, provision for life, even the good and enjoyable things, not merely the bare necessities, health and security. To speak about the blessing is to move into the sphere of God's providence, God's provision of the continuity of life and the matrix of existence in which life is both possible and good. The allotments of land to Israel, and indeed to other peoples such as the Edomites, Moabites, and Ammonites, manifest that provision for life. This has been the divine intention from the very beginning of creation (Gen. 1:28–30) and all along the way (e.g., Gen. 12:1–3; cf. Miller, "Syntax and Theology").

It is important to note that at the conclusion of chapter 11 both blessing and curse are mentioned, but they are not pronounced upon the people to take effect in the very pronouncement, as is the case, for example, in Noah's blessing and curse

127

upon his sons (Gen. 9:25–27) or Isaac's blessing of Jacob and Esau (Gen. 27), or Jacob's blessing of his sons (Gen. 49) and Joseph's sons (Gen. 48:8–22). Here Moses sets the blessing and the curse *before* Israel, in front of the people. These are not parental words upon children but the sanctions of the covenant that identify the possible outcomes of either obedience or disobedience to the covenant. There even seems to have been a ceremony of covenant renewal in which blessing and curse were actually set before the people at Shechem on the mountains of Gerizim and Ebal (11:29; chs. 27–28).

So a choice has to be made. Blessing and curse, the possibilities for life or death, are out there before Israel; it is up to the people now to choose. In a preaching manner, and consistent with the character of covenant, Moses calls for a verdict by the people; their choice will determine what the future holds for them—obedience to the Lord's will and way in the land, which will open up all its possibilities for life and blessing, or disobedience, which will bring loss of the land, its rich abundance, its provision for life, and thus will lead to death.

Again Israel, whenever it hears this word, is placed on the boundary between land and landlessness, life and death. A people of later generations, enjoying all the benefits of life on the land, are carried back to that moment when all or nothing lay before them; as that happens, they are reminded of the way of obedience and the way of disobedience. In the manner of their life before God in the sphere of divine blessing, God's people will shape their future as they decide between obedience and disobedience.

Deuteronomy 12–26
Further Rules and Regulations for Life

Having set forth the primary commandment, the most important words, Moses now presents further instruction: specific cases and rules that spell out the basic guidelines set forth in the commandments and the summary word of the Shema (6:4–5). Not all of these statutes and ordinances can be related directly to the Ten Commandments, but one may see a move now to show what the guiding principles set forth in chapters 5 and 6 mean for specific matters that arise in the lives of people in community with one another and God.

The section begins (12:1) and ends (26:16–19) with a call to obedience and a reminder. Israel's fundamental allegiance to the Lord is its covenantal obligation and the context in which the rich blessing of life in the land is possible.

Toward a New Order: One Worship of the One God (12:1–32; 14:22–29; 15:19—16:17)

At the beginning of the specific rules and cases that Moses teaches Israel for ordering its life—many of which echo earlier statutes and ordinances of Exodus 21–23 but are revised to fit changing social and historical circumstances (see von Rad, *Deuteronomy*, pp. 12–15)—is one of the matters most crucial to the Deuteronomic understanding of the right relationship with God: *the proper worship of the Lord.* In particular, the chapter is concerned with how and where such worship goes on, because that is integrally tied to the more basic concern of *who* Israel is to worship.

Placement of the instruction about worship at the sanctuary in first position indicates clearly its priority for Deuteronomy, which assumes that the starting point for the proper, full, and exclusive love of the Lord (the primary demand of the first and second commandments and the Shema) is found in the way Israel carries out the activities of worship. The radical and unyielding demand for a total commitment to God does not regard the practices and details of worship as incidental or secondary to other matters. Whatever else such commitment involves, it begins in the service of worship.

In studying chapter 12, one should keep in mind 14:22–29, which is closely associated with that chapter, as well as the related material in 15:19—16:17. The units of chapter 12 represent a logic that is not difficult to perceive. The two sections (vv. 1–7 and 8–12) provide the primary definition of and the rationale for correct worship of God, the first section setting this against Canaanite worship practices and the second section contrasting the way Israel is to worship the Lord in the land with how it has worshiped up to this point. Verses 13–19 provide the earliest and in some sense primary definition of right

129

sacrifice, which is expanded in verses 20–28. The concluding section (vv. 29–32) returns to the primary concern, resistance to the allure of the Canaanite gods and worship practices. In so doing it provides a transition to chapter 13, which gives further rules for guarding against such practices and safeguarding maintenance of the first and second commandments. Chapter 14:22–29 continues the regulation of sacrifice and worship but does so in terms of tithing. Chapter 15:19–23 sets forth similar rules but with reference to the firstlings of the flocks. Chapter 16:1–17 regulates the three major festivals—Passover and Unleavened Bread, Weeks, and Booths—along similar lines as the preceding regulations.

Looking closely at these units, one perceives some similarities and repetitions that reflect a generally common structure, or at least shared elements, which by their repetition identify basic themes of these statutes. This is particularly true in the first three units, as well as in 14:22–29:

	12:1–7	12:8–12	12:13–19	14:22–29
A prohibition	v. 4	v. 8	vv. 13 16–17	——
A command using the sanctuary formula	v. 5	v. 11	vv. 14, 18	v. 23a
Sacrifice and offerings	v. 6	v. 11b	vv. 14b, 17b	vv. 23b, 26, 28
Eating	v. 7	——	vv. 18–19	vv. 23b 26b, 29
Rejoicing	v. 7	v. 12	vv. 18–19	v. 26b
Allusion to God's blessing	v. 7	(implicit)	v. 15	vv. 24, 29
Concern for inclusiveness	v. 7	v. 12	vv. 18, 19	vv. 27, 29

Recognizing common threads running throughout these units serves two purposes. One is to identify basic themes of these chapters, and the other is to make the point that the concern of this part of Deuteronomic law is not simply a matter of making sure that all worship of the Lord is centralized in Jerusalem. One may be led to accentuate that note when these chapters are read against the historical background of Josiah's reform (see II Kings 21—23). But there is in fact no reference to Jerusalem here; one must listen to what the text says rather than merely labeling it the law of cult centralization. This makes it a matter largely of historical interest, and even then for a fairly brief period of Israel's history. The fundamental claim of this text is once again a reiteration of the basic instruction of the Book of Deuteronomy: that is, total allegiance to the one Lord, your God. In that sense the passage introduces no new divine regulation, now long obsolete and of historical interest only, but echoes what we hear at every point in this book, an insistence on the exclusive worship of the one God. The text is a radical claim for the lordship of the God of Israel and a total rejection of the claim of any other deity to Israel's worship. The total rejection is found in the opening verses (vv. 2–3), where total obliteration of every dimension of the worship of other gods—place, practices, and name—is called for. Destruction of the name parallels destruction of the place. Over against destruction of the names of the other gods with their sanctuaries is set the word about the Lord making the Lord's name dwell in the place where Israel is to worship.

Replacing one divine name with another serves two functions. First, it indicates that here we deal with the fundamental question of the functioning reality of the other gods. Their names are gone; one may no longer call upon the name of any of those gods. They may not be acknowledged or worshiped and are thus rendered ineffectual as far as Israel is concerned (cf. the sentencing of the other gods to mortality in Ps. 82). Further, negating one group of names and establishing another name in effect calls for a new order, a transformation: a shift from an order where there are multiple claims for human allegiance and where the worship of god or gods is done in arbitrary and accidental fashion (v. 2b); where any place and paraphernalia can function in that way; and where human design determines the place and nature of worship. This order is to give way to another, wherein divine control is placed over human worship and one name replaces all other names. Here is the significance of the Lord's choosing a place for the divine name to dwell: The emphasis is not upon *one* place so much as it is upon the place *the Lord chooses.* That is clarified in verse 13, where the people

131

are warned against offering burnt offerings "at every place that you see," like the other nations who serve their gods "upon the high mountains and upon the hills and under every green tree" (v. 2). The central activity of Israel's life, the worship of the Lord, is fully shaped and determined by the Lord. That worship will take place "in one of your tribes" (v. 14; cf. v. 5), but the choice is open. It will be the Lord's choice, and it may change. The point is that there is an appropriate place where the Lord may be found and worshiped, but that place is not arbitrary and anywhere. In the Lord's order, the Lord will choose and reveal the locus of dwelling and encounter with human life and with God's people.

As it sets forth the way it is to be when Israel inherits the salvation gift of the land, a place for life as God's people, the text before us is a kind of *anticipation of the Kingdom of God*. That is, it knows a present situation but anticipates imminently a quite different one in which the Lord's name and the Lord's order will be established. Even the seeking language of verse 5 anticipates the New Testament language about the Kingdom. The distinction between the present situation, where one does what is right in one's own eyes (v. 8), and the new situation is a sharp indication of the shift to a new order and a new kingdom. Verse 8 needs to be placed against verses 25 and 28 as well as 13:18. Even for people who worship the Lord, the present reality is shaped by their own designs more than is appropriate for the Kingdom. The shift from the old order to the new is not only a move from the claims of other gods to the exclusive claim of the Lord. It is also a shift from doing what is right in one's own eyes (v. 8) to doing what is right and good in the eyes of the Lord (12:25, 28; 13:18).

The text also has the character of Kingdom anticipation in that one sees here in Israel's regular life the seeds of the Messianic banquet. The community is called to gather with all its gifts before God to eat, rejoice, and celebrate the blessing of God with no member of the community unprovided for or left out. The primary activity at the place of the Lord's choosing is the bringing of gifts and sacrifices. But these are not seen as provision for upkeep of the sanctuary or the worship apparatus. Nor are they tied to sin and its expiation, though the later legislation of Leviticus 17:10–16 understands the prohibition against eating the blood that bears the life as due to its being set by God for atonement of sin. The Levitical understanding

132

leads directly into the New Testament christological claim that there is no forgiveness of sins without the shedding of blood (Heb. 9:22), which is given upon the altar by God (Lev. 17:11) in the death of Christ (Rom. 3:25; Eph. 1:7). The Deuteronomic instruction about worship, sacrifice, and festival (15:19—16:17) leads more toward the eucharist as a thanksgiving meal and toward the eschatological banquet, where people will come from east and west, from north and south, and "sit at table in the kingdom of God" (Luke 13:29). In thanksgiving and celebration, all shall partake of the blessing of God.

One can hardly avoid—nor should one hold back from—placing this text in juxtaposition with the one place in the New Testament where the Deuteronomic teaching about the proper place of worship is reflected; this occurs in the conversation between Jesus and the Samaritan woman in John 4. The woman alludes to the prior worship of her people on this mountain, Samaria (or Gerizim), and the Jewish worship of God in Jerusalem (vv. 20–26). Jesus appears to and does in some sense reject that notion for the future by indicating that worship shall be neither in this mountain nor yet in Jerusalem; the true worshiper shall worship God in spirit and in truth. This has often been understood as a breaking away from the particularizing of Jewish worship into the more universal spiritualized worship of Christian faith. Karl Barth has responded properly to that understanding by noting what follows in the story in the Gospel of John. The Samaritan woman answers Jesus with the words, "I know that Messiah is coming" (v. 25), and Jesus says to her, "I who speak to you am he" (v. 26). Barth says at this point:

> This does not mean that the freedom of the divine dwelling had suddenly ceased to be the freedom of an actual dwelling of God, and that its relativity would now rule out its reality. It does not mean that the divine presence in the world had suddenly become that of a mere undifferentiated ubiquity, and not of definite and distinct places. . . . On the contrary, we have only to glance at the way in which the terms "spirit" and "truth" are used elsewhere in St. John's Gospel and we shall see at once that it is worship of God mediated through Jesus as the one who makes everything known to us. . . . On the contrary, the reality of the definite, distinct dwelling of God in the world is now made clear in this true but not abstract antithesis, in which it can be said: "The Word . . . was made flesh, and dwelt among us, and we beheld his glory" (Jn. 1:14). This was what underlay Beth-El and Sinai, Jerusalem and Shiloh, but not the temples of the heathen gods or Gerizim ("Ye worship ye know not what").

133

... Salvation is really of the Jews. But it is really salvation; and when it has actually come from the Jews and been rejected by the Jews as such, it is no more simply for the Jews, but from the Jews for all, Jews and Gentiles, who are ready to be worshippers of this kind, in spirit and in truth, as the Father wishes them to be. We are dealing with the fulfillment of the Old Testament predictions of the divine dwelling, and not their annulment. ... What the Old Testament had said about the special nature of all these places still obtains—indeed now.... All these places in their special concrete and distinctive character stood for the special nature of God's place, from which His Word, His Law and His salvation always go forth in the special way that corresponds to the special nature of God Himself, that He may now be in His special place for us too in the world, that He may be seen and heard and tasted and believed by men with human faculties and senses. Now that the concealment of the Messiah has passed and His revelation by the people of Israel as such is repudiated, so that this people is no longer the isolated bearer of the covenant, the time has also passed of God's dwelling at those special places whose special nature was bound up with the conditions that have now lapsed. It has passed like the time of the sacrifices and the whole Law of Israel as such (II/1, 481–482).

The Deuteronomic word about the Lord's choosing a place for God's name to dwell in the midst of the people is not vitiated. It is confirmed, but that happens now in the One whom God sent, who has become the center of worship, the One before whom all the thanksgiving offerings are laid in joy, the One who presides at all the feasts of the people of God, the One in whom the fullness of God was pleased to dwell (Miller, "Way of Torah").

The Sabbatical Release (15:1–23)

In this important chapter the sabbatical principle, the ground of which is laid in the sabbath commandment, is given its fullest expression in Deuteronomy. It is one of the clearest expressions in the whole book of the love of neighbor and the humanity of the Deuteronomic instruction. Like the sabbath, the laws of release in the seventh year have remembrance of God's redemptive activity as an aim (15:15) but are fundamentally set to provide rest and release from large burdens and obligations that otherwise would indefinitely oppress and enslave those so encumbered. The revolution of freedom, which is one of the prominent threads in human history, receives a large impetus in this text and those associated with it (e.g., Lev. 25). The land was a provision for freedom in space, the sabbath a provision for freedom in time.

The "release" *(šemiṭṭah)* first appears in Exodus 23:10–11 where the land is "released" and lies fallow in the seventh year, presumably for the sake of the land but expressly for the sake of the poor and the wild beasts who are allowed access to what grows of its own (cf. Lev. 25:2–7). The weekly sabbath rest for animals, slaves, and aliens is directly tied to this early law in Exodus 23:12. So also the Deuteronomic sabbatical release is seen as analogous to the sabbath rest. As one "does the sabbath day" (5:15—RSV, "keep the sabbath day"), so one "does a release" (15:1—RSV, "grant a release"; NRSV, "grant a remission of debts"). As the fourth commandment calls for a *šabbat lyhwh*, "a sabbath to the LORD" on the seventh day (Deut. 5:14), so Deuteronomy 15 calls for a *šemiṭṭah lyhwh*, "a release to the Lord" (Deut. 15:2; NRSV, "the Lord's remission") every seven years. The force of the sabbath rest is now carried forward from the agricultural sphere of Exodus 23 into the economic sphere; the burden of debt can be stopped (15:1–6) and even bond slaves can gain release and freedom (15:12–18). The latter provision is specifically grounded in the same motivation or aim as the sabbath commandment: "You shall remember that you were a slave in the land of Egypt" (15:15). In fact, generally the laws that explicitly call for justice and compassion toward the weaker and powerless members of the community are motivated in exactly the same way (Deut. 16:9–12; 24:18, 22).

The movement of thought in 15:1–11 must be observed carefully. It begins in verses 1–3 with the statement of the ordinance for releasing debts in the seventh year. (Note that the law applies only within the community. It does not apply to outsiders [v. 3a], even as the slave law of 15:12–18 applies to Hebrew slaves only and not to captive slaves.) There has been much discussion over whether the release is a temporary release of interest obligations or a full remission of the loan. In light of the parallel law in 15:12–18 and the explicit language of verses 2–3, the latter would seem to be the case—a full release. Verses 4–6 are a qualification indicating that there should be no poor if only you obey the Lord. As in Deuteronomy 7:12–16, the abundance of the Lord's blessing is available if there is obedience. In that case there would be no poverty and

135

thus no need to worry about economic release. The point of these verses makes some real sense. Failure to live by the Lord's way did increase the poverty in the land, as Amos, Micah, and Isaiah make clear and as the Deuteronomist(s) well knew.

After a hortatory reminder in verses 4–6, the law of verses 1–3 continues in verses 7–11. Recognizing the human reality that there probably will be poor people ("If there should be a poor person among you" v. 7; author's trans.), here is how you are to act in regard to them. There follows a series of prohibitions—do not harden your heart or shut your hand or give grudgingly—and commands—open (the Hebrew is emphatic here in vv. 8 and 11) your hand, lend what is needed, give freely (again the Hebrew is emphatic, v. 10)—prescribing the proper way. Three things of note about these injunctions carry over into the law about release of slaves. One is the *prominent use of body language*—hand (vv. 1, 2, 7, 8, and 11), heart (vv. 7, 9, and 10), and eye (v. 9, 18). Such language indicates to the hearer that both attitude and action, disposition and conduct, are involved in relating to those who are poor. How you look upon "your poor brother [or sister]" is a matter of concern, but even more important is the attitude of the heart and mind (Hebrew *lebab* includes both). Do not set your mind against one who is poor: that is, create intellectual and rational reasons for ignoring the poor person in your midst. Nor should you be hardhearted and without compassion toward such a one. Compassion and openheartedness are the order of God, attitudes that work themselves out in the action of the hand, which, like the heart, must be open and not closed.

A second feature of the text is one we have noticed elsewhere (see the discussion of Deut. 2), and that is the regularity with which *the poor person is described as neighbor* (v. 2) *and especially "brother"* (vv. 2, 3, 7 [two times], 9, 11, and 12 [which makes it clear that "brother" is not a gender-exclusive term]). This is in part to distinguish conduct toward members of the community from that toward persons outside. But the frequency of usage (cf. the repeated use of "brother" in Gen. 4:1–16) indicates an emphasis on the relationship, precisely because it is a moral category. Those with whom one lives as brother and sister always have a proper claim upon one's compassion and care. Where that term—brother and sister or neighbor—is applicable, then enmity, disdain, negligence, and disregard are out of order. Compassion, care, and concern characterize the way with one's brother and sister or with one's neighbor. It is precisely this point that Jesus elaborates, even as he extends the definition of the neighbor, in the parable of the good Samaritan (Luke 10:25–37).

The other feature most noticeable in the instruction about the treatment of the poor and of released bond slaves is *the call for liberality and generous giving.* The hand is to be open to the poor brother or sister. You must loan whatever your poor brother or sister needs. You are to give liberally (vv. 10 and 14) out of flocks, grain, and wine. The literal expression in verse 14 is "You shall make a rich necklace for him (or her—the law explicitly refers to females as well as males; cf. v. 12) out of your flocks, threshing floor, and your wine press." That is, you shall richly load her with products from all your personal resources. The released bond slave is to be given the means of establishing a place in society again. A generous spirit and generous deeds, therefore, are what is required in the face of poverty and hardship, not a grudging, reluctant, half-hearted response.

A word needs to be said about verse 11, a verse that appears on the lips of Jesus (Matt. 6:11//Mark 14:7//John 12:8) and is sometimes taken as an excuse for ignoring the poor: that is, that there is always going to be poverty. That, of course, is exactly the opposite of what this text says. For one thing, verse 11a should be translated, "For the poor will never cease *off the earth.*" As verse 4 has indicated, in a land enriched by God's blessing and filled with those who obey the Lord's instruction, there will be no poor. That word is to be taken seriously. Equally serious and realistic is the awareness that such conditions do not operate throughout the world. Deuteronomy shows the way it should be even as it acknowledges the human reality. The manual for life on the land that is the Book of Deuteronomy is precisely to prescribe a way of life in community that provides for all and gives security to the whole. If it is at all utopian, it is also the way things are meant to be in God's intention.

In any event the implication to be drawn from the fact of continued poverty is clearly stated here and reiterated by Jesus: Open your hand wide to the poor (v. 1b) and do good to them (Mark 14:7). The First Letter of John makes the Deuteronomic point with equal clarity and directness:

137

> But if anyone has the world's goods and sees a brother or sister in need, yet closes one's heart against him or her, how does God's love abide in such a one? Little children, let us not love in word or speech but in deed and in truth (I John 3:17–18; author's trans.).

The existence of poor brothers and sisters is not a basis for acquiescence in the way things are. It is a call to generosity and liberality consonant with the blessing one has received.

So in this chapter about the sabbatical release—and in all similar words in Exodus, Leviticus, Deuteronomy, and the prophets—one encounters a principle that builds into the relentless movement and burdens of human existence regular times for release and recouping, for freeing from the chains and burdens that bind members of the community, especially to provide equity and opportunity for those members of the community who in varying degrees do not have it. Here is one of the most revolutionary forces for the creation and ordering of human community that the Lord's way with Israel set loose, because it did not simply stop with the seventh day, or even the seventh year, but opened up all kinds of ways in which the human situation is stopped and changed.

Two of our most common assumptions about the nature of human existence—that time is linear and not cyclical or repeatable, and that the causal nexus of events cannot be broken or interrupted—are shattered on the sabbatical principle of the Old Testament. For there is one way in which time is stopped and repeated, one way in which Israel broke out of the ongoing chain of events and went back to the beginning. That was in the sabbath occasions, whether the seventh day or the seventh year, or the fiftieth year (see Lev. 25), when the land was returned to its original ownership, when the land lay fallow, when debts were cut loose, when slaves were set free. On those sabbath occasions the word of the Lord was, in effect, "Stop and recover! Stop and recover freedom for slaves, stop and recover fertility for the land, stop and recover food for the poor, stop and recover property to its original owner." The sabbatical principle says no to the relentless movement of events that seems unchangeable; no to the assumption that, once circumstances have led a person into bondage or slavery, there is no release and the chain of cause and effect must keep going on; no to the economic system that ties people inexorably in debt; no to the claim that the land belongs completely and forever to

those who acquire it; and no to the relentless cycle of poverty
that is accepted easily as a fact of life. Every seven days, every
seven years, every fiftieth year, time that has brought bondage,
weariness, debt, poverty, and landlessness is to stop. There is to
be a break and liberty. Things do not just go on as they had been
before the Lord's release. They start afresh and refreshed.

This was not merely a noble ideal that was neither realistic
nor to be taken seriously. Jeremiah 34:13–16 gives a prophetic
condemnation of failure to carry out the law of release as well
as of a proclamation of release that was carried out only to be
followed by reinstatement of slavery:

> Thus says the LORD, the God of Israel: I made a covenant with
> your fathers when I brought them out of the land of Egypt, out
> of the house of bondage, saying, "At the end of six years each
> of you must set free the fellow Hebrew who has been sold to
> you and has served you six years; you must set him free from
> your service." But your fathers did not listen to me or incline
> their ears to me. You recently repented and did what was right
> in my eyes by proclaiming liberty, each to his neighbor, and you
> made a covenant before me in the house which is called by my
> name; but then you turned around and profaned my name
> when each of you took back his male and female slaves, whom
> you had set free according to their desire, and you brought
> them into subjection to be your slaves (Jer. 34:13–16).

Nor did the sabbatical principle, especially in its Deutero-
nomic character and radicality, die out with the Old Testament.
Jesus affirmed it explicitly in his claim that the sabbath was
made for human beings, not human beings for the sabbath.
Even more significant, the sabbatical principle is set forth in
that programmatic declaration of the nature of ministry which
Jesus gave through his reading of Isaiah in the synagogue at
Nazareth (Luke 4:16–19, 21):

> The Spirit of the Lord is upon me,
> because he has anointed me to preach good news to the
>   poor.
> He has sent me to proclaim release to the captives
> and recovering of sight to the blind,
> to set at liberty those who are oppressed,
> to proclaim the acceptable year of the Lord."
> . . . And he began to say to them, "Today this Scripture has
>   been fulfilled in your hearing."

139

Two texts from Isaiah have been brought together by a
single catchword—the Greek word *aphesis:* release, liberty—

the Greek translation of the Hebrew word for the release of the
sabbath principle. This is the key word of the Scripture read by
Jesus and becomes in Luke the defining category for interpreting Jesus' work. That release of which Isaiah speaks and which
is embodied and enacted in the Lord's sabbath is the intention
and goal of Jesus' ministry. The word *aphesis,* however, in the
New Testament is also the common word for another kind of
release, *forgiveness,* the release from the bonds and chains of
sin and guilt.

For us to hear this word is to be given the sabbatical principle as a hermeneutic, a way of understanding Jesus as the one
who fulfills and carries out the purpose of God as set forth in the
Old Testament and as interpreted by Luke and other New
Testament writings. The Old Testament presses us to understand that which God began in Jesus not simply as setting free
from sin but all those concrete kinds of physical, social, and
economic release and rest of which Deuteronomy, Exodus, Leviticus, Jeremiah, and Isaiah speak. And the New Testament
strongly confirms this. At the same time, however, the New
Testament gospel does not allow us, any more than the Old
Testament, to assume that those things which oppress and bind
the souls and lives of people are wholly tied to their physical
situation. The gospel reminds us that the freedom God intends
through Christ is also a release from the power and burden and
bondage of sin in our lives that frees us to love the Lord with
our whole beings (Miller, "Human Sabbath" and "Luke").

Leaders and Institutions (16:18—19:21)

Positions of leadership and associated institutions are the
subject of a group of laws following those that have to do with
the sabbatical and festival occasions (14:22—16:17). As the latter
may be regarded as developing out of the sabbath commandment of the Decalogue, so the former are to be associated with
the fifth commandment call for respect for parents. "These
rules proclaim the authority figures of the nation just as the
Fifth Commandment proclaims the authority of the parent
within the family" (Kaufman, p. 133). Here the Mosaic instruction delineates the major positions of leadership in the community, some indication of how such positions are filled, and
something of the characteristics one should look for or expect

140

in such leaders or matters having to do with their spheres of authority or jurisdiction. The leaders set forth and ordered in these laws are judges, kings, priests, and prophets.

Religious and civil affairs were bound up together in ancient Israel, as is reflected here in the congeries of positions established by law. In some cases their interaction is explicit, as in 17:9 where judge and priest make a decision. The aim of this legislation, however, is not unlike constitutional law, as we know it from Montesquieu and the framers of the Constitution of the United States, in that it is foundational law intended to assign various functions in governing the people; this is to assure that responsibilities are divided and to a large extent separated and that the role of the people in selecting or recognizing (16: 18; 17:15; 18:22) the leader and the leader's authority is clear (cf. Lohfink, *Great Themes,* pp. 55–75). No position of authority is placed under or subject to control by any other. All are placed under the torah, or instruction of God, and totally controlled by it. That is explicitly stated with regard to priest and judge (17: 11) as well as king (17:18, 19). It is also true of the prophet, as is clear when 13:1–5 is brought into the picture. The possibility that the king might have the final say in most matters does not seem to be envisioned in the Deuteronomic law. The way that each of these positions is discussed, with the law of the king in the middle and on a par with laws having to do with other authorities, suggests just the opposite. Assigned functions, separated spheres of authority, and limits on autocratic tendencies are characteristics of this system of government.

It is not entirely clear what stage of Israel's history this section of legal material reflects. Indeed, there are signs here as elsewhere that the present form of the legislation is a composite of various stages of ancient Israel's governmental and judicial history. Reference to "the elders" in 19:12 as well as in other texts having to do with the administration of justice (21:2–9, 19–20; 22:15–19; 25:7–10) suggests a time when judicial matters were handled by the elders of each town at the court held in the city gate. The appointment of specific judges and magistrates in each town (16:18; cf. 1:9–18) as well as the existence of a central court may reflect the results of Jehoshaphat's judicial reform in the ninth century (II Chron. 19:5–11). The present form of the text, however, reflects Deuteronomistic editing in the time of the exile. Norbert Lohfink has suggested quite plausibly that that is the context in which this collection of laws about the authorities was brought together and given its present shape and character:

> The kingship should be a precisely limited institution with a balanced system of various, independent, and constitutionally balanced powers. That had been Yahweh's desire from the beginning. Since they had not stuck to that, the monarchical institution had brought them to ruin. It had to be that way. By the same token, they now knew what they should do about it in the future. If ever again they were to be able to establish a state, they must create a new system of government, which would assure the Separation of Powers. For that was the only way of assuring that Yahweh truly ruled over Israel, through his *tora,* and through the prophets who proclaimed it. Thus the deuteronomistic constitution, with its sophisticated division of powers, served as an ideological therapy to cure a crisis in Israel's belief during the exile (Lohfink, "The Deuteronomist," p. 21).

If this analysis is correct, this "constitution" about the governing authorities only partially reflects actual practice in ancient Israel. It is an ideal, a program for the future, to describe the way things ought to be among God's people in the land God gives.

Judges and the Judicial System (16:18—17:13; 19:1-21)

The opening chapter of Deuteronomy gives a clear indication of the importance given to the judicial system and the administration of justice in this book. It is not surprising, and probably not accidental, that judges and the operation of a system of justice are placed at the beginning of this set of laws about the leaders of Israel. Indeed, looking at these laws and those of the chapters that immediately follow, one sees that more attention is given to the functioning of the courts than to any other institution. That reflects a concern for justice and the procedures that guard it that is no less characteristic of Deuteronomy than it is of the prophets. A good life in the good land is possible only if there are workable systems to ensure fairness and redress of situations of unfairness within the community. To that end, judges were to be elected in each community (16:18-20), procedures established for uncovering the truth in court and carrying out the court's decisions (17:2-7 and 19:15-21), a central court set up for handling difficult cases (17:8-13), and a provision for sanctuary created to ensure that revenge did

142

not take precedence over justice (19:1–13). The system here of judges and courts is probably to be associated with the system ascribed to the wilderness period in chapter 1 and that which was set up by Jehoshaphat in the ninth century (II Chron. 19:5–11.). In all three cases, judges are appointed and distributed among the communities and a central court is established to deal with difficult cases. In the case of Jehoshaphat's reform, the king set up the system of judges in the towns and may have actually appointed them. For Deuteronomy, however, there is a clear democratizing bent in chapter 1 and 16:18. The people are to select their judges, so that they are accountable to the people and trusted by them. There is no indication in the law of the king (17:14–20) that power of judicial appointment is given to him.

Only one thing is required of the judges: right judgments (16:18*b*). This requirement is hedged by prohibitions forbidding particular kinds of actions that will pervert justice and fairness; specifically, they were not to show partiality to anyone (literally, "recognizing faces") or to take bribes. Both actions are said to be uncharacteristic of the Lord (10:17) and so also must not be a part of the ways of those who are responsible for the Lord's justice in the community. These instructions are to guide the conduct of the judges (cf. 1:16–17). At the same time, they also instruct the community, as is indicated by their direct address, "You shall not pervert justice," in distinction from the third person, "They shall judge the people with righteous judgment." The system of courts will not produce fairness, justice, and righteousness if the judges alone are fair and resist bribes. All who participate are under the same constraints. Indeed, the requirement is so strong and universal that the opening section concludes with an emphatic call for justice as a sine qua non for life in the land (v. 20), a call that is echoed again and again in the words of the prophets.

The demand for fairness is signaled also in the specific case set forth in 17:2–7. The impact is felt in these verses of the primary commandment to worship/love the Lord your God alone and serve no other gods or idols. The specific legislation instructing Israel in the way that judges and the courts should operate is also a piece of case law dealing with violation of the prohibition against other gods, here described expressly as a breach of covenant (v. 2*b*). The example of how a case is handled in the courts is in fact the primary case, the most important

143

one, a violation of the fundamental stipulation of the covenant. A similar crime, of enticement to idolatry, is treated in 13:6–11. In that case, as in chapter 13 as a whole, it is clear that the entire focus is on obedience to the primary commandment (the Shema together with the prologue and the first two commandments), as one can see from the language (vv. 2, 3*b*, 4, 5*b*, 6*b*, 10*b*, 13*b*). That is, the statutes and ordinances of chapters 12–26 begin with cases having to do with the first commandments.

In the case of 17:2–7 and 9, or in the handling of such a case in the court, two concerns are uppermost: *fairness* and *responsibility*. The former is signaled in the instruction that the judges (cf. 19:18*a*) are to search diligently for the truth, the facts of the case, and the explicit requirement that an adequate number of witnesses agree on the testimony before a conviction can be sustained, a point made even more directly the subject of a statute in 19:15–21. There we can see that the insistence on a plurality of witnesses is precisely a safeguard against the possibility of false witness (the ninth commandment), and by implication the possibility of witnesses showing partiality and taking bribes. The requirement of two or three witnesses is not an infallible guarantee of justice, but it is a foundation stone of any system designed to maintain justice in the human community as it tries to guard against the danger of the system's breaking down through either human fallibility or human sin.

The concern for responsibility and accountability on the part of the community is reflected in the demand that the witnesses be the first to carry out the sentence, followed by the rest of the people. The members of the court are not allowed to separate themselves from the implications of their actions. They and the community as a whole are responsible for the whole process and demonstrate their integrity and that of the process, the justice of the matter, by being the ones responsible not only for conviction but also for execution. Obviously, this is a far cry from most contemporary systems of justice, where the responsibility for carrying out the sentence is handed to representatives of the community who have no direct involvement in the case. In a complex society a demand for accountability as direct as one finds in Deuteronomy may be difficult; but, according to Deuteronomy, that is how the integrity of the judicial process is upheld. This point is scored quite directly in 19:16–20, where a false witness receives the punishment he or she would have caused to another.

Consistent with Moses' instruction to the people in the wilderness to bring the difficult cases to him (Exod. 18:22; Deut. 1:17), the Deuteronomic legislation sets up a central or supreme court in the place that the Lord will choose. This was not so much a court of appeal as it was a court to handle the more complex cases (17:8). In some sense the matter is placed before the Lord (cf. 19:17). The court appears to have been set at the central sanctuary (v. 8c), where both lay and priestly officials decided the case. Their judgment was final, and contempt of this court was an act that came under penalty of death (17:12).

Provision for such a court reflects again the careful concern for justice in the community and the detailed regulations and instructions necessary to bring that about. Deuteronomy proposes all the ingredients of a system for the administration of justice: codes of judicial conduct; diligent inquiry into the facts and the search for truth; sufficient testimony to guard against error or malicious testimony; accountability on the part of the members of the court; access to those capable of handling more difficult matters by virtue of wisdom and experience, as well as knowledge of the torah or instruction of the Lord; and respect for the decisions and authority of the court.

Within these laws, other matters having to do with ensuring justice in the community are spoken of. One in particular needs to be lifted up at this point. That is the *provision for sanctuary* (19:1–13; cf. 4:41–43). The notion of sanctuary in Deuteronomy is limited to someone who has killed another person. Its aim is justice and humaneness more than mercy, and it is tied to the ancient practice of family revenge, whereby the kin of a slain person could go after and kill the killer. This practice is not eliminated by the Deuteronomic law, but it is restricted so that it can serve the purpose of justice only. Certain cities were to be designated as sanctuaries. They were to be distributed geographically throughout the land and made easily accessible by roads. Whoever killed another person unintentionally and without malice could flee to one of these cities and be given refuge. If the act did not merit a judicial sentence of death (v.6: "deserve to die"—"judgment of death"), then a relative of the dead person could not in anger and a spirit of revenge kill in turn. If the one seeking sanctuary did in fact kill out of malice and premeditation, then the penalty of death was appropriate justice and the "avenger of blood" could exact it (19:11–13). Even that, however, could not be done in anger and without regard for the judicial safeguards effected by the sanctuary system. There is no "wild justice" here. The relative of the dead could not go into the sanctuary. Only after the elders of the city, the responsible authorities, had decided the matter and brought the murderer out could the avenger of blood have the right of execution. Thus does human vengeance give way to justice in the Mosaic instruction. Vengeance, though not yet out of the picture completely, is subordinated to and controlled by the claims of justice.

It might appear that the final verse of chapter 19 contradicts what has just been said and builds vengeance into the system with its regulation of the *lex talionis:* the requirement of life for life, eye for eye, tooth for tooth, hand for hand, and foot for foot (19:21). Often this legal principle has been seen as the essence of Old Testament law, but that is clearly not the case, whatever may be the force of the principle. It appears in only three places (Exod. 21:23–25; Lev. 24:19–20; and Deut. 19:21) and never functions as a form of punishment in any of the individual statutes except those involving execution of a murderer. Mutilation as a form of punishment is absent from the statutes themselves except in one case (Deut. 25:11–12), the only legal statute in the Old Testament that has any relation to the *lex talionis* except those that require life for life. That is clearly what we have in Deuteronomy 19:21. While no specific crime is used to illustrate the danger of malicious witness, the contexts of the chapter dealing with possible cases of unjust execution suggest strongly that verses 15–21 also have in mind primarily the malicious witness who would cause the death of another person. The Deuteronomic expression "so you shall purge the evil from your midst" (which occurs immediately before the *lex talionis* in v. 19), commonly concludes statutes that call for the execution of a person for crimes such as murder, adultery, and dishonoring of a parent, those forbidden by the Decalogue (17:7, 12; 19:13, 19; 21:21; 22:21, 22, 24; 24:7).

The origin of this principle is uncertain. If it arose in a nomadic context, as has often been suggested, it may have been a way of limiting the extent of injury that takes place as a form of judicial punishment. It served thus to ensure that justice was done and not vengeance or a punishment greater than the crime itself. What is primarily suggested by the sporadic presence of the principle of *lex talionis* is a concern for proportionate compensation—that the punishment be appropriate to the

146

crime—as a principle underlying the law of Israel. This principle is reflected in an explicit fashion elsewhere in Deuteronomy (25:1–3), where proportionality is required but also controlled from being excessive and humiliating.

The Obedient King (17:14–20)

It is highly unlikely that placement of the law of the king after laws governing judges and the court system is accidental. The latter are fundamental in the Mosaic instruction in a way that the former is not. The way of the righteous judge reflects the way of the Lord (cf. 16:18–19 with 10:17). The way of the king in Deuteronomy is not a reflection of the deity but a model of the true Israelite.

The profile of the king in these verses is undoubtedly reflexive of historical experience under kingship. But, as has been suggested above, it is not simply a description of the way kings were at any one period in Israel's history. On the contrary, the picture here is an ideal, tempered by all the history of kingship. It betrays the ambivalence that existed around this institution from the start. The king is the result of divine acquiescence to human desire, not a requirement for life in the land under God (v. 14). Yet firm and emphatic permission is given for such a position (v. 15, "you may indeed set as king"). Kingship clearly is modeled after the practices of the kings round about Israel (v. 14b), but the typical prerogatives of such kings are prohibited (vv. 16–17). The king is "set over" (v. 15) the people, but his heart may not be lifted up above his compatriots (v. 20).

Out of that experience-based ambivalence and the constant conversation between God and the people through the centuries of monarchy is forged an ideal charter for kingship that is consistent with the character and content of the Mosaic instruction in the rest of this book. To whatever extent such a position of leadership is appropriate for life under God in the land, here is how it fits in the whole. That is what the Deuteronomic law seeks to convey.

The charter for kingship is a fairly simple one. While dynastic rule is clearly assumed ("his children," v. 20), the king must be chosen by the Lord and the continuation of the dynasty depends on his obedience to the Lord's requirements. The king must be an Israelite, a stipulation that does not so much reflect prejudice against non-Israelites as it guards against the encroachment of outside religious forces that would not conform

147

to the requirement of the basic commandment to worship the Lord alone. As to the prerogatives and functions of the king, the prerogatives are highly limited and the functions are reduced to one. He may not go the way of most kings, acquiring great wealth, many wives, and many horses (the last referring to a large professional army of horses and chariots [cf. I Sam. 8:11; I Kings 10:26]). His one positive responsibility as stated in the text is to have with him at all times a copy of "this law," the Deuteronomic law; he is to read and study it constantly and adhere diligently to all its instruction. Nothing is said here about military leadership. Judicial and religious matters are in the hands of other officials. Administrative oversight of the kingdom was presumably a royal responsibility, but in this royal charter one thing supersedes all others—careful obedience to the divine law.

Three conclusions may be drawn from these admonitions. There is, first, a clear *limitation on power,* to avoid tyranny and the danger of the king's assuming the Lord's rule of the people. The perquisites of power—wealth, wives, and military might— are explicitly denied. Royal responsibilities are limited and separated from important functions carried by others. The democratizing tendency of Deuteronomy restricts even, if not especially, the king, whose heart may not be lifted up above his brethren (v. 20).

Second, these restrictions and injunctions serve the main purpose of Deuteronomy, *to enjoin a full and undivided allegiance to the Lord.* The primary commandment is everywhere present in these verses. Limitation of horses and wealth had definite religious implications, drawn out by the prophets, particularly Isaiah 2:7–9 and Micah 5:10–15, where horses along with wealth (cf. 17) are seen as the things that lead to pride, to a loss of awareness of the need to trust in Yahweh, and so to unfaithfulness and apostasy (Mayes, p. 272). The danger that foreign wives will turn the king's heart away from following after the Lord is explicitly stated in verse 17 and echoed by the historical example of Solomon in I Kings 11:1–8 and Ahab in I Kings 16:29–33. The purpose of the king's constant reading of the torah is "to learn to fear the Lord his God," a positive formulation of the first commandment (cf. 6:13; 10:20). The law of the king is, like all Deuteronomic instruction, a guard against apostasy and idolatry.

Finally, the law of the king places upon that figure the

148

obligations incumbent upon every Israelite. In that sense, Deuteronomy's primary concern was that the king *be the model Israelite*. This is seen especially in the fact that the essential responsibility of the king is to read and study the law constantly (cf. 6:7 and 10:19), "that he may learn to fear the LORD his God, by keeping all the words of this law and these statutes, and doing them" (v. 19). This is the word that Moses constantly places on all Israel throughout his speeches. The warning "that his heart may not be lifted up" echoes the same warning to Israel in 8:14, even as the prohibition against multiplying silver and gold (v. 17) is reminiscent of the words of 8:13–17 about Israel doing the same thing and then forgetting that it is the Lord who has given the wealth. So also the warning not to "turn aside from the commandment, either to the right and or to the left," is the same as or similar to words addressed to each Israelite (cf. 5:32; 11:28; 17:17; 28:14; 31:29; Josh. 23:6) or to other leaders (e.g., Josh. 1:7). The fundamental task of the leader of the people, therefore, is to exemplify and demonstrate true obedience to the Lord for the sake of the well-being of both the dynasty and the kingdom. King and subject share a common goal: to learn to fear the Lord (v. 19).

Much has been written about the way the messianic passages of the royal psalms and Isaiah point us to and find their actuality in Jesus of Nazareth. It is possible we have overlooked the text that may resonate most with the kingship he manifested; he was one who sought and received none of the perquisites of kingship, who gave his full and undivided allegiance to God, and who lived his whole life by the instruction, the torah, of the Lord.

The Ministering Levite/Priest (18:1–8; cf. 10:6–9)

The central religious figure in the society envisioned by Deuteronomy is the Levite, or priest, whose functions and prerogatives are described in these verses and who has already been identified as the religious official involved in the "supreme court" at the central sanctuary (17:9). The history and character of the priesthood in ancient Israel is a complex matter, and there is no single depiction of it in the Old Testament. Changing conceptions or a developing history give us different views, especially in the literature associated with the Priestly document or stratum and the Deuteronomic. In the former, the tribe of Levi constitutes the priesthood, with those Levites who

149

are descendants of Aaron having the privilege and responsibility of carrying out the priestly office at the altar, while the rest of the Levites are assigned subordinate duties as a kind of support system for the sanctuary and the officiating Aaronic priests. As a tribe the Levites in the Priestly document are given an allotment of forty-eight cities in which to live.

The picture of the Levites, or priests, in Deuteronomy is rather different and is summarized in these verses. They do not have any special territory. Rather, their status is that of sojourners in the towns and villages of the land. They are supported by sacrifices (vv. 3–5, 8) as well as by the people as they are included in the various festive occasions (e.g., 14:29; 16:11, 14). Deuteronomy may know some distinction between priests, as reflected strongly in the Priestly writer, but the distinction, such as it is, seems not to be a matter of fixed status, role, or rights; rather it is that of areas of responsibility. Some Levites serve in the towns throughout the land (18:6) while others serve at the central sanctuary (v. 7*b*). Any Levite, however, may serve at the central place of worship. Rather than set forth or claim particular differences within or between priestly groupings, the Deuteronomic legislation gives the following profile of the priest or religious leader.

1. The religious or cultic leadership of Israel is assigned by the Lord to the tribe of Levi (cf. 10:8; 27:9, 14; 31:9–13; 33:8–11), whose responsibility is "to stand and minister in the name of the Lord" (10:8; 18:5). The members of this tribe are the priests in Israel, those who lead the community in the service and worship of God (cf. 21:5). Teaching (33:10; cf. 31:9–13), judicial (17:9; 21:5), and military (20:2–4) functions also are assigned to the Levites or priests.

2. The Levites are presented as brothers to all the other Israelites and thus are entitled to the provision and benefits of the good land that God gives even though they possess no special territory or tribal allotment (McConville). Instead of land, "his inheritance" (18:1–2; RSV, "his rightful dues") is the Lord and the dues or offerings presented by the people. But this "inheritance" is sufficient to sustain the Levite, or priest, as the inheritance of land does for all his fellow Israelites.

3. As with the pictures of king and judge (see 16:18–20), the Levite, or priest, is in some sense also the typical, ideal, or model Israelite, a point expressed well by McConville (p. 151):

The Levite in Deuteronomy is meant to be prosperous, therefore. His prosperity, however, is realized in dependence. He personifies the dependent spirit. His dependence on Yahweh is more conspicuous than that of his brethren, because he does not have private property in the same way that they do. His prosperity depends on the day-to-day factor of his brothers' continued obedient giving of cultic offerings. His security is therefore less evident than that of his brethren, and yet in reality they too can only be prosperous in dependence. The Levite, whose perennial dependence is ever before his brethren's eyes, yet who is prosperous, is a constant reminder of this basic principle.

The True Prophet (18:9–22; cf. 13:1–5)

The last of the leaders of Israel presented in this section is the prophet. What is said about this figure in verses 15–22 is set over against the prohibitions of verses 9–14, where Israel is specifically instructed not to practice any of the means of divination common among the peoples of the land. Seven different ways of trying to discern the future or the will of the gods are mentioned here (sacrifice of a child was probably a separate kind of abominable practice from divination). All of these represent human efforts and initiatives using various devices to figure out in some magical way—by casting lots, divining with arrows, reading dregs in a cup, observing natural phenomena as omens, or consulting dead spirits—what is going to happen. The list is long enough to indicate clearly that *all* the customary ways of discerning the divine will or plan by magic or divination are rejected. That naturally raises the implicit question, then, of how the people can divine or discern what God is going to do.

The answer is clearly set forth: The Lord will raise up a prophet. Two things stand out in the contrast between the way of the nations and the way Israel is to go. One is the emphasis on *the divine initiative* over against all the human devices mentioned in verses 10–11. *I* will raise up for them a prophet . . . and *I* will put *my* words in his mouth, and he shall speak to them *all that I command him* (v. 18; emphasis added). Such an emphasis is completely consistent with the thrust of Deuteronomy; for example, in chapter 12 all the various and human devices for worshiping God found among the inhabitants of the land are rejected because *the Lord* will decide when and where and how Israel is to worship. The prophet is a central part of the

151

new order that is set forth beginning in that chapter, the leader through whom the divine will is made known.

The other obvious feature that contrasts with the way of the Canaanites is again characteristic of the Deuteronomic polity, and that is its emphasis on the "word" (vv. 18, 19, 20, 21, 22). Revelation of the divine will, for the future as well as the present, is through the word of the Lord. "Word" is the overarching category in Deuteronomy for speaking about the Lord's instruction for life and God's intention for the future. Indeed, as Deuteronomy 4 indicates (see commentary), it is virtually a theologoumenon, a manifestation of the reality and presence of the deity. Thus it is through God's *word* communicated by the prophet that the divine rule is carried out.

But if there is to be one through whom God speaks the word that is to be obeyed and the word that uncovers the future work of God, how will the people know who that one is, especially if there are various persons, as indeed there were in the community, claiming so to speak? The problem of false prophecy was a real one. Who speaks the word of the Lord, and how does one discern the true prophet and the true word when there are conflicting words and claims? The issue arises a number of times in the Bible. First Kings 22 is an account of kings inquiring of the Lord through prophets before battle to see whether or not God will give victory. The kings of Israel and Judah question whether the prophets are giving them a true word and so send for another prophet, Micaiah; he gives them an unpleasant counter-word of defeat and declares that the Lord has put a lying spirit in the mouths of the other prophets. Jeremiah contended with false prophets frequently (e.g., 5:10–17; 14:13–16; 23:9–40). Chapters 27—29 describe a conflict between Jeremiah and other prophets, particularly Hananiah. Hananiah announced peace and God's victory over Babylon; Jeremiah declared that the Lord would put upon the neck of Judah and other nations an iron yoke of servitude to the king of Babylon.

Deuteronomy 18:20 identifies two kinds of false prophet: the one who speaks falsely in the name of the Lord and the one who speaks in the name of other gods. The latter danger reflects Deuteronomy's continual concern for resistance to the intrusion of other gods seeking Israel's ultimate allegiance. But it is clear from verse 21 and the stories mentioned above that the critical issue the people faced was the fact of differing prophetic words all claiming to come from the Lord. Verse 21 reflects the

152

problem and verse 22 addresses it. The criterion is a rather simple one: The authentic word of the Lord is a word that comes to pass, comes to reality (v. 22). This criterion is part of the view of history reflected in Deuteronomy and the Bible generally: to wit, that history is in God's control, both announced and effected by God's word. The authentic divine word is the one that is worked out in history. The Books of Kings reflect this understanding in that one of the main threads binding that history into a whole is the movement from prophecy to fulfillment (cf. von Rad, *Studies in Deuteronomy*, Ch. 7). In Isaiah 40–55 the decisive difference between the Lord and the Babylonian gods is that the Lord alone is the one who declares beforehand—through the prophets—what is to happen (e.g., Isa. 41:25–29). In the conflicts among the prophets mentioned above, the criterion set forth in Deuteronomy 18:22 is operative. After Micaiah has countered the favorable word of Zedekiah and the four hundred prophets with a vision of the defeat of the king of Israel, he directly submits his prophetic word to the test: "If you return in peace [i.e., victorious], the LORD has not spoken by me" (I Kings 22:28). And Jeremiah in his encounter with the false prophet Hananiah says, "As for the prophet who prophesies peace, when the word of that prophet comes to pass, then it will be known that the LORD has truly sent the prophet" (Jer. 28:9).

The criterion of true prophecy is what it should be—truth, the correspondence between the prophetic word and the realities of history. Both Old Testament and New Testament demonstrate that correspondence again and again for the prophetic words they contain. Indeed, it is those words proven true by this criterion that have become a part of the canon of Scripture. One must acknowledge, however, that the ability to decide is somewhat retrospective from this point of view. Thus other criteria come into play in the biblical reports: for example, the authenticating calls of the prophets that testify to their prophetic role as operating out of the Lord's compulsion and often against their own desires, or the consistency of the word of a prophet with that of prior prophets (Jer. 28:6–9; cf. 26:16–19), or their participation in the divine council of the Lord (Jer. 23:21–22; I Kings 22:19–22; Isa. 6:1–13, esp. v. 8). Deuteronomy itself in another passage sets forth the matter of consistency as a basis for knowing if a prophet is not truly proclaiming the word of the Lord (13:1–5). Here, however, the consistency is not

153

with other prophecies but with what Moses' instruction has declared to be the word of the Lord. Chapter 13:1-5 seems at first to contradict the criterion of 18:22, for it envisions a false prophet giving an omen or portent ("a sign or a wonder") that *does* come to pass. But the point of the passage is that such a word could never be a true word from the Lord if its result is to draw the people away from the exclusive worship of the Lord. Divine control of what happens is still to be assumed. In this case, however, the divine act is a testing of the people's faithfulness, not an authentic word about the future. Thus chapters 18 and 13 serve to give the people two criteria for distinguishing between true and false prophecy. The authentic divine word on the lips of the prophet is one that is confirmed by history and consistent with all the Lord's other words as set forth in the Mosaic instruction and focused in the demand for exclusive worship of the Lord.

EXCURSUS

Moses the Exemplary Prophet

The portrait of Moses sketched in Deuteronomy reaches its climax in the portrayal of him as the model for any future prophets (18:15, 18) and as the greatest of all prophets (34:10–12). In some sense Moses' role as prophet incorporates the other characteristics emphasized by Deuteronomy—suffering servant (see commentary on 3:12–29), teacher (see commentary on 5:1–5, 22–33 and 6:1–3), and intercessor (see commentary on 9:25–29 and 10:10–11). All of these are in some way found in the life and work of prophets. The central characteristic that identifies Moses as the ideal prophet is his function as the mediator of the divine word. That is indicated explicitly by verse 18 as well as the reference in verses 16–17 back to chapter 5, where Moses was given that role by the people and God. Implicitly the whole Book of Deuteronomy underscores the identification of prophecy with the communication of the divine word that is commanded, by depicting Moses primarily as such a spokesman. Once again, therefore, the priority of the word of God as the vehicle of divine presence and rule is affirmed by Deuteronomy; and Moses is the prophet par excellence, not only because

154

of the great signs and wonders (see 13:1) that the Lord empowered him to do (so 34:10-12) but primarily because of his faithful speaking of the word and will of God to the people. Indeed, as chapter 34 indicates, no other prophet like Moses has arisen or has been raised up by the Lord, if one uses the criterion of mighty deeds and signs and wonders as a basis for comparison. But one can expect that the Lord will raise up a prophet (or prophets) who, like Moses, will faithfully convey God's word to the people and in so doing represent God's rule in the new order being created by God in and through this people.

One issue that arises from looking closely at this text is whether in verses 15 and 18 Moses alludes to a single prophet whom God will call or raise up sometime in the future or to a line of prophetic figures, such as seen in the Old Testament. In light of the history of prophecy at the time this book took shape, as well as the inclusion of the law of the prophet in this charter for Israel's leaders, it is likely that the Deuteronomic law envisioned not one future prophet but prophets (plural) like judges, kings, and priests—although the language "God will raise up for you a prophet like me" does suggest that this is an occasional position of authority and not a regular continuing office, a figure raised up by the Lord when a new word is in need of being spoken.

Chapter 18:15–22 does, however, seem still to stand in some tension with chapter 34:10. The Lord *"will raise up* for you a prophet like me" (18:15) contrasts rather sharply with *"And there has not arisen a prophet since* in Israel like Moses" (author's emphases). The tension, as suggested above, is partly resolved by distinguishing between speaking the word commanded by the Lord (future prophets like Moses) and great signs and wonders (none since like Moses). There is something else happening here, however. Chapter 34 was added to Deuteronomy after the formulation of the law of the prophet in chapter 18. When that took place it served to elevate Moses' role, not only as a spokesman of the Lord but also as wonder-worker, as prophetic mediator of the Lord's power, so that the absolute claim was made that no prophet like Moses has arisen since. Once that claim is made—that *down to the present* (the time of the narrator) there has been no prophet like Moses—one can hardly see 18:15–22 in terms of a continuing line of prophets through Israel's history. The only way to resolve the tension between chapters 18 and 34 is to project *into the future*

155

the announcement that God will raise up a prophet, which is what eventually happened in Judaism and Christianity (John 1:21, 25; 6:14; 7:40). That shift from many prophets to one prophet in the future is created in some sense by the Book of Deuteronomy itself.

In some streams of tradition, the expectation is for the coming of a prophet like Moses; in some it is like the anticipation of the coming of Elijah, an expectation of the return of Moses himself. It is not surprising that such a hope was associated with Jesus, either indirectly through John the Baptist (John 1:21) or directly as a new Moses (so the Gospel of Matthew) or in early Christian preaching as the prophet God had raised up (Acts 3:22–26). When verse 22 of Acts 3 is compared with verse 26, one sees how Jesus is identified with the anticipated prophet both in having been "raised up" by God and as the Lord's servant. Now the words of Deuteronomy are understood to have their fulfillment and reality beyond the history of Israelite prophecy in one who, like Moses, is the Lord's servant, suffering vicariously for the people, intercessor in behalf of a sinful people, proclaimer and indeed embodiment of the Word of God, and even one who was raised up, not merely as prophetic spokesman but as the realization of God's delivering power to which the prophetic word continually attests, the inaugurator of that new order that is the Kingdom of God. (Miller, "Moses." For a helpful and extended discussion of the relation between Jesus as prophet and Jesus as Word of God, see Barth, IV/3, pp. 38ff.; for a brief presentation of the relation between the Deuteronomic Moses and Jesus, see E. Achtemeier, pp. 45–47.)

The Rules of War (20; 21:10–14; 23:9–14; 24:5)

It is not surprising to find in the Book of Deuteronomy, with its evident martial air, some statutes and ordinances dealing with the conduct of war. These are set primarily in chapter 20 but appear also in several other places in the final chapters of the legislative code (chs. 12–26). In both 21:10–14 and 23:9–14 the statutes begin in a fashion similar to chapter 20: "When you go forth to war against your enemies." The regulation in 24:5 does not so begin, but its content is similar to 20:7: the freeing of an engaged or newly married man from combat duty to enjoy the delights of his marriage. Several features of these military statutes should be noted: the presence of an idealized type of holy war, the continuing force of the Deuteronomic insistence on a devotion to the Lord alone together with a concomitant concern for purity, and the manifestation of some humaneness and compassion in the midst of the barbarism of war.

The Holy War. The directions for war that appear in this chapter are hardly what one would find in a manual of arms or a textbook on military tactics and strategy. What we find is rather an understanding that echoes the ideology of war in the earliest period of Israel's history, when the people engaged in holy war or "Yahweh's war" against their enemies. The instruction set forth here is consistent with the Deuteronomic claim that all that happens is by the power and direction of the Lord (see commentary on 2:1—3:11). The key ingredients in the accomplishment of victory are signaled in the opening verse of the chapter and then elaborated and underscored in the next several verses.

The one who fights and wins the victory is the Lord (v. 4), as was the case at the beginning of Israel's story when the Lord brought Israel out of Egypt (v. 1). The instructions always attribute victory over the enemies to the Lord's doing (vv. 4, 13, 14, 16; cf. 21:10; and 23:14). Particularly in engagements with the other nations, Israel asserted the rule and sovereignty of the Lord over all that happened. Indeed, the victory is not a human endeavor at all. God's power makes it possible to overcome the power of other peoples and enjoy the blessings of rest in a good land (cf. 8:17–18). The ideological character of this material (see the conclusion to the commentary on 2:1—3:11) should not keep the reader from seeing this primary claim of the text: Israel's life and death were totally held within the divine provision; whether it was a matter of surviving in battle or surviving daily in the land, everything was provided by the Lord and accomplished by the Lord's power (cf. 1:30–31).

The divine control of events does not mean the passivity of Israel. Quite the contrary: Israel has *one* responsibility. What is laid on Israel in its instruction for war has already been signaled in its experience of war in chapter 1. Israel is to trust completely in the power of God and to be unafraid before the power of the enemy. That word is given as a piece of instruction or command in 20:1 and then as an assurance in the words of the priest in verse 3. In the latter case, a powerful emphasis is given to trust as being the only "stratagem" Israel is to take up. Deuteronomy's use of four different expressions underscores the assur-

157

ance that Israel has no reason to fear when God is in their midst. The Immanuel word is heard again in this text (vv. 3 and 4): Do not be afraid, for the Lord your God is *the one who goes with you.* From the beginning to the end of the biblical story, this remains the perduring word of assurance and the ground for Israel's hope of living in the world in the midst of all its vicissitudes and threats. But as Israel found out time and time again, the presence of God was never something so self-evident that Israel could avoid the necessity of trusting in God's power. So in this case the "fear not" is given to the people as a word of command in their law (v. 1), an assuring word in the face of the enemy (v. 3), and as a warning in the rules for levying soldiers (so that no fearful soldier might cause the hearts of others to melt [v. 8]). The biblical insistence that life under God is impossible apart from the conviction and faith that God is controling and shaping events, and that the human responsibility is to live faithful to God and trusting in the Lord's power and providence, is sounded once more in all these rules of war.

The Lord Alone. The one word declared through Deuteronomy to the people who read it in different times was the insistence in the Shema that there was no other god for Israel but the Lord and that each person and the community as a whole must give its total loyalty and devotion to "the LORD our God" (6:4–5). The contrast between the way Israel was to engage in battle with the peoples far off (v. 15) and the way they were to treat the nations in the land itself (vv. 16–17) is a further reflection of that most important word and claim. Israel could and should make peace, if possible, with other nations outside the land God was granting to them. And if war was necessary, the handling of captives was to be carried out according to the standard practices of the day (vv. 13–14), killing the male warriors, who would continue to be a threat if left alive, and taking the women, children, and goods as booty (cf. 21:10–14). But as for those cities and peoples in the land itself, they were to be totally destroyed (see the discussion of the ban in the commentary on chapter 2). Here as elsewhere the ground for that harsh dealing is made clear: The continued presence of these people in your midst would mean that you would be drawn away to their gods and religious practices and forget the one who is your Lord (v. 18). This insistence on the purity of Israel's worship of the Lord, a purity that brooked no compromise and was always on the verge of dissolution (as the Deuteronomists well knew

158

from history), is heard in another form in the laws of 23:9–14, where rules for keeping the war camp pure are set forth on the ground that the Lord was in the midst of the camp and thus it must be kept holy. The holiness of God reflected in the holiness of the people (7:6) was not simply an abstract notion. It was to be manifest in all aspects of Israel's life, especially in the people's keeping totally separate from the temptations of the religious practices of their neighbors and even keeping pure and clean their own camp where the Lord "walks" (23:14).

Compassion and Humaneness. One notes in the midst of all the instruction here that a significant amount of it reflects a compassion for persons and nature that is not systematic but echoes similar notes elsewhere in the book. The sifting out that the officers are to do before battle (vv. 5–7) is designed to allow those whose possible death in battle would cut them short from enjoying newly received blessings to withdraw and go home. Of course, the death of anyone will cut short the enjoyment of wife and family and home, but the text recognizes a special sense in which the failure ever to enjoy the love of a spouse one has just married or a home one has just built or crops one has just planted is tragic and suggests that even in the conduct of war special dispensations are necessary. Even in modern times, deferments and discharges from military service have been granted for reasons of compassion. An explicit ecological concern also appears here, in rather surprising fashion. Indeed, in what is probably the most direct biblical expression of sensitivity to human destruction of the natural environment, verses 19–20 place a restraint on the assumption that anything goes and that defoliation and natural destruction are unlimited when one is at war. A rationality charged with compassion ("Are the trees in the field men that they should be besieged by you?") restricts the sweeping devastation of the natural environment that regularly accompanies war. It also requires a compassionate dealing with a captive woman who is physically desirable. Rape is not a rule of war, not even humiliation of women.

The text thus presses us to ask if it is possible to find avenues of compassion, human concern, and care of the natural order in the midst of the death and destruction that is intrinsic to war and assumed by these very texts. Such moves resist the disintegration into sheer barbarism that every military engagement faces and, in the face of the annihilation of individual existence,

159

insist that it is still worth something; home and family, the enjoyment of life, and human regard for other persons are not ever to be set totally aside. Something here is quite at odds with the enterprise of war. Deuteronomy does not reflect on it; it simply holds to a concern for individual humanity in the midst of its undoing. Perhaps such rules are not viable or realistic for war. They may undercut its purposes or create impossible contradictions. If so, that would hardly be all bad.

Some Spheres for Moral Direction (21—25)

The final chapters of the Deuteronomic code contain a collection of statutes and ordinances that are less obviously organized around particular concerns than is the case in the previous laws. It may be that the Decalogue structure has helped to shape this section, as well as earlier parts of the code. Stephen Kaufman has followed earlier interpreters in so perceiving this material. He has suggested that laws growing out of the sixth commandment are found in 19:1—22:8, the seventh commandment in 22:9—23:19, the eighth commandment in 23:20—24:7, the ninth commandment in 24:8—25:4, and the tenth commandment in 25:5–16. Clearly, some of these statutes can be seen in relation to the Ten Commandments. The connection of a number of them, however, is more difficult to perceive. More useful as a way of getting at the varied and often quite brief regulations is to recognize that several areas of moral concern are touched upon in these chapters, though not in a systematic or logical fashion. The primary areas discussed are purity of land and people, marriage and family relations, and the protection and care of others, particularly those outside of or in weaker positions in the community.

Purity of Land and People

The concern for purity of the people and the land is signaled in the first unit of this section, chapter 21:1–9. Here the problem of what to do in the case of an unsolved murder is taken up. In one sense, therefore, the Deuteronomic code at this point is finishing off matters having to do with judicial procedures, an area dealt with primarily in 16:18—17:13 and 19:1–21. The need to purge the guilt from the land, a need reflected in those earlier statutes on judicial process, is lifted up here and accentuated. In this situation there is no criminal or trial but a problem—unsolved murder—that would simply be ignored in many societies. It cannot be ignored in Israel, however, because criminal guilt pollutes the community, and therefore the community must be cleansed of that guilt.

The purity of Israel was an obligation that grew out of its existence as a holy people (7:6; 14:2, 21). Such purity was not primarily a matter of ritual activity but a quality of life belonging to this people's being set apart as the people of the Lord and the Lord's way. As one interpreter has put it, "Purity, according to the book of Deuteronomy, . . . is not the prerequisite of holiness, but rather an obligation which holiness imposes upon the Israelite" (Weinfeld, p. 228). Because the people were chosen by the Lord as a people and set apart to a special relationship of service and obedience, purity as a manifestation of holiness was not confined to certain spheres, persons, or institutions, like the priesthood or the sanctuary, but was a requirement for all the community of Israel and was to be manifested in their moral life, their worship of God, and their daily practices and customs. So in the instance of the unsolved murder, the moral guilt that comes from the existence of such in the community has to be dealt with. That happens through a ritual of purification (washing the hands over a heifer who is sacral in the sense of not having worked or pulled the yoke) and prayer for God's forgiveness for the sin that has been done in the community. Act and word together evoke God's forgiveness and thus maintain the moral purity of the community. In chapters 17 and 19, when the community is given a judicial procedure for dealing with crimes and told that by following such directions they will purge the guilt from their midst (17:7, 12; 19:13, 19), such regulations were designed to maintain the moral purity of the Lord's holy people. The earlier regulations of chapter 14:1–21, having to do with self-mutilation (a practice of the Canaanite worshipers of Baal; cf. I Kings 18:28) and the prohibition against eating certain animals regarded as unclean, are rooted explicitly, at the beginning and the end of the sequence, in the claim that Israel was a people holy to the Lord, set apart to the Lord out of all the peoples of the earth (vv. 2, 21; cf. Exod. 22:31; Lev. 11:44–45; 20:22–26).

When one asks what being set apart in this way means, Deuteronomy answers by identifying modes and acts that manifest a purity and cleanliness of life and action. Various reasons have been suggested for the insistence on dietary laws, including hygienic (some foods were seen as not being good for a person's health), religious (some foods were prohibited because of their place in the customs and practices of the Canaanites), and moral reasons (restricted access to animal life as food teaches reverence for life [Milgrom, p. 296]). But whatever the reason, dietary regulations were a part of the daily practice of purity, itself a part of the moral life and a reflection of the holiness of God. The prohibition against cult prostitution or the payment of a vow to the Lord with what one commentator has appropriately called "dirty money" (Craigie, p. 301) served the same aim (23:17–18). The Lord is not to be worshiped in ways arising from acts of sexual impurity.

While in Deuteronomy the concern for purity is rooted in Israel's existence as a people holy to the Lord (7:6), the maintenance of purity arises also out of the presence of the Lord in the midst of the people (23:14) and out of awareness that the land is the gift of God and as such is not to be polluted (21:23). One of the ways the purity of the people is to be maintained, one that sounds rather strange in the contemporary world, is the insistence that *things be kept in order and not mixed up inappropriately.* Regulations found in 22:5, 9, 10, and 11 prohibit men and women from wearing each other's clothing (a regulation whose deeper meaning is ignored by simply marking it as a prohibition of transvestism), the use of two different kinds of seed in a vineyard or field (so Lev. 19:19), the teaming of different kinds of animals to pull a plow (it has been suggested that the plowing refers to sexual activity, but that can not be determined definitively [cf. Lev. 19:19]), and the weaving together of different kinds of materials. As with the dietary regulations about which animals could or could not be eaten, interpreters have speculated about different religious, health, or practical reasons that may have lain behind these prohibitions against mixing. What is clear, however, at least with regard to the regulations about seeds, plowing animals, and cloth materials (which are often ascribed quite different motivations), is that what holds them together as a series is the resistance to intermixing things that belong to different categories. The regulations thus introduce into the life of holiness and purity a concern for the order and structure of things, the recognition of difference and sameness, and a desire to maintain things as God has created them. Nahmanides, a Jewish interpreter of the Middle Ages, saw in these statutes an effort to preserve the

162

integrity of creation. Order, social and natural stability, continuity, and coherence as they operate in various spheres of life are maintained by such regulations (Wieseltier, p. 36). Purity as a concomitant of holy existence is not confined simply to obvious matters of clean and unclean; it encompasses the moral life and the structure and order of the world that God gives. Martin Luther discerned this direction within the text when he saw here a kind of fuller sense (it was not for him the allegorical meaning, which he connected with the simultaneous teaching of faith and works in the church), a "proverbial and general maxim" through which Israel was taught to be of

> one heart and mind, simple, pure, without divisions and party spirit. . . . For God, who loves simplicity and purity, does not want first fruits or tithes of various kinds of seed to be offered to Him. So He also wants His citizens to be simple and wholly of one mind in feeling and manners. They should not plow with ox and ass together, use mixed clothing, and confuse everything (p. 221).

Marriage and Family

A series of statutes beginning in 22:13 and running through the rest of the chapter (22:13–21, 22, 23–27, 28–29, and 30) all deal with the marriage relationship and are clearly specific cases in which the implications of the basic guideline provided in the seventh commandment are spelled out. The commandment prohibiting adultery is designed to protect the marriage relationship. Here, then, are cases of how that protection works. In the first instance, the marriage is protected by prohibiting a husband from falsely accusing his wife of not being a virgin, and thus of having violated the marriage relationship, and by prohibiting a wife from entering the relationship claiming not to have had sexual relationships with another man. What such statutes make clear is that the commandment in a sense "means business." The intimacy of sexual relationship is at the heart of the enduring commitment of a man and a woman and the creation of a family. It is not to be taken lightly but is to be jealously guarded (see the discussion of the seventh commandment). The statutes that follow confirm this as they prohibit adultery on pain of death of both parties (vv. 22 and 23–24—a betrothed or engaged person was regarded as married as far as the adultery issue was concerned), rape of a married or engaged person (vv. 25–27), and incest (v. 30).

163

While the statute of 24:1–4 seems to be a law regulating divorce, it actually tells about divorce procedures on the way to restricting remarriage to a former husband or wife. The regulation per se is in verse 4, forbidding a man from taking back his former wife after she has been married to another man. It is not altogether clear what lies behind this prohibition, but it is most likely that the potential remarriage was seen as allowing the possibility for a kind of legal adultery in that the woman would have had sexual relations with her second husband and then with her first. The second marriage, while legal, would end up being a violation of the relationship to her first husband when the two were remarried (cf. Craigie, pp. 305–306). It is also possible, however, that in a paradoxical way the remarriage was seen as a kind of incest. The wife would have become a part of the family of her husband in a permanent way when they were married the first time. The remarriage would have the husband now marrying someone who in some sense was a sister in his family, and vice versa (Wenham). Both ways of understanding the grounds for this statute suggest guarding the marriage relationship and concern for the proper order of things, including not violating the order of family relationships. The law indicates that divorce was possible in ancient Israel and tells us something of its procedures, but it does not really indicate anything about what sort of moral judgment was made about divorce in general. Here, as elsewhere, one sees that the male takes the initiative and has primary control of the situation. Within the essentially patriarchal structure of Israelite society, the wife is not given the same right to initiate divorce that her husband is provided.

The statute of 24:1–4 is explicitly taken up as the basis for a theological metaphor by Jeremiah in 3:1. The prophet, like Hosea, uses the imagery of wife and husband, of harlotry and adultery, to speak about Israel's violation of covenant. The notion of "returning," which has in mind repentance and a turning of the ways in Jeremiah while meaning literally "to turn or take again" in Deuteronomy (24:4), is the linchpin of the Jeremianic appropriation of the Deuteronomic text. Citing the legal precedent from 24:1–4, Jeremiah says that if a man may not take back a wife who has been divorced and remarried, then surely Judah, who has whored after many lovers (the Baals), can not expect to return and be taken back by the Lord. As in Deuteronomy, the land is polluted by such action. Israel's faithlessness has prevented the "return."

The one exception to the various prohibitions against marriage within family relationships is provided in 25:5–10. When a man died without male heir, the law required that the brother of the dead man take the widow as his wife, procreate, and thus provide children for the man who had died. This practice is often called *levirate* marriage, from the Latin word *levir*, meaning "a husband's brother" (See "Marriage," *Interpreter's Dictionary of the Bible* [IDB]). The stories of Ruth (Ruth 2–4) and Tamar (Gen. 38) are examples of the custom (though in the case of Ruth it is not a brother who performs the duty of the next of kin). The primary aim seems to have been to carry on the name of the deceased, but the word "name" in the expression "that his name may not be blotted out of Israel" probably refers to the inheritance or property of the dead man as well as the family name (Num. 27:4; 2 Sam. 14:4–7; Ruth 4:10), suggesting that protection of the property of the deceased was also in view. By safeguarding the property and providing a husband for the widow, the law of levirate marriage also served to protect the widow, who was obviously in a vulnerable position. The ancient Jewish historian Josephus has expressed in succinct fashion the aims of this law:

> When a woman is left childless on her husband's death, the husband's brother shall marry her, and shall call the child that shall be born by the name of the deceased and rear him as heir to the estate; for this will at once be profitable to the public welfare, houses not dying out and property remaining with the relatives, and it will moreover bring the women an alleviation of their misfortune to live with the nearest kinsman of their former husbands (*Antiquities* 4.8.23).

If, as the statute indicates, the surviving brother could not be forced to marry his sister-in-law, the text makes clear that this was a neglect of duty and an occasion for reproach and implied the consequent freedom of the widow to find another mate outside the family. Here, therefore, is a statute that seeks to protect and provide for widows (on such laws of protection see below), but it does so within an essentially patriarchal concern to provide for a male lineage.

This Deuteronomic statute becomes the basis for the effort of the Sadducees to trap Jesus with the question about resurrection (Matt. 22:23–33; Mark 12:18–27; Luke 20:27–40). It is made to order for their purposes. If a woman has been widowed several times and had to marry several brothers, then whose wife would she be in the resurrection? The assumption implicit in the question is that the resurrection idea will not work; it is ridiculous to believe in it. The Sadducees, however, trap themselves by another assumption, that life in the resurrection is simply a carbon copy of this present life. Jesus says, in effect, that those who rely on Moses in one thing (levirate legislation) should draw upon him in other matters (resurrection). In so doing they will be confronted with the power of God to give life to the dead. The Scriptures thus trap those who would trap Jesus by the Scriptures. The Mosaic legislation of Deuteronomy is a guide for life under the exigencies of the human situation in this age and in this mundane world; as such, it is to be taken very seriously. In no sense, however, does it exhaust the power of God and God's word. To read it in such a manner is once again to misunderstand the law, God's instruction for our life.

Several of the statutes in this section deal with *relationships between parents and children.* In 21:15–17, the right of the firstborn son to the major portion of inheritance is guarded against rivalries, affections, and personal preferences that might provoke the father to ignore the firstborn's right. While the statute belongs to the body of family law in Deuteronomy, it also is consistent with those numerous regulations in the book designed to safeguard the rights, protect the lives, and take care of the needs of members of the society (see below). Indeed, that is true of several of the family laws just discussed.

The fifth commandment gets its most explicit specification in Deuteronomy in 21:18–21, where procedures for dealing with a "stubborn and rebellious" son are set up, procedures that culminate in execution of the son who will not obey father and mother. The association of the statute with the basic command to honor father and mother is self-evident from the content of the law but is further indicated by the fact that both parents are explicitly referred to and by the fact that the punishment for disobedience is death. The punishment seems not only inhumane but incredible to contemporary readers, who may wonder whether parents could every carry out such requirements. (No examples are known from the biblical story, and it is generally assumed by commentators from earliest times until today that the statute was probably not used.) Indeed, those who cite Scripture's legislation of capital punishment as grounds for its contemporary practice will rarely propose that it be used in such a case as this. It seems barbaric.

While the contemporary reader will properly abhor the

notion that parents would submit their own child to execution, it is possible to comprehend to some extent how such a requirement had its place in the Deuteronomic system. Two things are important to keep in mind. One is the relation of the statute to the fifth commandment. While no punishment is prescribed for any of the Ten Commandments, they were viewed as absolute, so fundamental to the well-being of the community that most of the specific statutes concerning obvious examples of disobedience of one of these commandments require the death penalty. Elsewhere, dishonoring of parents receives the same sentence or a pronouncement of curse (Exod. 21:15, 17; Deut. 27:16). The seriousness with which the community viewed these basic guidelines, the commandments, is nowhere more clearly indicated than in that fact. While a modern reader would not set such punishment and would view it as too harsh for the crimes (except possibly in some cases, and that is certainly debatable), Israel found in these basic commandments a sine qua non for its very existence and regarded the treatment of God and parents with the same seriousness as the treatment of neighbor.

The second feature of this statute is the way in which it reflects what was suggested in the discussion of the fifth commandment: that the treatment of parents is in some ways comparable to the way in which a person is supposed to respond to God. The respect for parents—and here it is important to note that the mother has no less a place in this regard than the father—is a refraction of one's honoring the Lord. The parents are the first rank of persons whose authority must be acknowledged in order for human community to work in behalf of goodness and peace.

It is no accident that the language describing the rebellious son (21:20) is similar to the language describing rebellious Israel before God (Jer. 5:23; Ps. 78:8) or that the image of a disobedient child functions in Scripture as a way of imaging the relation between the Lord and the Lord's people (e.g., Isa. 1:2; Hosea 11). In Deuteronomy 9:7 and 23 the Lord through Moses threatens to destroy the people because Israel has been "rebellious" and has failed to "obey his voice." Only the intercession of Moses prevents the destruction of the people.

In the statute concerning the rebellious child, such rebellion is clearly regarded as resistance to divine direction as mediated through parental authority and teaching. That behavior

167

is not simply a bad thing but is representative of a festering sore in the midst of the people, a corruption that can undo the community's devotion to its Lord and its continued attention to the Lord's way. While the sin or crime takes place in the context of the family and the parents are given the responsibility for initiating action as the ones who know of and are the recipients of the child's rebellion, the community is clearly the context and vehicle for all the judicial action that takes place. The statute, therefore, bears testimony once again to Deuteronomy's setting of the love of the Lord and the Lord's way as not only the highest good but an absolute necessity for the people to live as God's people and to enjoy God's blessing. Punishment is not determined by how much explicit harm has been done to individuals but by the depth of the wound to the body politic and religious when the fundamental directions of the Lord's way are violated.

The existence of a body of family law in the legal corpora of the Old Testament is worth noting. The fifth commandment set the family as one of the central spheres of moral concern. From the statutes of the Pentateuchal laws to the various pieces of proverbial wisdom of Proverbs and other parts of the Wisdom literature, the family was a matter of central attention. Its governance, order, and harmony were not a matter of individual preference and attention. If our life and death are truly with our neighbor and the treatment of the neighbor is the measuring stone of moral conduct, it must be recognized that Israel saw the neighbor first and most immediately in the members of the family circle. It did not regard the family sphere as one of "private morals" outside the sphere of community law. Quite the contrary; community depended on the stability of marriage, the harmonious life of the family, and the direction given by parents to their children.

One other piece of "family legislation" should be noted: Parents shall not be put to death for the sins of their children and vice versa (Deut. 24:16). As the command indicates, each person is responsible for his or her own sin. The principle of individual accountability, which is here made a feature of the judicial system, is fundamental. A contemporary reader tends to take that principle for granted. But being able to do so is rooted precisely in the Bible's insistence on the principle. Vicarious punishment was not unfamiliar in the ancient Near East. In Israel there are instances of family and city punishment

168

where the guilt is held to be corporate and the family or the city is punished (Gen. 19; Josh. 7; II Sam. 21:1–9). Such accounts may reflect an earlier system that did not insist on individual responsibility and restrict corporate punishment, but it is clear that the legal codes and the prescribed legal system found in them never allow for vicarious punishment or corporate punishment unless in fact the whole community is guilty, as in the case of Sodom. The Deuteronomic insistence on this principle is underlined in the Deuteronomistic History in II Kings 14:6, where Deuteronomy 24:16 is quoted directly to explain why the children of royal assassins are not punished. Both the legal corpora and the prophets insist that each person *must* be held responsible for his or her actions while insisting with equal vigor that no other persons—within the family or outside it—be held accountable or punished for someone else's sin (cf. Ezek. 18; Jer. 31:29–30). Both parts of that principle are fundamental to the nature of biblical law and its understanding of the relation of individual to community and the nature of moral responsibility.

The Protection and Care of Others

Many of the statutes of Deuteronomy have a concern for the protection of the person or the rights of individual Israelites, some of which have been noted in the preceding discussion, and several laws in this section of the book seem to have that as their primary focus even if often in relation to other matters also.

Several sections in chapter 22 focus on protection and care. Deuteronomy 22:1–4 deals with one's attention to and care for the property of another member of the community when that property is jeopardized or in some kind of danger of loss or destruction. It is indebted to the earlier regulation of Exodus 23:4 but represents an expansion in several ways. The earlier legal statement required an Israelite to return a straying animal to its owner even if that owner were one's enemy. Deuteronomy extends the law to make clear that protecting and safeguarding the lost property of another is something to be done for any and every member of the community (your brother or compatriot; v. 1). While that may have been implicit in the Exodus regulation, Deuteronomy makes it explicit. The law is further expanded within Deuteronomy to indicate that *any* property of a fellow Israelite was to be looked after, whether one encountered it as lost property or, in the case of animals,

169

as property that was in difficulty. Whether the property of the neighbor was lost or in trouble, the requirement of the statute was the same: You may not hide yourself (the literal meaning of the Hebrew). The regulation seeks to guard against the very human tendency not to get involved in another's problem or go out of one's way to help (Craigie). The verb chosen is a singularly appropriate one, for it points to the tendency to act as if one has not seen the problem and therefore can not be held accountable. As the statute recognizes, such claims may conceal the fact that one has really *chosen* to disregard the lost or incapacitated animals so as not to have to go to the trouble of tending to or caring for them.

The point of the statute is raised to the human level in Jesus' parable of the man who, having been beset by robbers on the road between Jerusalem and Jericho, was bypassed by priest and Levite but aided by a journeying Samaritan. Jesus' intention was to define the neighbor, but his example refers to kinds of actions long before set in Israelite law. They had to do with regard for the welfare of persons, but they were also to ensure ordinary human decency in caring for the property of another, especially for animals that were a means of livelihood for one's neighbor. This was the original force of the statute, as indicated in 22:1, 4.

In a somewhat different way, verses 6 and 7 protect animals also; but, as in the case of the regulation about lost livestock, the protection seems ultimately for the sake of the human community. Like the law protecting fruit trees (20:20), this statute allows members of the community to take young wildfowl and eggs for sustenance if they happen to find them. But the mother bird may not be taken, because she is the guarantor of the continuation of this food source. It is worth noting that only here and in the commandment to honor parents, as well as in one other general exhoration to obedience (4:40), do we encounter the double motivation to keep the statute "that it may go well with you and that you may live long." As in the case of the fifth commandment, the motivation clause makes some sense; the law recognizes that for this source of food to continue to be available for the good and long life of the community, the source of the food, as represented by the mother, must be protected. Both the law protecting fruit trees and the law protecting wildfowl are examples of early environmental protection regulations. These cases are not simply for the sake of the

170

natural environment but because of its existence as a habitat for the human community. The regulations remind the reader of the interface of the natural and the human; the welfare of both are inseparable.

The welfare of animals as well as human beings is specifically provided for in the statute of 25:4 prohibiting muzzling an ox while it is treading out grain. The animal ought to be allowed to eat while it is working hard. One notes that while this statute does not occur elsewhere in the Old Testament, it is cited twice in the New Testament (I Cor. 9:9; I Tim. 5:18). There, however, the Torah is cited as Scripture, not as a literal regulation for Christian conduct but as indicative of the *general principle* that one who works deserves to be properly rewarded. That principle is indeed a part of the force of the original regulation in Deuteronomy, but its use in the New Testament illustrates how principles operative in these Old Testament statutes continued to guide the Christian community whether or not they may have been followed literally. And for Paul, the regulation has its primary force analogically, with reference to human beings rather than the animals involved (a reference shared by the other statutes having to do with flora and fauna discussed above).

The statute in 22:8, requiring a parapet or protective wall to be constructed on the roof of a new house so that no one will fall off accidentally, reminds one of contemporary building code safety regulations. Without such a safety factor, the owner would be liable (blood guilty) if someone fell off. Such a regulation was especially important in an era when the roof of a house was much used for sleeping and other functions. The statute thus protects life and identifies in a particular and important case the minimum responsibility of a citizen in safeguarding the lives of others.

A number of regulations in chapters 23 and 24 deal specifically with the protection and care of the marginal or weaker members of the community. The prohibition against kidnapping a fellow citizen for slavery or sale (24:7) is a specific manifestation of the eighth commandment and thus carries the absolute punishment of death (see the discussion of the eighth commandment). The law providing sanctuary for an escaped slave from another country (23:15–16) is an important one for comprehending Israel's attitude toward slavery. Previous regulations about slavery, for the most part, have had to do with

171

Hebrew slaves or, more precisely, bonded servants, persons who have indentured themselves because of debt. Here, the text has in mind slavery of other sorts, outside the provisions for working off debts. The term "escaped," sometimes translated as "sought refuge/protection," is the same verb used of God's delivering Israel from slavery. The slave who seeks deliverance may not be handed over. For those who had already been delivered by God from slavery, another person in bondage was a brother or sister, bound in a relationship of care and protection. And the fleeing slave, according to the statute, is as free to choose a place to dwell as the Lord is free to choose a place for the Lord's name to dwell. The language is the same. There are no conditions here. As in the case of the bonded servant who has served six years, the initiative rests with the one who has been in servitude to decide what is best for him or her: in one case deciding whether to continue in bondedness because of its economic benefits (15:16–17), and in the other case deciding what area looks best to settle in (23:16). The statute thus helps to undercut slavery even in a setting where it was practiced. It also sets into the legal system the provision for sanctuary, not only for those members of the community seeking to avoid blood vengeance (cf. ch. 19) but also for persons who come from outside seeking sanctuary against oppression. The sanctuary is obligatory. The fleeing slave may not be handed over. Rather, the community must make provision for the well-being of the one who flees oppression in another land.

In chapter 24:6, 10–13, 14–15, 17–18, and 19–22 there appears a series of statutes designed to protect persons from economic oppression that would keep them from securing the basic needs for life. They particularly prohibit injustice and oppression of the less protected and less secure members of the community, specifically the widow, orphan, sojourner, and poor person. One notes two things in general, however, about these statutes. First, they are not confined only to the poor and the weak. All members of the community are protected against acts that would jeopardize their access to the basic needs of life (see vv. 6 and 10, which make no reference to the poor and the like). Second, they not only speak generally about oppression and injustice (vv. 14 and 17), which can cover a multitude of sins, but the particular actions enjoined against might appear quite legal and indeed appropriate except for one thing: They do not help secure the basic needs of food, clothing, and shelter. Three specific areas are identified and addressed: loans, wages, and gleaning.

1. *Loans* in Israel were not commercial loans, made as a means of developing or using economic capital; seeking interest from a fellow Israelite was prohibited by statute (23:19). Loans were a provision to help the poor, as is indicated in the parallel laws in Exodus 22:25–27 and Leviticus 25:35–36, where the poor are explicitly mentioned as the recipients of loans and interest is excluded. Presumably this would be, as Craigie suggests (p. 302), because such a move would further the poverty of the individual and reflect ingratitude and selfishness on the part of the one able to make the loan because of God's provision of economic well-being. Where, therefore, the statutes in chapter 24 refer to pledges received for loans (vv. 6, 10–11, and 17), they have in mind temporary loans to help a poor person, loans secured by collateral or a pledge of some sort, rather than interest-bearing loans.

But even as one may not abuse or oppress a person in difficult straits by taking interest, so the handling of such pledges must also be humane and not endanger the individual's access to the necessary goods for life. Therefore, taking a millstone as collateral is prohibited because, as the regulation specifically says, such an act would deprive the borrower of the means of life, the means of making bread for the family to eat. So also clothing may not be taken in pledge from a widow (24:17). If clothing is taken from a poor person, it must be returned by nightfall so that the poor person has something for protection from the cold (24:12–13). The subordination of economic proprieties to the protection of basic needs is indeed deemed to be an explicit indicator of righteousness before God on the part of the members of the community (v. 13). Failure to conform to this divine instruction was, unfortunately, a reality (at least in the eighth century when Amos prophesied; cf. Amos 2:8), and was a part of the reason for God's judgment against the people of the northern kingdom, Israel. A Hebrew letter from the time of Josiah actually tells of a man's petition to have his garment returned to him, though in this case it was not necessarily taken in pledge for a loan (Pritchard, p. 568; Cross). The practice of taking garments in pledge or fine or punishment is thus attested, as well as the failure to return them to their owner.

2. *Wages* are to be paid promptly. Work properly done

173

should be properly—that means readily, in this case—rewarded. Here again, the rationale of the statute lies in the situation of the poor person. The wages are necessary immediately because such a person does not have accumulated wealth or other resources. Without immediate payment there will not be food to eat or clothes to wear.

3. *Gleaning* laws appear in chapters 23 and 24 to protect owners of fields and vineyards and to provide food for the poor and needy or the hungry traveler. One is allowed to go into a field or vineyard to get grain or olives or grapes to sustain oneself (23:24–25). Indeed, the owners of such fields must not overharvest a crop but must leave some for those who do not have fields to pick up (24:19–21). But one is not allowed to exploit the right of access to the goods of others for the sake of basic sustenance (23:24–25). The laws, therefore, at one and the same time protect the goods of the members of the community even as they open them up to help provide for the needy persons. Such a system to provide for the welfare of all was rooted in the experience of slavery, when freedom and access to the goods of life were not available to the Israelites (24:18, 22; cf. Miller, "The Human Sabbath"), and was a mark of the proper relationship with God as well as neighbor (24:13).

A look at many of the ordinances in chapters 21–25 confirms what Dean McBride has said in summary about this section:

> Matters treated in this division bring into relief the social policies that the covenant community is sworn to protect, above all the sanctity of life and the worth of individual personhood. If these statutes seem more wide-ranging, formally diverse, and discretely focused than legislation in the preceding divisions, so much the better to show that it is not enough for society to affirm humanitarian ideals in the abstract. The quality of justice is measured by responsible procedures and specific results. Egalitarian justice, like political life itself, can only be practiced in a social arena where basic values collide and concrete decision must be made between divergent human interests. So it is that most of the statutes in this division deal with issues of conflict in which individual lives, livelihoods, and personal liberties are directly at stake. The consistent witness throughout is that each member of the larger community—whether male or female, child or adult, native born or sojourner, culprit or law-abiding citizen, landowner, laborer, or refugee slave— must be treated with the dignity due someone whose life is infinitely precious. Whenever society acts, as it must to prose-

cute and punish those guilty of grievous offenses or even to pursue its well-being through warfare, the worth of all living things has to be respected. In short, this division more than any other segment of the constitution shows us in sensitive detail just what it means for the covenant community to claim identity as a "people holy to Yahweh your God" (7:6; 14:2, 21; 26:19); for if holiness involves corporate apotheosis, setting Israel apart from all other nations, it does so by making sanctification of life at once the prime objective of the whole social order and the political prerogative of everyone who resides in Israel's midst ("Polity," pp. 242–243).

Some Unsettling Relationships

McBride's reference to "setting Israel apart from all other nations" calls attention to a dimension of these laws that many readers find disturbing. In chapters 23:3–8 and 25:17–19, statutes having to do with specifically named other nations are taught (note also the general permission in 23:20 to lend money to foreigners, allowing the building of capital at the expense of those outside the community). The first set of these regulations has to do with who may enter the assembly of the Lord, the worshiping community gathered before the Lord, and thus suggests that the references to Ammonites, Moabites, Edomites, and Egyptians have in mind in this instance such persons as may be present as sojourners within the community of Israel. These ordinances in 23:1–8 are equivalent to criteria for membership or formal participation characteristic of most religious groups. Several things may be noted in the ones governing membership in the Israelite congregation.

1. Not surprisingly, in the light of other dimensions of this instruction, purity was required, as indicated by the specific prohibitions against participation by eunuchs (23:1 does not have in mind accidental mutilation) and children of sexual unions prohibited by the Mosaic teaching (23:2): for example, incestuous unions.

2. The fundamentally male character of the Israelite cultic community, to which women were only marginally or mediately related, is suggested by a statute that refers to male sexual mutilation (v. 1; cf. 16:16 and P. Bird).

3. The ethnic and political history of Israel's relationship with other peoples affected the degree to which they were given access to the worshiping community of Israel. Both positive and negative outcomes are indicated in these verses. Posi-

175

tively, the Deuteronomic emphasis on the category of brother or sister as determinative of a special relationship is reinforced by the access of Edomites to the assembly because they are "brothers" or kin (cf. 2:1–8 and the commentary there). Further, the Deuteronomic recognition of the special care for the sojourner and the motivating power of empathy for the marginal on the part of those who have themselves been in such a position is seen in the access given to an Egyptian(!) of the third generation who seeks to be a member of the congregation (23:7–8). While Israel experienced slavery in Egypt, the people were also resident aliens among the Egyptians—so the Joseph story (cf. Deut. 26:5)—and that experience should make them open to Egyptians who would sojourn among them, even as their experience of slavery should make them sensitive to the needs of the oppressed and the weak and powerless.

But the statutes here speak negatively about others, specifically the Ammonites and the Moabites. And the treatment of these peoples is relatively mild compared to what is said about Amalek at the end of this section of the Deuteronomic code (25:17–19)! The Ammonites and Moabites are forbidden access to the worshiping assembly, to the covenant community. Such a prohibition probably reflects a history of conflict between Israel and these two peoples. Even though they were kinfolk and recipients of the Lord's blessing (cf. 2:9 and 19), they did not have the claim of close kinship as did the Edomites, the descendants of Esau, the brother of Jacob/Israel. The rationale for the prohibition (v. 4) may well be a later addition to the statute, providing an ideological rationale for it. The Ammonites' failure to provide bread and water for the wandering Israelites is seen as an act that incurs lasting hostility on the part of Israel (v. 4a), although nothing is said in the accounts of the wandering in Numbers or Deuteronomy to confirm that claim. The Moabites' sending of the seer Balaam to curse Israel is recorded in Numbers. But conflicts with these peoples were of such long standing that other rationales might well have been provided had these not been available. What is surprising is that conflict with Edom and Egypt did not lead to similar prohibitions of access to the assembly of the Lord.

The words about Amalek at the end of chapter 25 are the most unsettling of all. They are not really a statute and they do not reflect the varied relationships with the other nations in Deuteronomy. Here we have testimony to an enduring hostility

176

toward another people that goes beyond that held toward any other group, including the Canaanites generally. Its roots lie in the conflict with Amalek recorded in Exodus 17, where it is said that the remembrance of Amalek will be blotted out forever. Conflict with Amalek is recorded in a number of other places also (Num. 24:20; I Sam. 15 and 30; I Chron. 4:41–43). The intensity of animosity, bordering on genocide, however, outruns what one might expect even in these many stories of belligerence and battle (see Levenson, "Is There a Counterpart in the Hebrew Bible to New Testament Antisemitism?"). It has been suggested that the note about Amalek cutting off stragglers in the rear is an addition to the tradition to try to account for the level of animus and the extreme demand for destruction. When other peoples are spoken about negatively in the biblical tradition, other more favorable perspectives toward them are usually also somewhere in the tradition (see Levenson), but that is not the case with the Amalekites. Even the hated Haman of Esther is given an Amalekite genealogy as a descendant of Agag (Esther 3:1; cf. I Sam. 15:32–33).

Whatever the actual or supposed rationale for this hatred of Amalek, the ancient or contemporary reader must not find in it any kind of final direction for the community's conduct toward any other people. Even Luther heard in these words a dangerous sound and cautioned that what was spoken of here was God's vengeance through human agents and not human revenge. The many words in the Old Testament and the New Testament about the blessing among the nations, the rule of God over the other peoples, God's providential care of even Israel's enemies, and the injunctions to love not only your neighbors but your enemies serve as a critique and a relativization of these words. Whatever their source, their outcome is vitiated by other divine words and deeds that show another way for the people of God to deal with those with whom they have experienced conflict.

Concluding with Liturgy (26:1–15)

The code of Deuteronomy, the statutes and ordinances given by God to Moses to teach the people (chs. 12–26), comes to an end in this chapter. Instruction will continue to be given, 177 for that is the nature of the book, and Moses does not cease speaking, teaching, and exhorting the people until his death in the last chapter. But the specific rules and regulations for the life of the people conclude here with two sets of instructions having to do with liturgy, more specifically with individual offerings prescribed for the people. This section of the book, spelling out specific cases and rules for the basic guidelines set forth in the commandments, began with directions for worship in chapter 12. In a similar manner it now comes to a close.

The particular matters taken up in chapter 26:1–15 have already been touched on in earlier regulations, the firstfruit offering (26:1–11) in 18:4 and the three-year tithe offering (26:-12–15) in 14:28–29. But now these matters are not only spelled out in more detail, they are set in the context of the entry into the promised land; they function as concrete exemplars and demonstration of the attitudes of *thanksgiving* and *obedience* that are to be characteristic of those who have been redeemed and provided for by the Lord, who have received the salvation gift of God. That is not a new word in this teaching, but it is underscored and offered as a kind of coda to all the many directions that have been set forth in these chapters. "When you come into the land" (v. 1), this is what you are to do.

The two acts of offering in verses 1–11 and 12–15 are readily discernible to the reader. They are discrete and separate. But their combination in this context invites a listening to the resonances between the two sections that are clearly there. In both cases offerings are presented before the Lord accompanied by affirmations declared by the offerer. The statutes as encountered in their present form tell of *two* offerings presented, *three* declarations made when the offerings are presented, and *four* implications growing out of the offerings and the declarations. These offerings, declarations, and implications are the primary ingredients of the two statutes contained in 26:1–15 and provide an appropriate structure for thinking about their meaning.

Firstfruits Offering (26:1–11)

Essential clues to the meaning of this statute are given in the opening temporal clause, "When you come into the land which the LORD your God gives you for an inheritance." These clues are (1) the temporal setting for the enactment of the statute and (2) the thematic word "gives," a verb that occurs with the Lord as the subject, the land or its produce as the object, and Israel or its individual citizens as the indirect object—the recipients of the Lord's gift (vv. 1, 2, 3, 9, 10, and 11).

As noted above, the point at which this regulation is to be carried out is at the beginning of one's life on the land. Symbolic actions upon entering a new land or territory are not unfamiliar to us. Sometimes the new arrival will kiss the ground, as if there were some sort of personal relationship with the soil. Often new arrivals in a land—and one must remember that there were then and always are previous inhabitants—have planted a flag to claim ownership of the land for themselves or their country. In this text the symbolic action is of a different sort. It does not take place upon setting foot on the new land but only after the people have settled in and have had a chance to enjoy its good and rich benefits. But as soon as that happens, each member or each family representative is to take some of the first of all the produce that the land has yielded and bring it before the Lord at the sanctuary. Such an act has nothing to do with any personal relationship with the ground or the land, nor does it represent any kind of claim over the land; precisely the opposite. As indicated by the *first declaration* that is made ("I have come into the land," v. 3) and the way the land is always described (as the gift of God [six times]) it is clear that this offering is an act of response and gratitude. The act acknowledges that the land and all its rich benefits come from the Lord as a gift, undeserved and unearned. Thus it expresses deep gratitude to the one who is the source of all the provision for life that comes from this gift. To say "I have come into the land" is in effect to say "I have received the gift." It is equivalent in meaning and function to what one hears in a familiar folk blessing frequently sung at mealtimes: "The Lord's been good to me, and so I thank the Lord."

In the Lord's provision of a place to live in freedom under the rule of God and with opportunity to enjoy the rich blessings of the land, Israel found its salvation gift from God. No theme so permeates the book as does the word of God's gift of land and place and provision for life. It is the presupposition of all the instruction. Indeed, all the law is given to Israel to enable this people to maintain the kind of community and relationship with God that will keep God's good gift perduring through the ages. It is no accident, therefore, that the Deuteronomic code closes with a provision for the people to express at the beginning and always their gratitude for God's "inexpressible gift," their being set free and given an abundantly rich life. In a most fundamental way this regulation defines forever the purpose of

179

those offerings that God's people bring out of their labors and offer as a reflection of God's provision of the possibilities for life.

The gift of the land is to the people as a whole, but its benefits are for each individual member. Here, as throughout the Book of Deuteronomy, one encounters that sense of the way life under God is to be lived in a corporate existence, always by and for the sake of each member of the community. The direct address in the singular second person that runs throughout Moses' speech to the people and is constant in these verses, along with the "I" speech of the offerer, indicate that the demands of life under this Lord and the care provided by this God rest upon each individual. At every turn, the reader is reminded that the requirements and the gifts are both comprehensive and particular. One of the features of Deuteronomy that has most puzzled scholars (but is not discernible in translation) is the way hundreds of second-person pronouns jump back and forth between singular and plural. Whatever the reason for this vacillation, its effect is to cause the reader to perceive the text as addressing a corporate body whose sense of responsibility and experience of weal and woe are thoroughly shared by one and all, while at other times the instruction and the promises come very personally and directly to each individual. The one who participates in the group is neither lost nor hidden.

It is a matter of debate as to whether the offering of first-fruits set forth in verses 1–11 is commanded as a onetime gift, when the people first settle down in the land, or is meant to be a regular offering. The choice is unnecessary. The statute tells Israel how to acknowledge the gift of the land and its blessing when that has been received. But that acknowledgment does not cease anymore than the blessing of firstfruit of a new harvest ceases. Israel is to come before the Lord in gratitude then and always.

The *second declaration* accompanying the offering of first-fruits has the same rationale as the first one. It expresses a "response" (v. 5) of gratitude to God. Its form, however, is different. It does not simply acknowledge the gift of God but in a confessional way tells the story of how Israel received the gift of the land. The meaning of this offering is spelled out now in detail, and the offerer claims to be a part of the large story of God's redemptive and gracious purposes with this people.

The words uttered here are often called a "credo," and with Deuteronomy 6:20–25 they provide the earliest examples of

180

members of the community of God's people confessing their faith, declaring before God and each other what God has done in their behalf. Here, therefore, is the precursor of all the creedal activity of the later communities of faith. In these two cases it is clear that the confessional activity is rooted in the memory of a people. It is the telling of the story of God's way of goodness with this people. In Deuteronomy, the function of the credo is catechetical (ch. 6) and liturgical (ch. 26). The story is told to teach the next generation what God has done with them and why they live a life of obedience, and it is told to express gratitude to God for all the Lord's gifts. These purposes are not separate, of course; as the story is remembered and told again and again, the next generation can make the confession its own in bringing the fruits of *their* labors in God's good and productive land before the altar.

The details of the credo merit closer attention, even though the story should be quite familiar to all hearers and readers of Deuteronomy—past and present—by the time they reach this point. For this succinct summary of all that has happened from the beginning until now, the story that is contained in the five books of the Torah, identifies what really matters and is fundamental for the faith of this people.

The credo begins with the origins of Israel's story with the Lord by recalling the lives and experiences of the patriarchs, specifically Jacob. What is remembered about the fathers and mothers of Israel, however, is that they wandered about: that is, they did not yet have a place and a land. In other words, the credo recalls how it was at the beginning and how different it is now that Israel has come into the land, into the Lord's allotment. The wandering about of the patriarchs is implicitly contrasted with the "I have come into the land" (v. 3) and "now I bring the first of the fruit of the ground" (v. 10) of the later posterity to show how God has brought this people from its difficult beginnings to the rich possibilities of the present life on the land.

The journey of Jacob and his sons into Egypt is remembered next. The ambivalence of Israel's relation with the other nations is never more sharply seen than in this central core of the credo that focuses upon the time in Egypt. Egypt was the place (note the repetition of the adverb "there") where Jacob and his family were able to sojourn and survive the famine; it was also where the promise of God was fulfilled that the descendants of Abraham and Sarah, though very few at the beginning, would become a populous people. Here again we perceive a contrast between the way things were at the beginning and the way they came to be by God's blessing. But ironically that blessing of many people led to disaster when the Egyptians began to oppress the Hebrews, afflicting them with slavery at hard labor.

At this point, at the center of the credo, we come to the heart of the matter; we hear not simply the story of the Exodus but within that story the paradigm of God's way with God's people. When the victims of oppression and suffering cry out to the Lord, God hears their cries of pain and sees their trouble and comes to deliver them. That was indeed the liberation event that enabled this people to enter into the salvation gift of a good and productive land. It was also an indicator of how God deals with humankind, a way that is attested from the first outcry of human pain when Abel's blood cried out from the ground, through the cries of the victims of Sodom and Gomorrah, the people under oppression in the time of the Judges, an exiled people in Babylon, and the suffering ones whose voice is heard in the psalms of lament, to the cry of abandonment of God's righteous sufferer on the cross. Indeed, it is precisely because of this biblical conviction of the proneness of God to hear and respond to the cries of the people that such a horror as the Holocaust seems to strike at the very heart of the biblical faith.

While the credo of these verses is not itself a prayer, it is not unlike the songs of thanksgiving found in the psalms (e.g., Pss. 18, 30, 34, and 116) where an individual who cried out to God for help gives thanks and sacrifices of thanksgiving (Ps. 116:17) and recounts what God has done to deliver the suffering one from affliction. Thus the presentation of an offering of firstfruits served as a pattern for Israel's response of gratitude at all times, even as the Exodus experience of suffering seen, heard, and dealt with reflected God's persistent way in the world. In this statute, therefore, a people who had experienced that way were called to remember it and demonstrate their gratitude with offerings. Their memory was a memory of suffering, of powerful deliverance, and of blessing and providential care. To remember that experience and tell that story is what it meant to confess one's faith.

Because it is true, the story has *implications for life*. They are stated succinctly in the verses that follow. The first of these has been indicated from the beginning of the chapter. It is the fact that those to whom the gift has been given now present their own gift in gratitude to God, thereby acknowledging in that act who is the source of all good (v. 10*a*). Second, the power and will of God to work this way in behalf of the people demonstrates the claim of this God to the full worship of those who have been so redeemed and cared for (v. 10*b*). But gratitude and worship are not alone the implications of this story. It is meant also to evoke a *joy* and celebration of all the good given by God to these people, a good that is available to the whole community, even to those who have no direct access to the fruit of the land, the Levite and the sojourner (v. 11).

Tithe Offering (26:12–15)

A final implication of the story that is told and the faith that is confessed in Israel's credo is found in the second offering regulated in this chapter, the tithe. Grateful offering, worship, and joyous celebration are what this story means for those who have participated in it in deed, in memory, and in faith—but also in *obedience,* obedience that in turn is the means by which the blessing continues. The third confessional statement, or *declaration,* appears in connection with the completion of the tithe. It is a lengthy one and different from those in the first eleven verses. The meaning of the three negative statements in the first half of verse 14 is not altogether clear. They seem to have to do with the proper carrying out of the tithe offering ritual. The force of those statements, however, is quite clear from the final confessional statement of verse 14 and the preceding verse. The Book of Deuteronomy regularly calls the people to hear and obey the voice of the Lord and to be careful to do all that the Lord through Moses requires. In the structure of the book, that obedience is the "therefore" of chapters 4–25 that grows out of the story of God's redemption and providence recounted in chapters 1–3. Here that obedience is both demonstrated (in the presenting of the offering and its manner of presentation) and acknowledged (in the verbal statements that the worshiper makes before the Lord). The implications for faith of the experience of God's salvation and blessing are thus clear and complete: offerings of gratitude, worship of God, joy and celebration, and obedience to the Lord's instruction.

It would be remiss of the reader, however, to ignore the character of the offering regularized in these concluding verses.

183

Its purpose is stressed by being referred to twice, in verses 12 and 13. The law of the tithe in 14:28–29 succinctly identifies the purpose of this offering as providing sustenance for those persons or groups who do not have access to the land and its goods, specifically Levite, sojourner, widow, and orphan. That point is reiterated in 26:12–15, thus lifting up at the conclusion of the Deuteronomic code another of its fundamental themes: the importance of making available the goods of God's blessing to *all* members of the community. No member of the community was ever free to ignore those persons who lacked the necessities of life. All members were expected to provide a portion of their income to provide for such sisters and brothers. The ordinance for the tithe in chapter 14 sees in this process the way to continue the blessing of God. So in 26:15 the ritual of the tithe concludes with a prayer to God to bless Israel and the ground from which the produce comes. One notes that while 14:29 seems to suggest that blessing will automatically come to those who bring the tithe for Levite, sojourner, orphan, and widow, the prayer in chapter 26 reminds us that blessing is not a computerized signal built into the universe but is a gift out of the free will of God, to be sought in prayer and facilitated by the community's attention to the needs of all.

The Covenant Concluded (26:16–19)

The presentation of the commandments and the statutes and ordinances that will guide Israel's life in the land is over now. Verse 16 serves as a concluding bracket around chapters 5—26, matching Moses' introduction to the whole in 5:1 as well as his introduction to the section setting forth the statutes and ordinances in 12:1:

> 5:1   Hear, O Israel, the statutes and ordinances that I am addressing to you today; you shall learn them and observe them diligently.

> 12:1   These are the statutes and ordinances that you must diligently observe in the land.

> 26:16   This very day the LORD your God is commanding you to observe these statutes and ordinances; so observe them diligently with all your heart and with all your soul.

(NRSV)

184

So a signal is given that Moses has finished teaching the rules and regulations for life. But this conclusion is not simply a literary end. As in all of Moses' teaching, the final word urges full obedience to the divine instruction, reminding hearers and readers again that what matters ultimately is not simply the setting forth of the law or polity but what the people will do with it. To underscore the fact that these laws are the means by which Israel lives out its relation with the Lord and in the keeping of which it can receive and experience the rich blessing of God, the final verses of this chapter record the oaths that bind the Lord and Israel to each other. As Dean McBride has put it, "this is the constitutive act per se, the ratification ceremony, formally inaugurating, or reinaugurating, the covenantal bond between Yahweh and Israel" ("Polity," p. 234). While these verses do not explicitly refer to "covenant," they describe clearly a contracting together of two parties with mutual obligations and expectations. The parallel and formal character of verses 17 and 18–19 suggest the legal or juridical character of what is set forth here.

There is some uncertainty about how precisely to translate the first few words of verses 17 and 18. They mean something like: "Today you have accepted the LORD's declaration to be your God" (v. 17) and "Today the LORD has accepted your declaration . . . to keep all his commandments" (v. 18). In verse 18 the Lord's oath to be this people's God is made in a single statement, followed by three clauses that delineate the implications for Israel of its assenting to the Lord's intention. The three clauses in verse 17*b* spell out what God receives from Israel for having made obligation to be their God. Israel's declaration that it would keep all the Lord's commandments (v. 17*b*) is assented to by the Lord (v. 18*a*), and three clauses indicate what Israel will receive from the Lord for accepting this obligation (vv. 18*a* and 19). The following translation, adapted from that of Norbert Lohfink (*Great Themes*, p. 26), may best represent what verses 17–19 are saying. (The basic declarations or obligations by each party, first the Lord and then Israel, are italicized.)

v. 17   Today you have accepted the Lord's declaration. He has declared to you:
   He will be your God,
   and you are to walk in his ways,
   keep his statutes, his commandments and his
       ordinances,
   and obey his voice,

185

v. 18
> and today, the Lord has accepted your
> declaration.
> You have declared to him:
> Because you wish to be his people, his
> personal possession,
> as he has promised you,
> *you will keep all his commandments,*

v. 19
> that he may set you high above all nations
> that he has
> made, in praise, and fame, and honor,
> and you shall become a people holy to the
> Lord your
> God, as he has promised.

With these words, the covenant is concluded, literally, legally, and liturgically. The obligations taken on by the parties involved, the Lord and Israel, and the implications for each one are made very explicit. The Lord makes obligation to be the God of this people, to be the one who watches over their existence, providing for life, protecting from enemies and harm, and guiding them in all the vicissitudes of their dwelling on the land. That obligation, of course, is not something new to the relationship at this time. It has been God's way with Israel up to this point. Indeed, one notes that God's actions with and for Israel justify a claim over them. The reader might well assume that obviously the Lord is Israel's God, whether the people like it or not. But the covenantal structure reveals that this is also an offer Israel accepts or contracts for, that having the Lord as Israel's God is the relationship that creates for this people the possibility for life and good. They are not forced into the relationship. They have been led into it by the gracious, redemptive work of God; but they formally acknowledge and agree to the relationship that the love of God has initiated. The one who responds to the suffering cries of the people makes obligation to be there for them as their God, redeeming, blessing, and requiring on into the future.

What the Lord seeks in return is indicated in the three concluding clauses of verse 17 and is in fact what Israel, for its part of the covenant relationship, obligates itself to in verse 18—keeping all the commandments, the statutes, and the ordinances. Israel in effect makes an oath to do what God desires. The primary formulation of that obligation is "keeping his commandments (and statutes and ordinances)" (vv. 17, 18). What that means from the Lord's angle is indicated by the language of the other clauses in verse 17—to walk in the ways of the Lord, to follow the direction that the Lord sets, and to obey the voice of the Lord: that is, to heed the divine instruction and teaching. In these clauses stipulating Israel's responsibilities in the covenantal structure and relationship, we have three primary biblical motifs for describing from a human perspective that relationship and its requirements: *way, law,* and *word.* The impact of the covenantal structure for understanding the life of the people of God is thus seen to be large and formative. The *way* of the Lord is one of the most fundamental images of Scripture for speaking of ethics, discipleship, and the human pilgrimage. Psalm 1 sets it as a metaphor for understanding what all the psalms are about. In the New Testament "the way" is a christological definition (John 14:6) and one of the earliest names for the Christian community (Acts 9:2). The *law* or *commandment* is the concrete specification of the covenantal life. It is the definition of the way, the guideposts to keep one from falling by the wayside or wandering in another direction. The *word* or *voice* is a constant reminder that whatever relation the commandments and the statutory rulings have to other expressions of law or statutes governing nations and people, this law is rooted in the divine will and intention for the human community. Its authority does not come from human structures. It may or may not conform to human definitions of appropriate rules for ordering life (though for the most part its continuity with other bodies of laws and regulations is clear and important). In Deuteronomy alone, one may find several reasons for keeping the commandments. In these verses, there are at least two grounds. One obeys the divine instruction because it is just that, God's word and way, and because the members of the community have solemnly obligated themselves to do so in the enactment of a formal relationship containing obligations and benefits for both parties.

This text, as so many others, raises the question of why it is that God would seek a people to be obedient. Like all questions that ask why of God, answers are difficult to come by. The best clue is from the story as a whole, which reveals the need for someone in the world to help demonstrate, bring about, and maintain a good world whose character is compatible with the character of God. In Genesis 18:19, the story of Israel begins with an indication that this people have been known or chosen "to keep the way of the Lord by doing righteousness and jus-

187

tice." That is God's way. Deuteronomy spells out a similar way for Israel, and the covenant ratification binds this people "today" (three times in these verses) so to live.

Israel's willingness to keep all the commandments of the Lord has significant implications for their place in the world. They shall become the Lord's special people, a status and relationship that is spelled out three times in verse 18, echoing the earlier claim of Deuteronomy 7:6 (see commentary on 7:6). The one distinction between the two passages is that in 7:6 Israel is chosen as God's treasured people *out of* all the peoples of the earth. In 26:18 the Lord promises to *set Israel high above* all the nations that the Lord has made. The note of separation and distinction from all other peoples is reiterated and here made a fundamental part of the covenantal relationship. But in this context the sense of status that is implicit in being separated out and explicit in the reference to Israel as "treasured" (NRSV) or "his own possession" is underscored by Moses' claim that the Lord will set Israel *above* the other nations *"in praise and in fame and in honor"* (emphasis added). The force of this extravagant offer and its role in the covenantal relationship with the Lord is best seen by looking at the two other places where the identical expression appears, Jeremiah 13:11 and 33:9. In 13:11, the Lord announces judgment against Judah and Jerusalem and gives this rationale:

> I made the whole house of Israel and the whole house of Judah cling to me, says the LORD, that they might be for me a people, a name [or fame], a praise, and a glory [or honor], but they would not listen.

The special status of Israel and the fame, praise, and honor that accrue to them are not ends in themselves or, perhaps better, not simply for Israel's sake but *to the glory of the Lord of Israel.* One actually hears an anticipation of such fame, praise, and glory heaped upon Israel by the other nations but *because of its God* in 4:5–8, where the nations shall say of Israel that it is a wise and understanding people. The reason for saying that is because their God is near when they call out and because the Lord has given them such righteous laws.

This understanding of Israel's glory being a reflection of the glory of God and ultimately for God's sake is further indicated in Jeremiah 33:9, where healing and forgiveness and restoration are promised to Israel and Judah after God's judgment:

188

> And this city shall be to me a name [or fame] of joy, a praise and
> a glory before all the nations of the earth who shall hear of all
> the good that I do for them; they shall fear and tremble because
> of all the good and all the prosperity I provide for it.

The "specialness" of Israel is a constant theme of the biblical
story. It was experienced in the love and faithfulness of God.
But it seems always to have been more a matter of function than
being, those who knew themselves to be God's treasure as a
holy people in the world through whom the Lord's way could
be demonstrated and the Lord's blessing manifest, a vivid testimony of the power of God to provide goodness and peace in this
world.

Deuteronomy 27—28
Ceremony and Sanctions

After the long central discourse setting forth the stipulations and regulations of the covenant, these chapters deal with
two rather obvious matters that need to be taken into account
in order for the possibilities envisioned in God's way with this
people to come to fruition. If this law is to be the constitution
or polity of the people that will guide their way, there must be
some way of preserving it, holding it before them, and keeping
them mindful of its particulars. Chapter 27 sets up a way for
that to happen. Further, if this law is to be maintained and is
a life-and-death matter, which Moses constantly insists that it is,
there must be some way of enforcing it, some way of ensuring
that the law will be followed. The last half of chapter 27 (vv.
11–26) and chapter 28 deal with that need through the divine
provision of a system of rewards and punishments, encourage-
ments and sanctions, a provision already anticipated in 10:12—
11:32 (see commentary there), and one that also concludes the
final speech of Moses in 30:15–20.

The historical origin of the materials in these chapters is a
matter of debate. Some see in parts of both chapters elements
of a fairly ancient pre-exilic covenantal liturgy. Others see here
language that sounds Deuteronomistic and suggests a later
composition, exilic or postexilic. What is clear from text and
possible contexts is that however one decides the question of

189

literary history—and because there seems to be much traditional material in these chapters, that may be difficult to do with much certainty—the matters addressed by the chapters were of importance at the beginning of Israel's history where the book sets them and much later in Israel's history as well. The need for continual recall and reaffirmation of the instruction of God and awareness of the implications of obedience and disobedience is just as sharp (if not more so) when these words address the generation that has forgotten the rules and regulations and has experienced the consequences in exile. On whatever side of the boundary marking the salvation gift of the Lord and the possibility of enjoying its goodness that the people find themselves, their need for reaffirmation and enforcement is real.

Recording and Confirming the Law (27:1–10)

The chapter gives an initial impression of containing a single ceremony consisting of various elements—building an altar, inscribing the law on plastered stones, sacrifice and celebration, exhortation and declaration, pronouncement of blessings and curses. A closer look suggests that the present form of the text may represent the pulling together of different pieces and their editing and re-editing. One notes that at the beginning of the chapter it is Moses and the elders of Israel who charge the people, while in verse 9 it is Moses and the Levitical priests who speak to the people. And in both cases the first person singular "I," rather than plural, is used, suggesting that only Moses speaks, which in fact is the case in verse 11, where we encounter a third introductory sentence with only Moses as the speaker. Some would see in the provision for setting up an altar in the Shechem area (where Mount Ebal and Mount Gerizim are located) signs of a ceremony that is older than the provision for setting up a sanctuary and altar only where the Lord shall cause the Lord's name to dwell (though technically this does not violate the way that regulation is set up in chapter 12). At the same time the double reference to "law" or torah in the first section of the chapter suggests a late edition of the text, for that term is used only in the later framework of the book.

Recognizing the complexities of the formation of the chapter and even possibilities of contradictions in its present formulation, one nevertheless encounters a text that has put all this

together in a way that suggests to the readers a single ceremony. Its primary purpose is to make sure that when the people
on the boundary of God's promise come into its blessing, they
do not forget that they are the Lord's people (v. 9; cf. 26:16–19)
and how they are to live as such. To do this, they are to inscribe
in permanent fashion (on the stones) all the law, the instruction
that the Lord has given through Moses. They are also to build
an altar of unhewn stones and, in good Deuteronomic fashion,
bring their offerings to the Lord and eat and rejoice there (see
commentary on ch. 12). The prescribed ceremony, therefore,
served to preserve the law in monumental fashion and to institute its obedience in the context of the regular worship of God.
The recording of the law takes place in the context of the Lord's
acknowledgment of the people and the land and of the enjoyment of the benefits of the land. However much the details of
the law may be common to good jurisprudence and originate
in statutory rulings, their religious ground and their divine
source are attested in the way in which they are recorded in this
ceremony in the context of worship. One may assume that the
laws would be visible whenever the people came to worship
and sacrifice. One is also reminded in the sacrifice, eating, and
celebration that such rules and regulations for life are the
means by which the blessings of God are ensured.

Placing this ceremony immediately after 26:16–19 is probably not accidental, even though the two texts may not have
referred to the same event. Here at the end of chapter 26,
chapters 27 and 28 are the materials that point to a confirmation and reaffirmation of the covenantal bond and a ratification
and cementing of the relationship and the requirements and
expectations that go with that relationship. The tie to 26:16–19
is sharpened by the fact that Moses and the priests go on (vv.
9–10) to exhort the people to an obedience by declaring that
they have "this day" become the people of God, a central aspect
of the covenantal relationship ratified in chapter 26. In these
two verses (27:9–10) we find, at the center of the ceremonial
confirmation of the covenant and its stipulations, the essential
structure of faith as Deuteronomy sees it, embodied in the
Shema (6:4–5) and reiterated time and again in the book. Israel
is called to hear and heed the dual word that (1) they belong to
the Lord and the Lord is their God and (2) that relationship and
identity as the people of this God means a total commitment of

191

themselves to live as the Lord has instructed them. Once again, the basic word of the whole book is set before the people in a way that calls for them to respond. This is neither the first nor the last time in the book that hearers and readers encounter Moses' call for a commitment on the part of those who hear and read, a commitment that is elsewhere characterized as love and whose content has been spelled out in all the instruction that has been given in chapters 5—26.

Two things are worth noting about the ceremony prescribed here. One is the fact that the tradition records the carrying out of these instructions after the people entered (Josh. 8:30–35) and with specific quotation and reference back to the words of Deuteronomy 27. The setting of this law at the beginning of Israel's life in the land as a guide for the years ahead was taken seriously. In Joshua 1 and then at the end of chapter 8, the book of the law is set before the leader, Joshua, and the people. The Book of Deuteronomy proclaims this law as a touchstone, a guidepost, and a measuring rod for the common life and daily conduct of this people. As the story of Israel's life in Canaan begins, it is clear that the claim of Deuteronomy is a most serious one and their way in the future will be measured by the criterion of conformity to the divine instruction set forth in it. At the beginning of that story, Moses' successor is instructed to live by this law and then sets it before the people as directed by Deuteronomy. At the end of the story, the last great king of Judah, Josiah, calls the nation to a repentance and a new obedience to the book of the law (II Kings 22—23) and himself is evaluated positively according to the norms it provides (II Kings 23:25).

The references here to Joshua and Josiah may give us a clue to the meaning of the elders joining Moses in charging the people to keep the commandment. That is a rather unusual note, for while the elders are mentioned more than once in the statutes and regulations, they do not customarily appear alongside Moses instructing the people. But here at the end of the book there is a consciousness that Moses is beginning to pass from the scene, as well as a recognition that others will have to give leadership in his place even if, or perhaps especially if, there is no new Moses. The awareness of the passing of Moses and the need for new leadership becomes explicit in chapter 31, but it is already suggested here, where a ritual is prescribed that will have to be carried out after Moses is no longer with the people.

Encouragement and Sanctions (27:11—28:68)

As verse 11 indicates, we have in the rest of chapter 27 something different from but connected to the ceremony described in the first part of the chapter. Verses 1 and 11 both introduce a ceremony with the words: "Then Moses [v. 1, "and the elders"] charged the people as follows." In verse 11, what Moses prescribes is said to be "on the same day" as the preceding ceremony, thus being distinguished from but associated with the ceremony of reaffirmation and inscription of the covenant requirements. In a similar way verses 11–26 are related to but distinguished from what follows in chapter 28. They are related by having to do with blessing and curse, with the sanctions of the covenant, as is the case with chapter 28. They are distinguished by being a narrative description speaking of Moses in the third person and setting forth the form of a community ritual, while chapter 28 in form is again speech of Moses and seems in some sense to be a continuation of the long speech in chapters 5–26.

In terms of its content, all this material has to do with setting forth the sanctions of the covenant, encouraging obedience to the divine instruction by pointing to the good things that grow out of that obedience, and discouraging disobedience by describing its disastrous consequences. We have an extended form of what is set forth more succinctly in 11:26–31 (see commentary there for discussion of blessing and curse). Several things are worth noting about the presentation of blessing and curse in chapters 27 and 28. In 11:26–31 and 30:15–20, Moses simply sets blessing and curse before the people as a choice and the focus is upon the call for a decision by Israel. Here in chapters 27 and 28, the focus is less upon the act of choosing, though that is certainly assumed, and more upon the specifics of what will happen dependent upon Israel's choice.

One notes, however, that the specifics are much more heavily in terms of the negative consequences of disobedience than the positive results of obedience. The latter do not appear in the blessings and curses of 27:11–26 and occupy only fourteen out of sixty-eight verses in chapter 28. That disparity is not peculiar to Deuteronomy. The background of these curses, or at least those in chapter 28, is most likely the treaty form of international relationships in the ancient Near East, where blessings and curses were placed at the end of the document as sanctions to ensure that the parties to the treaty would abide by its stipulations. It is just such a function that these blessings and curses fulfill in the covenantal structure that Deuteronomy sets forth to formalize, articulate, and enforce the relationship between Israel and the Lord. In the treaties of the ancient Near East, and especially in those of the second millennium, the curses often significantly outnumber the blessings (Hillers, p. 33); so Deuteronomy's form is consistent with the background models. At the same time, the reader may note that the primary focus throughout the book to this point has been upon the benefits and good that the people will receive in the land that the Lord gives. It is therefore not inappropriate to shift that emphasis now, especially in light of the fact that the book is transmitted in a time when the temptations to disobedience had not been very well resisted and the negative consequences had taken effect. The curses serve to give a theological rationale to the disasters that came upon the people. The disasters were real. What one hears in Deuteronomy is the claim that they grew out of the choices and actions of the people and were also part of the effecting purpose of God. The book and the story of Israel that was told according to its norms do not allow one to generalize about the effects of evil and disaster. They do teach that with this people in special relation to God there was a connection between the way they went and the way they would go, between the patterns of conduct they exhibited and their outcome—defeat, death, and exile.

The form and content of the set of curses in 27:11–26 and those in chapter 28 need to be distinguished. In the first case, we do not have descriptions simply of the consequences of disobedience to the divine instruction but specific moral instruction having to do with matters already anticipated in one form or another in the commandments, the statutes, and the ordinances. Indeed, the focus is not on the specifics of the consequences but on what sort of action is prohibited. A generalized statement of the fate—"cursed be the one who"—precedes the description of a forbidden act. The acts whose commission leads to being cursed echo those we encountered as prohibitions in the Ten Commandments (e.g., vv. 15, 16, 24, and 25) or else-

194

where in the legal traditions of Israel (cf. v. 17 with Deut. 5:19 and 19:14; v. 18 with Lev. 19:14; v. 19 with Deut. 24:17; v. 20 with Lev. 18:8 and 20:11; v. 21 with Exod. 22:19 and Lev. 18:23 and 20:15; v. 22 with Lev. 18:9 and 20:17; v. 23 with Lev. 18:17 and 20:14; v. 25 with Deut. 5:17; 16:19 and Exod. 23:8). The matters taken up are not a neat, ordered collection; they deal with fundamental aspects of the order of Israel's existence: the exclusive worship of the Lord, honor of parents, protection of life and property, justice for the weak and powerless, and sexual relations. These curses have often been regarded as a kind of ancient collection of laws analogous to the Ten Commandments, which have no curse expressions attached but do seem to have a sense of absoluteness implied and in other contexts are given the penalty of death.

There is a feature of these legal-curse formulations that may have to do with their being drawn together in this context. As has often been noticed, the particular nuance found in some of them explicitly, and probably implicitly in all of them, is the fact that they prohibit and place under judgment illegal and immoral acts done *in secret* (see vv. 15 and 24). Elizabeth Bellefontaine has suggested a possible rationale for this curse ritual in the midst of the assembly of the people:

> The curse ritual as such does not necessarily promulgate new demands. The deeds mentioned were already known to the community as liable to the wrath of God. It was the possibility of their secret commission, of the criminal's eluding of justice and the consequent fearful results for the people, that prompted the community's solemn invocation of divine retribution upon the criminal. . . . The curse brings into the legal sphere certain prohibitives whose violation in secret would escape the ordinary legal process. . . . The community, as sacral assembly, must solemnly invoke the action of the deity in such cases. The curse provides the prohibitives with the only punishment which can reach secret sins: the inescapable consequence of the vengeance of God. In the curse the prohibitive norm under the aspect of secret violation is made legal (Bellefontaine, pp. 58–59).

The curse ritual now concludes (v. 26) with what is probably an addition, but it is an appropriate ending to this list of curses. It is an all-inclusive judgment of curse placed upon *any* failure to "confirm," to establish this law solidly by doing it. The chapter thus appropriately balances the initial provision for a permanent record of the law by an insistence that it is established only

195

by the *doing* of it. No laws or statutes, no rules or regulations, have any solidity or meaning unless those for whom they are designed carry them out and do them. So one of Moses' most frequent exhortations is "be careful to do," which appears, in fact, in the very next verse of the book (28:1). The regular "Amen" response of the people is their individual and communal agreement to the stipulations that have been set forth here. The final one in this covenanting ceremony (v. 26) thus represents their formal consent to keeping all the laws, as they have already declared is their intent (26:18).

Chapter 28 continues the theme of the preceding verses. It shifts back to Moses' address in the first person to the assembly of Israel. In this way it presents itself as a continuation of what has just been described in the ritual on Mount Ebal and Mount Gerizim, because Moses continues to speak without further introduction and because the subject matter continues to be the consequences of obedience and disobedience. In this chapter we learn in more detail what those consequences are.

It is worth noting first of all, however, the language Moses uses to describe how all the blessings and curses happen. The source of them all is the Lord, as the formulations of chapter 28 indicate time and time again. But at the beginning of the blessings (v. 2) and of the curses (v. 15), it is said that "all these blessings/curses shall come upon you and overtake you" (cf. v. 45). The experience of disaster as pursuing and overwhelming one, almost as a kind of force at work, is a fairly common phenomenon; it is often encountered in the sensation of being undone by the consequences of some action that one has taken. That experience is suggested by the idiom in these verses, but it is not confined to disaster. Like the pursuit of goodness and mercy in Psalm 23, which appear there also like some personified forces but are clearly the work of God, goodness and blessing shall overwhelm the people as they live by the Lord's way and teaching just as disaster shall destroy them if they do not. At one and the same time, the Mosaic speech points to the divine agency in all things (see commentary on 2:1—3:12) and the equally inevitable and intelligible outcome of choices made and actions taken.

196 The blessings that follow from obedience have to do basically with three areas: fruitfulness of land and people (vv. 3–5, 8, 11–12), victory over enemies (v. 7), and an exalted place as God's people (vv. 1, 9, 10, 13—on this last theme see commen-

tary on 26:16–19). The Lord will provide a beneficial matrix for the existence of this people in nature and history. All of that depends on and grows out of adherence to the way and will of the Lord as spelled out in the commandments and statutes. At the beginning, at the end, and in the middle, the list of potential blessings is bracketed and punctuated by the condition of obedience to the commandments and walking in the ways of the Lord (vv. 1, 9, and 13–14). The list concludes with explicit placing of the demand of the primary commandment, the exclusive worship of the Lord, once again upon the people. The contemporary reactualization of these demands is heard expressly and repeatedly in the clause "which I am commanding you *today*" (vv. 1, 13, and 14). Because of its repetition, the emphasis of the temporal note cannot be lost. These teachings are being laid upon hearer and reader "right now," whenever that "today" is. The audience receives all the authority of the text as ancient Mosaic promulgation of the divine word, and at the same time it has all the contemporary force of a word commanded "today."

The much longer list of curses is a negative warning against disobedience alongside the positive promise of blessing for obedience. The same conditionality and contemporizing of the commandments (v. 15) begin the list, but with the reversal of the initial blessings. Death, plague, and destruction by enemies are the fate of a disobedient people. Much of the material here reflects traditional curse formulations known from Near Eastern treaties and elsewhere. Lists of various kinds of sicknesses and plagues, human enterprises doomed to futility, natural disasters, frustration of the blessing, exile, cannibalism—all these and other unfortunate fates are what a disobedient people may expect. The curses are clearly corporate and aimed at the people as a whole. Indeed, the reader would perceive that many of these things did in fact happen to the nation of Judah at the hands of the Babylonians. They make sense in the context of history. But the fate of the community is the fate of each individual. As the commandments are addressed to each member of the community, so the curses are experienced by those same individuals. The detailing of the consequences of obedience and disobedience are a sharp reminder of the interrelationship of individual and community. The divine instruction is set to show the people how to live together as the people of God. That will work, however, only as each person in the community is "careful to do" all the commandments. The outcome of living or failing to live this way is the fate of the people as a whole. But as the curses (which like the blessings are expressed consistently in the second-person-singular address) vividly indicate, that fate represents a suffering that happens to men, women, and children, sons and daughters. The covenantal structure with its encouragement to obedience and sanctions against disobedience is not meant to suggest a one-to-one correspondence between a single act and a single outcome. It is meant to claim a relationship in which choices and acts determine outcomes and consequences. The results are built into the structure of existence by the Lord of the covenant, who points the way the people are to go and directs the way that by their acts they choose to go.

PART THREE

Moses' Third Address: The Covenant at Moab

DEUTERONOMY 29—32

The third major section of the book and Moses' final address is found in chapters 29—32. This speech is given a heading at the beginning of chapter 29 (28:69 in the Hebrew text): "These are the words of the covenant which the LORD commanded Moses to make with the people of Israel in the land of Moab, besides the covenant which he had made with them at Horeb." Whereas Moses' memoir of the journey through the wilderness (1:1—4:43) is introduced as "These are the words" and his proclamation of the Deuteronomic law is introduced by "This is the law" and further explained by "these are the testimonies (stipulations), the statutes, and the ordinances" (4:44, 45), this section is introduced as "the words of the covenant." The heading therefore gives us an indication of what the chapters are about. Because we do not encounter another redactional heading until chapter 33, it seems that chapters 31 and 32 were also meant to be included under the rubric of covenant, even though they are not a part of the speech that begins in chapter 29.

On the assumption that these four chapters now have as their primary aim the presentation of the making of a covenant between the Lord and Israel, one that is explicitly differentiated from the Sinai covenant, Dean McBride ("Polity," p. 235) has accurately summarized what this section is about.

> Although aspects of this second covenant are strikingly similar to the first, there are some obvious differences. The main emphasis here falls on Moses' imminent departure and how Israel can survive without his unifying leadership. What the assembled Israelites now accept on solemn oath—on their own behalf

and that of their descendants, as individuals, as separate tribes, and as a federated nation—is full accountability for the maintenance of their common life (29:2[Heb. 1]—30:20). Furthermore, Moses does not leave them leaderless: Joshua will oversee the conquest of their homeland (31:7–8, 14–15, 23); and Moses' own guidance will remain forever with them in the form of the written constitutional *torah* (31:9–13, 24–26) together with his prophetic witness to its efficacy (31:16–22, 27–30; 32:1–47).

Deuteronomy 29—30
A Second Covenant

The question inevitably arises with this material: Why a second covenant at Moab besides the one at Horeb (Sinai)? That is especially acute with the realization that this covenant receives no further discussion or attention in the Old Testament after Deuteronomy. Readers of the Old Testament are familiar with the Sinai covenant, the Davidic covenant, and a new covenant sometime in the future. But only here do we have this covenant.

The chief clues for understanding this second covenant are found in recognizing the boundary character of Deuteronomy, the place of this covenant in the structure of the book, and Deuteronomy's concern for actualizing in the present moment the relationship between God and Israel and the demands and consequences of that relationship. Its connection both to the Sinai covenant and the new covenant is signaled in its opening section (29:1–9).

As Moses gives this third address and calls upon Israel to make covenant, an oath of allegiance to the Lord, the people are, as they have been all along in Deuteronomy, on the border between promise and fulfillment: before the land, off the land, not yet having received the land, or—if this text in its final form is exilic, as is likely the case—having lost the land. Participation in the salvation gift is possible only for those who bind themselves to the Lord of Israel. For a people who have frequently demonstrated faithlessness (a point that is one of the chief themes of the Moses memoir at the beginning of the book) and who at a later period in fact have lost the land, the call to a new oath of allegiance as a prerequisite for entering the land is singularly appropriate.

200

That call is also consistent with the way the book has presented the stages in Moses' leadership and his function as mediator and teacher of the law. The first four chapters of the book have recapitulated the difficult journey to the border, a journey characterized by the Lord's provision and Israel's lack of trust. In chapters 5–28, Moses has reminded them of the basic stipulations of the covenant at Sinai in the Ten Commandments and then has taught them at length the rest of the law as a guide for their life in the land. (Note how often Moses refers to the land in the paraenesis of the law.) It is time for them to covenant together to live by that instruction. As the people bound themselves at Horeb (Sinai) to keep the commandments throughout their history and at the moment of entering the gift of land and place and home, they bind themselves to obey those laws that spell out in detail the way they are to live in the land and enjoy God's blessing. The teaching Moses has given them is made a part of the covenantal structure of their relationship with the Lord. A people who have broken faith are given a fresh opportunity to bind themselves solely to the one who has redeemed and guided and punished them and whose large intention is to exalt and bless them.

As various scholars have noted, not only is this section of the book specifically called "the words of the covenant," it bears as clearly the marks of a covenantal structure as any other part of Deuteronomy. That structure can be described in different ways and does not agree precisely with any other. It is also permeated with Deuteronomic rhetoric and exhortation. The following outline is heavily indebted to the analysis of Dennis McCarthy (*Treaty and Covenant*, pp. 199–205; cf. Baltzer, pp. 34–36):

Superscription and Setting	29:1
Historical Prologue	29:2–9
Parties to the Covenant	29:10–15
Basic Stipulation	29:16–19 (esp. v. 18)
Curse	29:20–28
Preaching of Repentance and Restoration	29:29—30:14
Covenantal Decision	30:15–20
The choice (vv. 15–18)	
Witnesses (v. 19*a*)	
Call for a decision (vv. 19*b*–20)	

The two chapters are a genuine mixture, comprised of elements that are both pre-exilic and exilic, typical of the treaty genre and typical of Deuteronomic rhetoric. But in its present form, the whole has a movement and logic that holds the two chapters together and exemplifies the hortatory style, the liturgical context, and the covenantal structure that are basic elements of the torah that is Deuteronomy. A closer look at the various elements of this covenant speech will give the reader a glimpse of the perspective and theology of Deuteronomy in compact form.

Historical Prologue (29:2–9)

God's activity in behalf of the people provides the grounding for the call to obedience of the Deuteronomic instruction in the requirements of the covenant, a logic that is characteristic of the structure of covenant and of biblical faith in general. The recall of God's activity is formulated in a way that serves to identify the particular theological thrust of this second covenant under the impact of the experience of exile and prophetic theology. In its similarity and dissimilarity to other such historical prologues, basic notes are sounded that convey the intentionality of this covenantal act couched in the form of Mosaic speech.

The similarity to other covenantal prologues is seen in the way that the brief recitation recalls in three stages the way that God has tended to this people: (1) the deliverance from Egypt, (2) the guidance through the wilderness, and (3) the defeat of Sihon and Og and the taking of the land. (In this case it is only the Transjordanian part, but that has served to demonstrate the intention and power of the Lord to give the land to Israel.) The familiarity of these themes should not dull the mind to the significance of this reiteration of the structure of covenantal existence. Both the logic and the content are definitive for biblical faith.

Covenantal *logic* says that the most fundamental relationship of human existence is initiated from outside ourselves and created by the prior reality of loving-kindness. All the talk of demand and obedience, of sanctions and blessing and curse, does not come into the conversation until the people have been grasped and held by the powerful and loving hand of God. While there is considerable divine address in Scripture, and Deuteronomy is entirely God's address to the people mediated by Moses, it must never be missed or forgotten that God first listens and responds to the needs of the people (Exod. 2:23–25; 3:9). While the act of covenant making here and elsewhere (cf. Josh. 24:15) impresses us with its call for choice and decision, we must keep in mind that those who are called to choose have in some sense already been elected and drawn into covenant by what God has done in their behalf.

The *content* of the covenantal prologue is as important as the logic it opens up. What God has done is historical, in the sense that the covenantal community is not a Platonic ideal but one that has been created in human history in the experience of a particular people, and it is paradigmatic as well, in the sense that the way of God's acting with this particular people is indicative of God's way in the world. At least the biblical story suggests that the redemptive and providential work of God that is spelled out—the deliverance from oppression in Egypt; divine guidance in the difficult, unknown, and terrifying wilderness; provision of the needs for physical existence in this world; the securing of place for people to live their life under God's blessing and God's instruction—is not a historical peculiarity but reveals what humankind can expect from the Creator of heaven and earth. The covenant relationship assumes all that as a given and then indicates what God's way with the community means for the community's way with God. The whole Book of Deuteronomy has served to spell that out in general and in detail. Now, in the logic and movement of the book, it is time for the people to claim that way as their own by entering into the covenant with the Lord (29:12).

This prologue that is so like many others has its own particularity, however. This can be discerned especially in verses 4–6. First of all, these verses echo in explicit and implicit fashion the Deuteronomic understanding of the wilderness period as a time of testing and learning for Israel, learning that the Lord disciplines and teaches like a parent, learning that it is possible to live by whatever the Lord provides (Deut. 8:3–5). God's providential care is a gift to be accepted in gratitude. It is also a lesson to be learned, for it points to the one who is the giver of all good gifts, the Lord of all. The experience of being guided and cared for in the wilderness time is a way of coming to know who is the Lord. Providence in this perspective is not a mystery to be pondered but a testimony to the rule and character of God. In that context it was intended to elicit faith, to test whether the people recognized that security and well-being are not products of human achievement but manifestations of a caring God.

There is a danger in such words, for such conclusions may be reached too easily; one can assume that the gifts received from God are "natural" and to be expected. Deuteronomy seems to see a larger danger in forgetting the source of such gifts and believing that they are the result of one's own power and wealth. It may be that only in the wilderness without wealth and power could Israel come to know who is the Lord. Both Deuteronomy 8 and 29 suggest that a time of settled prosperity is a time when God's rule and care are easily forgotten and the measure of all things is human achievement.

The paradigmatic character of this wilderness experience became evident once again when Israel was cast off the land and into exile; without the resources and wealth of the land, they were forced to rely only upon the mercy of God. Nothing else was available. That Israel found it difficult to learn the lesson of the wilderness is suggested by the apparently contradictory words of verses 2–3 and 4. Three times reference is made to Israel's direct witness to the power of God in their behalf and against the Egyptians (vv. 2–3): "you have seen" (Hebrew emphatic expression), "before your eyes," and "which your eyes saw." But in an almost contradictory fashion, the next verse says: "But to this day the Lord has not given you a mind to understand, or *eyes to see,* or ears to hear." The tension between the verses is obvious. How is it to be explained?

One must remember that Moses' first speech (see the commentary on 1:19–46) demonstrated in sharp fashion that seeing is not necessarily believing, that the first generation of Israelites to see God's power over the Egyptians and God's protection in the dangerous wilderness still did not trust the Lord to be their deliverer in the face of new dangers. This peculiar prologue to the second covenant suggests that the problem did not end there, that *"to this day"* the Lord's people have lacked three things: a mind to understand (or, equally accurate, "a heart to know"), eyes to see, and ears to hear.

Deuteronomy is clear about what it is that Israel is to know, to see, and to hear. Indeed, what the people are to know, both in the sense of to comprehend and acknowledge, is indicated in verse 6: "that I am the LORD your God." In other places in the Mosaic instruction, Israel is called to know the same thing. In 4:35, Moses says with reference to the mighty acts of the Lord in Egypt, which were done "before your eyes": "To you it was shown, that you might know that the LORD is God, there is no other besides him." In 7:9, with reference to those same events, the command is given: "Know therefore that the LORD your God is God, the faithful God who keeps covenant and steadfast love." The particular phrasing of 29:4 is reflected in 8:5: "Know then *in your heart* that as a parent disciplines a child so the LORD your God disciplines you" (NRSV, emphasis added). And in 9:3, the call to know is given once more: "Know then today that the LORD your God is the one who crosses over before you as a devouring fire" (NRSV). All these texts make it clear that the people are to understand and acknowledge that the one they know as the Lord, who has acted powerfully, redemptively, and providentially in their history, is God and God alone.

That *acknowledgment* is one of the three basic things needed for life as God's people in the place God gives. The other two requirements are signaled by two additional phrases in 29:4. The expression "eyes to see" always has in mind the acts of deliverance and providential care (e.g., 1:19, 30–31; 4:3, 34; 10:21; and 11:7). But as we have seen throughout the book, the issue is whether the eyes that see will become eyes of faith that *trust* this God (who has delivered them) to be with them in the same way in the future. While such a response would seem to be self-evident, the biblical story—from Abraham to the redeemed slaves (who murmur in the wilderness and are afraid to go into the land) to King Ahaz (who would not trust in the promises of God [Isa. 7]) to the disciple Thomas (who had to touch the wounds of Jesus [John 20])—is replete with examples of those whose eyes have seen but who do not then act as if they trust the Lord of their past to be the Lord of their future. The problem of faith is indeed doubt, but the Bible does not praise that doubt. It calls those who have seen something of the grace and providence of God to live by what they have seen and known, being neither fearful before the future nor overly confident of their own capacities.

The final necessity for the community of faith as it lives under God's blessing is signaled by the phrase "ears to hear." That, of course, is what Moses has spoken about most. For what is to be heard and heeded is the voice of God, the words of the Lord, the instruction and teaching embodied in all the commandments, the statutes, and the ordinances. So along with *acknowledgment* that the Lord is God, and there is no other one or thing who can make such claim, and *trust* in the power and will of God to provide for the future as for the past, there is also the need for an *obedient* people, a community that will demonstrate the Lord's way in the world and be a holy people, the seekers of the kingdom, a locus of blessing and righteousness.

But "to this day," the covenantal prologue suggests, that has not really happened. More explicitly, and perhaps surprisingly, considering Deuteronomy's constant call to obedience and decision—reiterated in this very covenantal proclamation—the text indicates that the heart to know, the eyes to see, and the ears to hear are *a gift of the Lord* and one not yet received. Why is that?

Possibly the text means to suggest that these things are given by the Lord as Israel enters into covenant. Only now in this (cultic) act does the Lord give the grace truly to see, to hear, and to comprehend and acknowledge (Lohfink, *Das Hauptgebot,* p. 128, n. 5). Even more likely is the possibility that with its particular formulation this second covenant reflects the people's history of frequent failure and its devastating effects in loss of the land and exile. Up to this day, time and again the people of God have failed to know or understand, to see, and to heed. Now in this covenant it is suggested—nay, claimed—that God will have to *give* people knowledge, sight, and obedience.

In other words, we touch base here with that revelatory discernment in the prophets, such as Jeremiah and Ezekiel, that what it is to live as God's people under God's rule must come as a divine gift; it does not happen simply by human will. The experience of exile suggested that, and the clearest echoes of Deuteronomy 29:4 are found in the prophets' words about the possibilities that a gracious God will effect beyond punishment and exile. So Jeremiah declares (in 24:6–7) the word of the Lord with regard to those God has sent away into exile:

> I will set my eyes upon them for good, and I will bring them back to this land. I will build them up, and not tear them down; I will plant them, and not uproot them. *I will give them a heart to know that I am the Lord;* and they shall be my people and I will be their God, for they shall return to me with their whole heart (emphasis added).

206

The text speaks implicitly of a new or renewed covenant as it uses the covenantal formulary, "they shall be my people and I

will be their God" (cf. Deut. 26:16–19; 29:13). In phraseology
and theology, the prophetic oracle is reminiscent of Deuteronomy. Like Deuteronomy, it declares that God will give the
people a heart to know, out of which and through which they
will return to the Lord with all their heart. Jeremiah's oracle of
a new covenant sounds the same theme: "I will put my law
within them, and I will write it upon their hearts; and I will be
their God, and they shall be my people" (31:33). Nor will the call
to "Know the LORD" be necessary anymore, "for they shall all
know me" (31:34).

In similar fashion, Ezekiel declares the word of the Lord
that, after exile,

> *a new heart I will give you,* and a new spirit I will put within
> you; and I will take out of your flesh the *heart* of stone and *give
> you a heart* of flesh. And I will put my spirit within you, *and
> cause you to walk in my statutes and be careful to observe my
> ordinances.* You shall dwell in the land which I gave to your
> ancestors; and you shall be my people, and I will be your God
> (36:26–28; cf. 11:19–20; emphasis added).

Here again, the covenant formulary speaks implicitly of a new
covenant; and the language and theology remind one of the
covenantal prologue in Deuteronomy 29, suggesting that
knowledge and trust and obedience to the Lord's way will be
no less incumbent upon the people, but the *Lord* will work that
in the hearts and minds of the people. The transforming possibility of being the people of God is there, but it is possible only
as a gift of God.

Elsewhere in the text, the second covenant at Moab expresses this same thing in another way. In 30:6 where return
from exile is expressly announced as a future act of God, the
Mosaic voice declares, "And the LORD your God will circumcise
your heart and the heart of your offspring, so that you will love
the LORD your God with all your heart and with all your soul,
that you may live." This imagery of the circumcision of the
heart has appeared already as a call for purification and dedication of the mind and will to God (see commentary on 10:12—
11:32 for discussion of this symbolism and its relation to the
New Testament). What is important in the comparison of the
two passages is that in 10:16 the circumcision of the heart is a
command to the people, whereas in 30:6 it is a *divine act* that
enables obedience to the basic commandment—loving the
Lord your God with all your heart and with all your soul.

207

In this juxtaposition of human act commanded and divine act promised there is a fundamental and appropriate tension that is characteristic of the covenantal relationship in the biblical context. Circumcision of the heart is a way of speaking about conversion and transformation ("Circumcise therefore the foreskin of your heart, and be no longer stubborn"—10:16) and about identity as a member of the covenant community (Gen. 17:9–14; Rom. 2:28–29). The ambiguity inherent in the notions of transformation and conversion as they have been understood in Christian theology is reflected in these two texts. On the one hand, conversion is a human decision and commitment to direct oneself toward the will of God; on the other hand, its actuality is always accomplished by the gracious power of God. "For by grace you have been saved through faith; and this is not your own doing, it is the gift of God" (Eph. 2:8).

So identity as a member of the covenant community results from an act of commitment, but its ground is the grace of God that draws human beings into that commitment and that relationship. The possibility of a knowing heart, of seeing eyes, and of hearing ears is a gift of God. Its actuality still involves a human response, as the concluding words of this covenantal section make very clear (30:19).

The second covenant at Moab, therefore, anticipates or reflects the new covenant that the prophets announce out of the experience of exile and punishment by God for failure to live according to the divine purpose. That is probably why, in this formulation of the covenant, we hear of curse and punishment first (29:20–28) and then of blessing that will come after that (30:1–10), a blessing that is found in the restoration of Israel's fortunes after exile and the overthrow of their enemies who persecuted them.

Parties to the Covenant (29:10–15)

In this section we encounter the covenant formulary establishing the people as the Lord's people and the Lord as their God (v. 13). Two points related in significance stand out clearly: the detailed listing of the participants in the covenant and the reiterated "this day" (vv. 10, 12, 13, 15 [twice]).

208

The full force of the enumeration of all the participants can be felt only upon listing them. Twelve phrases are used to identify the ones with whom the Lord enters into covenant relationship: "all of you . . . the heads of your tribes . . . your elders . . . your officers . . . all the men of Israel . . . your little ones . . . your wives . . . the sojourner who is in your camp . . . the one who hews your wood . . . the one who draws your water (vv. 10–11); . . . the one who is not here with us this day . . . the one who stands here with us this day" (vv. 14–15). Two things are indicated by this extended list. First, the covenant is made with *every* member of the community. While it might be possible to come up with categories of persons not listed, the extent and detail of the list, as well as the final references to whoever is not here and whoever is here (v. 15), make it clear that all the members of the community are drawn into this relationship to live under God's blessing in the land and to live by the way set forth in all the Lord's words. The notion of "children of the covenant" has one of its roots in this text, which explicitly identifies the little ones as being a part of the covenant. Age and accountability are not factors in the community's relationship to God. To be a member of the community is to be drawn into covenant.

Second, the generalized categories in verse 15, "those who are not here with us as well as those who are here with us," serve to make the inclusiveness of the covenant community transcend the boundaries of space and time. The covenant made with the Lord is not restricted to the ones immediately present. The covenant is open-ended and includes those beyond this time and place, people who were not present when the covenant was first made and even generations unborn. By this means, the covenant is open to the later generations who read and were addressed by these words. Thus the community in the seventh century, for example, would hear itself potentially called to stand and make covenant with the Lord, which is just what King Josiah did when the book of the law, presumably some form of Deuteronomy, was read to him (II Kings 23:1–3). In like manner the community in exile and those returning from exile are also included among those "who are not here with us this day," but with whom the Lord makes covenant.

This explicit reference to those who are not present serves with the repeated "this day" to do what regularly happens in the Mosaic speeches of Deuteronomy: Past events are actualized in the present to take later readers of the book back to the border and include them in the address. They are made witnesses to the delivering and caring activity of God; they receive the Lord's teaching and are called to choose the Lord's way of life rather than the way of death (30:15–20). The covenant the Lord enters into with the people who have been redeemed is taking place *today*. The emphasis on the contemporaneity of the event is signaled by the repeated "this day . . . this day . . . this day . . . this day . . . this day." When the word of the Lord comes as direct address with that emphasis on the present and its openness to those who were not there at the earlier moment, no reader of Deuteronomy is left outside the Lord's intention to make covenant. Such formulation may reflect an originally liturgical act of covenant making, but even in its present literary speech form the actualizing of the covenant for the present community is clearly intended (cf. 5:3).

Basic Stipulation (29:16–19)

The words of the covenant do not in this case include a list of stipulations like the Ten Commandments at Horeb (Sinai). But they do include what is often characteristic of the ancient treaty and covenant formulations, the basic or primary stipulation. In this case the basic stipulation of the covenant is the same as it has been throughout the book: the exclusive worship and service of the one God, the Lord of Israel. What we have heard in the first commandment and then in the Shema has its place once again as the primary demand of the covenant. Here it is couched in negative but familiar terms, a warning against idolatry and the service of other gods (v. 18).

The formulation is of interest further because it speaks of the interaction of individual and community in relationship with God and points to the insidious character of disobedience, which expects to have little effect but ends up having ramifications far beyond the immediate act. The warning is first uttered against "a man or a woman" and then "or a family or a tribe." Accountability, therefore, is laid upon each individual for his or her acts and also upon the larger social units of which the individuals are members. That is one of the central facts of the covenant relationship. It is seen in the Decalogue, where the commandments are formulated in a singular address but given to the community as a whole. In a different way, the text shows an awareness of the individual as part of a larger whole when it refers to an act of stubborn disobedience and describes it as

210

"a root bearing poisonous and bitter fruit" that sweeps away "moist and dry alike." While the expressions are somewhat enigmatic, they suggest the picture of a disobedience that grows and whose outcome is bitter fruit, not only for the individual who disobeys but eventually for the whole community, "moist and dry alike" serving apparently as an image for totality.

Curse (29:20–28)

The interaction of the individual and the larger whole is carried further in the announcement of punishment that results from disobedience to the primary command of the covenant. In verses 20–21, punishment is specifically focused on the individual rebel who has secretly gone his or her own way. Such a person will bear the Lord's judgment. There is no dissolution of the individual's accountability or punishment in a judgment that comes upon the larger community. But the latter happens also, and hidden behind these words is the later history of Israel's failure to keep the covenant and live by the Lord's way (vv. 25–29). Verse 19 suggests that the wider punishment can come as the fruit of a single poisonous root, but the text reflects the fact that the problem was less the single individual than it was a widespread failure to keep the commandments of the Lord. So in language typical of the treaty curses of the Near East, the Mosaic speech announces punishment upon a sinful people who fail to keep the covenant God made with them. That failure, at its root, is once again seen to be the falling away from the service of the Lord and the shifting of allegiance to other centers of meaning and value and loyalty (v. 26).

There is a feature of this announcement of curse that echoes earlier words of the Mosaic speeches. It is an implication that while the surrounding nations appear primarily in Deuteronomy as Israel's foes, there is a larger place for them in the divine economy than is suggested by the hostile relationship. At least they also serve in this book as indirect witnesses and interpreters of what the Lord is doing. That is seen first in 4:6, where the peoples who hear of Israel's torah testify to its wisdom: "Surely this great nation is a wise and understanding people." In 9:28, it is said that they could interpret the Lord's destruction of the people as evidence of the Lord's powerlessness and hatred (a possibility Moses' prayer sought [successfully] to avert). Now in

211

the curse section of this covenant (29:24–26) there is a stereo-typed question-and-answer schema that appears elsewhere (I Kings 9:8–9; Jer. 22:8–9) and clearly belongs to the conventions of treaty and covenant (Long). This Deuteronomic form echoes the texts mentioned above in placing both question and answer on the lips of "all the nations." Burke Long sees in this schema "a peculiar sort of pedagogical historiography which sought to place the destruction in the context of a broken covenant and a realized covenantal curse" (p. 131). It may be too much to suggest the nations are Israel's teachers, but the work of God in Israel is once again set within the context of world history. Not only does that larger history serve as the plane on which God's story with Israel is worked out, but in these indirect ways the other nations are seen as witnessing, reflecting upon, and comprehending that story even though it is not their own. The divine word through the prophets draws those nations even more directly into the story, confirming the word at the begin-ning (Gen. 12:1–3) that Israel's way was never for its own sake alone but a part of God's purposes for all the families of the earth (for the nations as allotted to other gods and vice versa, see the commentary on Deuteronomy 32:8–9).

Preaching of Repentance and Restoration (29:29—30:14)

Once again, hortatory address and covenantal form blend together to carry the Deuteronomic message. The blessing that is inherent in the covenant relationship is now not an alterna-tive to curse but its successor. Verse 1 of chapter 30 suggests that this covenantal speech envisions a time when Israel has experienced both blessing and curse, but the rest of the chapter indicates that the curse is not the last word. The Lord will once again bless the people and enable them to live in obedience to God's way. That blessing is indicated in verse 3 with the prom-ise of restoration of fortunes and gathering from the nations. The specific language of covenantal blessing appears in verse 9 (cf. 28:4 and 11).

In this section, therefore, Moses addresses the people to say, with a word that probably arose in a time of exile and judgment, that beyond judgment you will return (Heb. *šûb*) to the Lord your God in full obedience and the Lord will have compassion upon you and restore (Heb. *šûb*) your fortunes. Israel's turning to the Lord (vv. 2 and 8), or repentance, is matched by the Lord's turning of Israel's fortunes (v. 3). That returning envisioned here will be one in which the essential requirement of Israel's life, to love the Lord with all your heart and with all your soul, will come to reality. It will happen by God's gift of a circumcised and dedicated heart and by the people's obedience: "The LORD your God will circumcise your heart" (v. 6) . . . "and *you* [Hebrew emphasis] will obey the voice of the LORD" (v. 8) . . . "when you obey the voice of the LORD . . . because you turn to the LORD" (v. 10). History by this time has indicated that such obedience cannot come without God's gift of a heart to know and obey. But the responsibility so to act as God's people is no less incumbent upon each individual (see comment on 29:2–9). The marvelous thing about this text is that it arises out of the harsh realities of disobedience, judgment, and exile and yet dares to assert the new possibilities not only of God's mercy and pardon but of the people's full obedience to the Lord's way. The church has called this justification of the unrighteous and sanctification. In the covenant at Moab, it is blessing for those who have been judged and obedience. Either set of categories confronts us with the powerful grace of God and the transformation of life that it can effect. Neither set releases us from the responsibility to love the Lord with our whole being, a point that is dramatized in the climax to this covenantal speech in 30:15–20.

Covenantal Decision (30:15–20)

In many respects, not only this third address but the whole book reaches its climax in these verses. There are some more things that Moses—and the Lord through Moses—has to say to the people, but the rest of Moses' words are set in the context of his leaving the scene and the transition to new leadership. What needs to be said has been said; now matters are in the hands of the people. To enter into covenant with the Lord is to make a decision, to commit oneself wholly to God and God's way (cf. Exod. 19:3–9; Josh. 24:15–24). That commitment is what the covenant is about and what Deuteronomy is about. Participants in Israel's liturgies of covenant renewal, listeners to the word of the Lord and the words of Moses, readers of Deuteronomy then and now are all confronted with one of the most

213

explicit calls for a decision that the Bible presents. Whether one stands before God in the context of worship or hears the instruction of the Lord or simply reads through this presentation of it, one cannot step aside or put the text away as if all that has been done, said, or read is simply information. The most fundamental choice of life lies before those who have come to this boundary line. Indeed, the choice is life itself—or death; blessing—or curse.

The opening words of Moses' first address were "See, I have set before you the land; go in and take possession" (1:8). Now, as his speaking comes to an end, those words are echoed: "See, I have set before you this day life and good, death and evil . . . therefore choose life" (30:15). Between those two addresses is all the teaching of the commandments, the statutes, and the ordinances. And therein lies the theological structure of Deuteronomy in a nutshell. Setting the land before the people who stand on the boundary is setting life before them with all its good possibilities. That is the fundamental kerygma of Deuteronomy: the offer of life on the land that God gives. However, the realization of that life and that good—indeed, *that good life,* which is God's gift to God's people—does not just happen automatically. The land given must also be a land taken; the life offered must also be a life lived out. And there is only one way to do that, a way that has now been spelled out in detail in the instruction of the Lord. It has to do with the manner of Israel's worship, purity of life, justice and fairness toward the weak and the poor and the slave, honor of parents, respect of neighbors, administration of justice, leadership of the people, treatment of the natural order, the practice of war, the treatment of women, and many other things. To live in the land according to the directions given about all these things in the torah of the Lord, God's instruction, is to create the possibilities for a good and blessed life. To live some other way, however, is to choose the way of death and catastrophe. Elsewhere, such negative results are ascribed to God's action. Here, that divine agency is specified only for the blessings. But from beginning to end in Deuteronomy, human choices and actions are fateful, creating their own positive and negative effects, and divine purpose and action are in control of history and Israel's destiny. To choose life is because life is effected this way, achieved by conformity to these rules and regulations, and equally because God gives life; to choose death is to bear the burden of what one has done and failed to do, to reap the whirlwind of disorder and chaos, but also to receive the punishment of God for disobedience (cf. the commentary on 10:12—11:32 and ch. 28).

The hortatory character of these final words in the covenantal speech is signaled in verses 19–20 when, having set the alternatives clearly before the people, Moses does not simply say "Choose!" His preaching is to the heart, a call to receive all God's good blessings by choosing life, by loving the Lord and obeying the Lord's voice. For, as Moses says, *that means life.* Whatever notions of the good life may exist as alternatives in a world where many gods, enticing systems of power, and hawkers of attractive elixirs of life contend for the loyalties of humankind, the Bible insists without qualification that there is really only one way to find life and good and well-being, in this world and in any other worlds that may exist. It is the Lord's way. So choose *that* way, follow *that* Lord.

Finally, the comparison with Exodus 19:3–9 and Joshua 24: 15–24 noted above is illuminating just at that point where this text differs from the other two. On those occasions, it is reported that the people made a positive response, committing themselves to the Lord and the Lord's instruction. But that is not the case here. Formally, the difference is because Deuteronomy is Mosaic speech, not historical or narrative report. But the effect of the silence of the text at this point is to leave the decision open. The response is not reported as a past act. It is to be given by those who read and hear these words—today.

A Note on the Law (30:11–14)

Just prior to Moses' call to the people to choose life, there is a brief discourse, almost a digression, in 30:11–14 on the commandment—or the law—underscoring the possibility of living according to the Lord's instruction. It is an important counter to ancient and modern assumptions that the law of the Lord cannot really be kept. It has already been noted that the passage connects with other places that suggest the nearness of God is found in the presence of the law among the people (see commentary on 4:1–8). But in this context, where the surrounding material gives so much attention to keeping the commandments, it is almost as if the failure of the people so to act, which is implicit in this covenantal speech, raises the issue of whether or not they *can* do so. The answer is firm and encouraging.

215

God's word in all these commandments and statutes is not in fact too difficult for human beings to carry out. Nor is it inaccessible. It is readily available in the teaching of Moses; when taught and studied and learned, that teaching can become appropriated and made a part of one's life ("in your mouth and in your heart"). Here the text echoes the instruction about the Shema, to speak about it and to lay it upon your heart. When that really happens, then (as the RSV translates) "you can do it" (v. 14). So to the questions "What does the Lord want of us?" and "Can we do it?" Deuteronomy answers unequivocally and reassuringly. You can discern in the word or teaching of the Lord all that the Lord wants, and it is not too hard for you to carry out. On the contrary, it is the very means of life.

The apostle Paul takes up this text in Romans 10:5-12 to speak about the word of the Lord that gives life and is always near and available. His appropriation is sometimes read as a counter to the Deuteronomic word, but that can hardly be the case when Paul is quoting Deuteronomy to make a point. For Paul, the word of God, the way of the Lord, the means to life are all so completely given in Jesus Christ, the end or goal of the law (Rom. 10:4), that what Deuteronomy means is crystal clear. Nowhere is the availability of God's gift of life more readily transparent and demonstrated than in the word made flesh and the word preached. This is not a counter to the instruction that God has heretofore set before the people, unless that instruction is understood to replace the grace and mercy of God as the primary ground of the relationship. Deuteronomy, however, has asserted that ground time and time again, while always maintaining that the people of God find their life in living by the word and way God has set before them. Paul reminds us that the way to life and the way to live are fully set before us in Jesus Christ, in who he was and what he said and did.

Deuteronomy 31—32
From Moses to Joshua

216   The divine instruction has been presented; the choice has been laid before the people; Moses' task is finished. Now the people will shape the future by the choice they make. All that

is left to do is pass the torch of leadership on to Joshua so that he may take the people into the land, the place of their testing. In these two chapters, that transition takes place, accompanied by final provisions for keeping and reading the law regularly before all the people, a common feature of the covenant formulary. With Moses' departure, two matters need attention: Who will lead the people, and how will they continue to have the instruction of the Lord to guide them? Chapters 31 and 32 handle these matters. The provision for reading the law, however, includes a significant feature. It is a song of testimony or witness against the people. They are to learn it and, when they have been faithless, are to sing it as a reminder of how, despite the Lord's care of them, they have neglected the commandments and the statutes and regulations.

A New Leader (31:1–8, 14–15, 23)

The setting of this book on the boundary between wilderness and promised land, between landlessness and landedness, is evident once again. This time it is reflected in the transition of leadership from Moses, who led the people out of Egypt and through the wilderness to the brink of the promised land, to Joshua, who will lead them into the land after Moses is gone. That transition is a significant theme of the book. It has already been signaled in 1:38 and 3:28, where Moses is commanded to charge and encourage Joshua. That is just what is done here at the end of the book, first by Moses and then by the Lord. The repetition of the commissioning within this chapter may reflect variants of the report of Joshua's taking over. But it also serves to impress into the record and upon the reader the significance of this event. Indeed, a further form of Joshua's commissioning occurs in Joshua 1.

The strong connection of the first eight verses of chapter 31 with the end of chapter 3 has prompted the argument that chapters 1–3 and this material about the commissioning of Joshua, as well as part of chapter 34, were connected originally and formed the introduction to the Deuteronomistic History of Joshua through Kings, which begins with a reiteration of Joshua's charge. In their present form, these chapters have had a more complex literary history than that argument suggests; the commissioning of Joshua has been worked into the covenant at Moab and functions now as a part of that rather than as an introduction to Joshua to Kings (on the literary history of this material, see J. Levenson, "Who Inserted the Book of the Torah?"). At the same time, it is clear that these chapters explicitly carry us a stage further into the future; if they are not now explicitly an introduction to Joshua through Kings, they are at least the transition to the next stage, which begins with Joshua. Further, the way chapters 31 and 32 anticipate a falling away of the people also points toward later developments in that history.

This whole section deals with the situation that confronts the people of God frequently in the pages of Scripture and beyond: What happens when the leader of the people moves off the scene? The community has been guided by an individual who led them when they did not know where to go, provided for them in time of trouble and need, and instructed them about how to live. The disappearance of such a leader is a traumatic event. The text of Deuteronomy tells us nothing of how the people felt in anticipation of the loss of their leader. What happens in these verses, however, gives us some basic clues.

The community is first given divine assurance that they will not be abandoned and that the Lord will go with them. That word needs to be said first, and it is said at some length in verses 3–6. The text accentuates, therefore, what the story has revealed over and over again: The guidance and sustenance the people have received has its source in the Lord. The first word is not an appointment of a new leader but the Lord's own assurance that the primary pattern of the past will continue: God will be there with you and will deliver you. Without the power of God at work, the question of a new human leader is moot—as the story will demonstrate repeatedly.

Thus the words of Moses testify implicitly to the anxiety of a potentially leaderless people and address that anxiety first with assurance about the *Lord's* presence. One is reminded of the words of Psalm 127:1.

> Unless the LORD builds the house,
>   those who build it labor in vain.
> Unless the LORD watches over the city,
>   the sentry stays awake in vain.

The confidence of God's people in the face of an unknown future is not *primarily* secured by the presence of a capable leader, though that ingredient follows. Overcoming anxiety and fear is found first in the realization of the Lord's powerful presence with the people. Where the sense of the presence of God in the ongoing life of the people is real, fear about "what will happen to us" can be set aside. Moses' word to the people at the end, as they begin to deal with his absence, is the same as at the beginning, when he was very much with them: Do not be afraid; the Lord goes with you. Then, it was a command to a timid people who would not act upon the evidence they had of God's power and provision (1:29). Here, it has become a reassuring word to a leaderless people (31:6), suggesting that anxiety is an authentic and appropriate response but need not persist. The fundamental ground rules have not changed. You are not alone. The Lord is in charge and will bring about the purposes set for this people. That being the case, you do not have to be afraid. The issue for faith, therefore, is the same as at the beginning. It is not primarily a particular set of beliefs, though Deuteronomy has frequently identified what the people should believe about the Lord in light of their experience. The fundamental issue for faith is how you face the future. Will the community's experience of God's care in the past ("as he did to Sihon and Og," v. 4) determine its attitude toward the future? There is no word more persistent and repeated in all of Scripture than this: The way it has been is the way it will be. The Lord goes with you now as before. That is what the faithfulness of God means. So take courage.

Such words, clarifying who the true leader is, are the primary assurance to a people faced with the loss of a human leader. But Deuteronomy always affirms the interaction of divine and human activity in the accomplishment of the Lord's purposes. That is no less the case here. God's leadership and guidance will be through the agency of a new leader. The people cannot make it without a human leader responsive to the Lord's direction, to whom the people can turn for direction. So Moses' successor, who has already been identified in chapters 1 and 3, is now formally given the responsibility of leading the people.

The repeated commissioning of Joshua in verses 7–8, 14–15, and 23 reflects what seems to be a formal procedure of *installation*, or *commission* (Heb. *siwwah* = "charge" [3:28; cf. I Kings 2:1–3] or "commission" [31:14, 23; cf. Num. 27:19]). It is a genre encountered in repeated fashion here and elsewhere in the Old

Testament (Josh. 1:6–9; I Chron. 28:10; II Chron. 32:6–8; 19:5–7; cf. McCarthy, "An Installation Genre"). It serves as a model for occasions of installation and commissioning of new leaders, and its constitutive elements are instructive. The commissioning or charge begins with *words of encouragement,* "Be strong and of good courage" (31:7, 23; Josh. 1:6, 7, 9; cf. I Chron. 28:10; II Chron. 32:7). The *primacy* of this element in the charge is indicated several ways. It is repeated precisely in each of the charges in this chapter; and it is repeated *three* times in Joshua 1; it is also the word of encouragement given to the people in 31:6. Furthermore, in 3:28, when Moses is told to charge Joshua, that is further defined as "encourage and strengthen him"; in 1:38 when Moses is first instructed by the Lord that Joshua will take his place, he is told to "encourage him."

The second element in the commissioning act is *the description or assignment of the task.* For Joshua, that task is twofold: bringing the people into the land and apportioning the territories to the tribes (31:7 [both tasks]; 31:23 [first task]; Josh. 1:6 [second task]). The third element is *the divine reassurance* or what has aptly been called an *assistance formula.* Its content is consistently the promise that "the Lord is with you" or "I am with you" (31:6, 8, 23; Josh. 1:5, 9). That word is indeed assurance of the Lord's assistance in the endeavors that lie ahead. It is thus the ground for both the charge to be strong and the assignment of the task. Confidence in taking up the assignment is rooted in the assurance that God will be with the new leader in carrying out the responsibilities laid out in the commissioning process.

Within this form of commissioning one can find the rudiments of a theology of leadership and the appropriate elements for all occasions when persons are given responsibility over the community of faith. Courage and confidence before the difficult tasks ahead is the starting point. The commissioning of Joshua sets this encouragement as both an *assurance* and a *command.* It is simultaneously a call to set oneself forthrightly to the job that is to be done and an assurance that one can do that work. The commission process sets the disposition of mind and heart to the fore but claims by its form that that confidence is both given and required. Hearing the words "Be strong!" or "Take courage!" both calls for and instills an attitude of confidence.

Along with the creation of a disposition is the specific identification of a work that is to be done. That is, the commission genre in the Old Testament is not really a way of calling persons to a general office. It is precisely commissioning one to do a particular work for the Lord. That task may be long and complex. Indeed, it was for Joshua; his leadership lasted for the rest of his days (Josh. 23:2; 24:29). But the leadership of God's people as it is reflected in this biblical type is not a generalized standing in the community or position of status. It is responsibility for carrying out work that needs to be done. Commissioning of the community's leader(s), therefore, as encountered in this model, is to a *task*, not to a position. Authority and standing are dependent upon the nature of the task, not vice versa.

Finally and fundamentally (in the literal sense of the word) is the promise of divine assistance, which is the only basis upon which confidence and the completion of the task are possible. The leaders no more than the people are to view themselves as either alone in carrying out their responsibilities or dependent utterly upon their own devices. Neither arrogant pride nor despairing anxiousness is appropriate, because the Lord is there and will not fail. It is the despair and anxiety, however, that these words particularly address. Indeed, one notes that what is said as a basic word of assurance to the leaders is equivalent to the repeated good news given to people in trouble: You do not have to be afraid, because the Lord is with you. You are not alone and will not be left alone. In that sense, there is no special word for the leaders of God's people. Their capacity to face what lies ahead is grounded in the same reality that elicits joy and praise from the sick and the dying, the troubled and oppressed—the powerful presence of God, who is there to help and will never forsake. At the conclusion of his ministry, Jesus gave just such a word of commission and assurance to the disciples, telling them not to be afraid, charging them to go into all the world, making disciples, baptizing, and teaching, and promising his eternal presence with them (Matt. 28:16–20).

Reading and Keeping the Law (31:9–13, 24–29)

Keeping covenant with the Lord means fulfilling the obligations and stipulations set forth in the whole law. But that is dependent upon a ready acquaintance with the law, a familiarity that makes its doing second nature. Two elements inhibit such familiarity. One is the forgetfulness of the people, a tendency well attested in the prophetic indictments as well as in the preaching of Moses in this book (ch. 8). The other is the coming onto the scene of new generations who were not there when the Lord and Israel made covenant and when Moses taught the people all the law and what it meant. For these reasons, provision is made for storing and preserving the law and for its periodic reading. Again the instruction stresses the inclusion of every member of the community, so that no one is without knowledge of what it means to love the Lord and especially so that the children who have not known the Lord's instruction will find out about it. Telling the story and what it means for their lives is the way the community of faith transmits to the next generation the faith and direction by which they have lived. The text at this point echoes the concerns expressed in 4:9–10; 6:5–9, 20–25; and 11:1–7 (see commentary on 6:20–25 for discussion of teaching the children in Deuteronomy).

Despite what may seem to be a rather simple and routine provision specified in verse 26 for permanent storing of the law, there is here a rich symbolism. The book or scroll of the law is to be placed next to the ark of the covenant. This juxtaposition indicates, first, the distinction and relationship between the Decalogue as the basic principles and guidelines and the statutes and regulations (chs. 12–26) as the specifics. That distinction and relationship, indicated by the literary shape of the book (see commentary on ch. 5), is symbolized here by the *separation* of the Decalogue, which is contained in the ark of the covenant (10:1–4), from the book of the law, which is then *placed alongside* the ark with the ten words (commandments) in it. What has been indicated literarily is now represented visually. They are not the same, but they are intimately related. The words in the ark are completed, spelled out, and specified by the particular statutes and ordinances in the book of the law.

Second, the juxtaposition of these two written or inscribed forms of the Lord's instruction symbolizes to the people a double function of that instruction. In the ten words set within the ark of the covenant, we have a sense of the law as the presence of God in the midst of the people (see commentary on 4:1–8), a powerfully positive function of the law. But alongside that, the book of the law is set now with a rather ominous function, one not previously ascribed to it. It is to be a witness against the people (v. 27). The whole thrust of Deuteronomy has been to set forth the law as the means to life. That thrust is at the heart

222

of the covenantal decision in the preceding chapter. Now, however, we hear a negative use of the law, one that anticipates in some ways the second use of the law in Christian theology. The law that is disobeyed stands as a witness against the people because its presence in their midst is a silent but articulate reminder of the way they are to live. When it is read to them periodically, presumably they will realize how they have disobeyed the Lord's instruction and will repent. The discovery of the "book of the law" (presumably some form of Deuteronomy) during Josiah's reign in the seventh century B.C.E. (II Kings 22—23) illustrates this possibility. The narrative reports that when the king heard the words of the book of the law, he rent his clothes and feared the wrath of God because he realized that for generations they had not been obeying its instructions (II Kings 22:11–13).

The provisions for reading and keeping the law are directly connected here to Moses' leaving the scene (v. 27). If the people have been stubborn and disobedient even under his leadership, how much worse is it going to be with Moses gone? The allusion is to their rebellion in the wilderness, recounted in Moses' sermon in chapter 9. The language used on that occasion is used here (9:6–7; 31:27). Moses, in effect, says that despite all the exhortation and teaching he has given them, past experience does not bode well for the future. A people who have known the protecting care of God in dire circumstances and still rebelled are likely to rebel when they are enjoying the divine blessings in the future. The ominous note of the law as witness has nothing to do with anything within the *law;* Moses knows what is within the *heart* of the people.

A Song of Witness (31:16–22, 30; 32:1–47)

The related themes just discussed—the law as a witness against the people and their propensity to disobedience of the Lord—are at the center of the introduction (31:16–22, 30) to what is commonly called the Song of Moses (32:1–47) and serve to signify the function of the song in the book. Like the torah, the Song of Moses is given as a witness against the people when they turn away from the Lord and toward other or, in the language of the song and its introduction, "strange gods." At every point in this chapter, the breach of covenant that took place in the time of the prophets is anticipated.

223

INTERPRETATION

The words of the Lord in 31:16–21 set forth one of the primary prophetic images for disobedience and turning from the Lord—harlotry. The image, while undeveloped here, is a potent one. It has less in mind the professional prostitute than it does the act of abandoning one's exclusive marital loyalty to a spouse to go after other lovers, perhaps because they seem more attractive or offer irresistible favors and gifts. Hosea 1—3 centers on this image as a way of expressing the disintegration of Israel's faithfulness to the Lord. The issue, as always, is obedience to the basic commandment as reflected in the Shema and the first commandment.

The consequence of disobedience is clear. It is expressed in two of the primary images for judgment in the Old Testament, the anger of God (v. 17) and the hiding away of God's face (v. 18). Because the presence of God is so tied to the reality and help of God, trouble and disaster (whether the inexplicable or undeserved trouble of the victim and the sufferer or the justified punishment of the wicked) are perceived as reflections of God's hiddenness. The one who is able to help and deliver is either absent without cause or has turned away in anger. A poetic justice is declared to be operative in God's scheme of things (vv. 16–17); those who abandon the Lord shall be abandoned by the Lord (Miller, *Sin and Judgment*). The anger of God is righteous; it rises out of the failure of the people to be the kind of community purposed by the Lord, a people whose center is the Lord and whose way is the Lord's way. The justification for this righteous anger is stated forthrightly in verses 16 and 20 and spelled out in more detail in chapter 32. The Lord cannot operate with a people who will not give their devotion to God. The purpose of the Lord to provide blessing for all the nations of the earth is thwarted when the agent of that blessing follows a way other than the one set by God.

The text reinforces the notion, suggested in 31:24–29, that the people are destined to fall away and abandon the Lord. Such an assumption may reflect the experience of a later community that knew of the failure of the divided kingdoms, Israel and Judah. In verses 24–29 the propensity for disobedience is assumed by Moses because of a history of such behavior. In verse 21, however, the text goes further and echoes a word first heard in the story of beginnings in Genesis 6:5 and 8:21–22: to wit, that there is within the human heart and will a tendency to disobey God. It is this tendency that the New Testament

224

seems to identify so clearly, especially in Paul, who analyzes it in some detail in Romans 1–3 and 7:13–25. That inclination is not a major theme within the Old Testament, but it is there and becomes more prominent, not only in the New Testament but also in Judaism's teaching of the existence of a good inclination and an evil inclination in each person. These closing chapters of Deuteronomy anticipate that tendency to fall away and make it clear that such inclination is already known to God. For this reason, the Lord gives to the people ahead of time a witness that will be both a reminder of what the Lord expected and self-incriminating testimony.

Not only will the people hear their condemnation in the regular recitation of the law they have neglected to follow, they will declare their own guilt in the words of the song Moses is to teach them. Like the reading of the law, the singing of the song has both a legal-judicial function and an educational one. It convicts as it instructs; it instructs as it convicts. Like the torah, it is to be written, taught, and put in the mouths of the people (v. 19). If it is sung regularly, like the law it will be not only a testimony after the fact but a warning beforehand. What happens, therefore, as the book comes to a close is that the people of Israel are being given both torah and song—torah to guide their life to blessing and as a testimony against them when they go another way and turn to other sources of good and claims to loyalty; song as testimony against them but also, in Deuteronomy 33, as blessing for Israel. The testament that Moses leaves as he passes off the scene is law and song. They serve similar functions, and Israel is to learn them both and carry them both into the land. Further, the song has now become a part of the torah. Israel, who is usually called to sing praise to the Lord for the Lord's deliverance, now is called to sing in order to bear witness to God's demand and its failure and to learn the obligations of the Lord. In good times it will be a warning; in bad times of trouble and sorrow it will be a reminder and a confession.

In his study of the poetics of Deuteronomy 32:1–47, Harold Fisch has aptly described the power and potential of this song that is to be regularly sung as a witness against a faithlessness not yet manifest:

> It will . . . act as a mnemonic, an aid to memory, because during the intervening period it will have lived unforgotten in the mouth of the reader or hearer, ready to come to mind when the troubles arrive. Poetry is thus a kind of time bomb; it awaits its

225

hour and then springs forward into harsh remembrance. . . . It will live in their minds and mouths, bringing them back, whether they like it or not, to the harsh memory of the desert sojourn. Once learned it will not easily be forgotten. The words will stick, they will be importunate, they will not let us alone (p. 51).

The song itself has been described with some aptness as a covenant lawsuit (Wright), a term that recognizes its juridical character as a witness and its appropriateness in the context of breach of covenant (31:16, 20). The latter connection, of course, gives it its place at the end of this third speech of Moses, "the words of the covenant" made in the land of Moab (29:1). While it is indeed a witness against the people's disobedience and breach of the covenant, it bears testimony also to all the faithful and caring ways of the Lord with this people, including their eventual vindication and deliverance beyond judgment.

A possible understanding of the structure of the song in Deuteronomy 32 and its components follows.

Introduction (32:1–6)

The introduction to the song is made up of two parts. The first is a *formal introduction* (vv. 1–3) that ties the song to two fundamental thematic structures of the book, covenant and Moses' teaching. In the treaties of the ancient Near East that seem to have formed a model for the covenantal structure of Deuteronomy, gods were invoked as witnesses to the treaty. While the invoking of other gods as witnesses to a covenant between the Lord and Israel would be impossible and indeed counter to the very point of the covenant to guard the Lord's exclusive claim on Israel, several times in Deuteronomy the Lord has called heaven and earth to witness against the people (4:26; 30:19; 31:28). It is likely that the address to heaven and earth—either as representing the totality of everything or spheres inhabited by various beings—here at the beginning of the Song of Moses reflects their role as witnesses to the covenant and, more specifically, to the fact that Israel has not lived by the covenantal requirements and the case is being laid in this song.

If, however, the covenantal structure and theology is pervasive in Deuteronomy, it is couched now in the form of Moses' speeches and teaching. The book is a book of instruction, not a legal document. Indeed, this song is supposed to be taught (31:19). So now the beginning of the Song of Moses sets it forth as a part of his teaching (v. 2). The hymnic character of the song as a testimony to the greatness of God, which is as much its purpose as testimony against Israel, is then signaled in verse 3. Its intention to evoke praise as well as confession is confirmed by the way this verse forms an inclusio with verse 43 around the main body of the song, calling for praise at its beginning and its end. One is reminded of how the Psalter begins as torah instruction (Ps. 1) but has become praise of God by the time it ends. Here also the song that is sung is both teaching and praise.

A *thematic introduction* is then provided in verses 4–6. The song, whose basic character is poetic narrative, laying out the ways of God with this people and their way with God, essentially begins with these verses but in the form of a presentation of the primary theme of the song. A contrast is offered between the Lord's work and ways and those of Israel. That contrast then is developed in the rest of the poem.

The theme is indicated in the first two words of this section, "The Rock," an ancient epithet for the deity that is repeated throughout the poem (vv. 15, 18, 30, 31; cf. 37). Its meaning is transparent and important, elaborated in the various adjectives that follow in verse 4. The image of "Rock" for God becomes an important one in the psalms, for it points to the steadfastness of God as an anchor and refuge in a tottering world. It is a poetic way of speaking of the faithfulness of God, who can be counted upon and trusted, whose ways are clear, straight, upright, and not devious or deceptive. The problem is that the Lord's way is matched ("requited," v. 6) by a slippery, perverse, unstable, undependable people. The covenant relationship depends upon the parties keeping faith, keeping their part of the agreement. But this song testifies that they have not kept faith. They have dealt corruptly, and thus foolishly, with the one who, like a rock, always deals faithfully. The poet expresses a kind of astonishment that a people would so respond to the one who created and made them. Here the notion of a rebellious child becomes the vehicle for speaking about how the people have acted. The parent-child imagery that appears at the beginning to speak about God's caring for Israel returns here at the end in a more extended fashion to portray both the caring parent and the disobedient child. A careful reading of the song will discern that, like the picture of God as rock, the parent-child relationship is a persistent image and theme, particularly in the first half of the song.

227

Recollection of God's Past Care of Israel (32:7–14)

Consistent with the modes of discourse in the speeches of Deuteronomy, the Song of Moses begins its elaboration of the Lord's care of Israel with a call to remember the past wonderful works of the Lord in behalf of this people (cf. 5:15; 8:18; 9:7; 15:15; 16:3; 24:9, 18, 22) and an instruction to the new generation to learn that story from their fathers and mothers. The song thus testifies once again to the importance of memory and telling the stories from one generation to the next in the covenantal community. That is how the new generation learns not only the facts of how they came to be, their story, but what that story means and implies for them in the present. For Israel it is a family story, and family stories are always told and retold to help new generations learn how they are to live.

The story here is a poetic recollection of the Lord's election of a people (v. 9) out of all the peoples brought into being by God's creative activity (cf. v. 6). No specific event is referred to until verse 10. The picture in verses 10–11 is an allusion to Israel's journey in the wilderness but may also have in mind the Lord's care of the people in Egypt. As in Exodus 19:4, the powerful and beautiful image of an eagle taking care of its young is used here to convey the continual providence of God. The wilderness time is portrayed as one of harsh life, where survival was possible only by the Lord's provision, where a young nation learned how to live, and where they were trained in the proper ways by the mother or father eagle (v. 11). They were protected from preying enemies. Verses 13 and 14 then recall God's giving the people the promised land (v. 13a) with all its rich produce and fertility of agriculture and herding (vv.13b–14)—one indication that composition of the song and its ascription to Moses were after the people had been long on the land. The pivotal verse 12 connecting wilderness with promised land makes the point so central to Deuteronomic theology, that Israel relies on no other power except the Lord. The declaration that there was no foreign or strange god with them anticipates and already condemns in an implicit fashion the reliance of Israel in the land on other gods, a condemnation that is the whole point of the song in its context (31:16, 18, 20).

228   The particular way Israel's creation is described in verses 8 and 9 is worth further note, for it lays out in more detail a perspective on the other nations and gods that has been hinted at but not developed in other places in Deuteronomy (4:19;

29:26). In these verses the other nations of the world are clearly understood as having been created by the Lord, with each apportioned its territory and each allotted to one of the gods, that is, set under the aegis of one of the gods. Deuteronomy 4:19 and 29:16 caution the people of Israel against worshiping other gods whom the Lord had not allotted to them and whom the Lord *"has* allotted to all the peoples under heaven." Here is the strange word that only vis à vis Israel are the other gods idols and condemned. Election by the "Lord your God" means no other god but the Lord of Israel for them. But from the perspective of the other nations and in the divine economy, it is another matter. They are accepted as belonging to the divine world ruled by the Lord of Israel even though they are criticized; indeed, they are actually allotted to the other nations by the Lord.

This word from the Old Testament is one we do not hear very often, one that gains some force by its coming from the same source that so vigorously prohibits the worship by Israel of any other god. Those gods that function as center of value and meaning for other nations have their place. The religions of that world were a part of the order set by the God of Israel. Not much is said in these verses, but a note is sounded three times, twice within the speeches of Moses and once now within his closing song. Deuteronomy thus opens up the possibility of a dialectic between the one and the many, between the one God of Israel, the God of Jesus Christ, who for Israel and the church is the only God, and the many gods who are worshiped to the far corners of the earth. From the perspective of Christian faith and theology, there may be a clue here to what it means to claim the universal lordship of Jesus Christ in a religiously plural world. We may not turn to those gods of other peoples who have their place under the lordship of Christ. Nor may we condemn, deride, or dismiss those whom the Lord has allotted to the peoples of the earth. To Israel it was given neither to worship nor to speculate about the other gods. Whatever goes on in the cosmos, humanly and religiously, is under the rule of God. Those who worship the Lord know that there is no other who can rightfully and truly claim their full loyalty and devotion.

229

Report of Rebellious and Idolatrous Response (32:15–18)

The narrative poem now shifts to the counter theme, the rebellion of the child so loved and cared for and blessed by the parent. What Moses has warned about in all the speeches has come to pass and now is described in a self-incriminating song of the people. Moving back and forth between direct address to the people and describing them in the third person, the song gives a litany of their sins, all of them anticipated or warned against in Deuteronomy: forsaking the Lord (28:20; 29:25; 31:16); provoking the Lord (9:7, 22); making the Lord jealous (see 4:24; 5:9; 6:15; 29:20); becoming fat and turning to other gods (31:20); doing abhorrent, abominable practices (7:25, 26; 13:14; 17:1, 4); forgetting the Lord (8:11, 19).

The fundamental fault, of course, is disobeying the primary commandment. Life in the land has acquainted the Lord's people with interesting and attractive gods they had not previously known, gods whose claim to provide fertility and blessing is very appealing. Old loyalties, like memories, die all too easily when newcomers hawk their wares and new experiences evoke fresh desires. The contrast between the people's fickle loyalties and the faithfulness of God is intimated by the repetition of the word "Rock" to speak of the God Israel has forgotten (vv. 15c, 18).

The parent-child imagery is carried through this whole section and becomes very explicit in verse 18. This verse is one of the places in the Old Testament where one can see its openness to using maternal as well as paternal language and imagery to speak of the Lord's creation and care of the people. While previously in the song the Lord has been spoken of as father, here the picture is of a mother giving birth. The imaginative freedom of the poetry is heightened by the fact that the subject of both the verbs describing giving birth is an inanimate object, the Rock. The use of birth imagery underscores the intimate and close relationship between the Lord and Israel, a relationship now betrayed by the people turning to other "mothers," or gods.

The Lord's Sentence of Judgment (32:19–27)

The divine speech indicting Israel turns now to pronounce judgment upon this people. The poetic images and eloquence that come forth in the description of the Lord's goodness to Israel and Israel's faithlessness continue in the announcement of judgment. A powerful picture of the wrath of God as a burning anger is elaborated in these verses. It is not pleasant and creates a tension in the mind of the reader, who is accustomed to hearing from these same pages and this same book of all the loving-kindness and faithfulness of God. But that very character will not allow the agents of the Lord's loving purposes to continue to be its inhibitors. The judgment is expressed as a clear provocation on the part of the people and a crime whose punishment fits. As they have stirred the Lord to jealousy with no god, the Lord will stir them to jealousy with no people. And as they have vexed God with their worthless things, their idols, they will be vexed with a foolish thing, a nation (Miller, *Sin and Judgment*, pp. 76–79). The imagery that follows is that of an event of war as the means of the Lord's judgment.

Then, however, there comes a kind of shift, a turning point. The Lord stops short of a full destruction of the people, wiping their memory from the pages of history. The Old Testament gives more than one reason for God's mercy and forgiveness, the Lord's holding back the full force of divine wrath. In this case, however, the reason is one that has been appealed to before. In chapter 9, Moses prayed to the Lord to withhold judgment on the grounds that the Egyptians might think this reflected God's weakness and inability to bring the people into the land. Here again the power and reputation of the Lord are the basis for a divine decision. This time the enemy might think that its victory over Israel was out of its own power and not the work of the Lord, and they might regard the Lord as powerless to help and protect the people. Such an outcome would itself thwart the purpose of God to demonstrate in every act that only one source of power, meaning, and direction is at work in this world. Thus the punishment of Israel, consistent with the Lord's nature and purpose as a covenant God, would, if carried to the end, lead to a result out of accord with that nature and purpose. The reputation of the Lord is no small matter in the biblical story. It is a frequent ground of appeal and basis for divine action. God will be God and will not allow human misunderstanding of that action to perdure. So even as the punishment is consistent with God's nature and way with Israel, so also is the decision not to let the punishment be complete and to vindicate God's people (v. 36).

The Stupidity and Corruption of the Enemy (32:28–33)

Now the point made about the enemy in the Lord's speech is elaborated by Moses. That enemy is never named in the poem. A particular foe may have been in mind in the original

231

composition, but it now stands as a more generalized and hopeful word about Israel in the midst of enemy nations. It has been proposed that the song originated at the time of Philistine domination in the eleventh century B.C.E. Such a date would be hard to prove in a convincing manner, and a later date is just as likely. But the perspective of the rest of the song is not unlike that of the story of the capture of the ark by the Philistines told in I Samuel 4–6. There, as here, Israel is defeated in a devastating fashion. The Philistines assume that the victory is a sign of their power and the power of their god Dagon over the Israelites. As the story makes clear, the Philistines' feat was God's judgment against the Israelites, and when they presume to think that they are in charge and put the ark of the Lord next to the statue of Dagon, all sorts of troubles come upon them at the hand of the Lord.

This part of the song, therefore, bears testimony to a conviction already discerned in Deuteronomic theology: All that happens is at the hand of the Lord. The imagery of God as the Rock comes in again to express the notion that the God of Israel is not unstable or unable to provide a secure foundation for the people against their enemies. They do not fall because their Rock is unable to hold them. Only by divine decision do they totter and fall. This section joins with I Samuel 4—6, Isaiah 10, and the Book of Habakkuk to make the case that while God may use a corrupt people or instrument in the divine purposes of judgment, that instrument is subject also to the Lord's judgment. It is no more autonomous or safe than Israel.

The Vindication of God's People (32:34–43)

The song concludes therefore with the good word that the vindication of God's power and rule (v. 33a) is also the vindication of God's people. Verse 34, which sets the Lord's punishment of the stupid and corrupt nation as a part of God's plan long before it is accomplished, is reminiscent of the note in Deuteronomy 29:29 alluding to the secret things that belong to the Lord our God. In both cases there is a recognition of the hiddenness of the divine purpose, the possibility of mystery and plan in the mind of God that is not discernible or not yet revealed. Both dimensions, the mystery never fully comprehended and the plan not yet unfolded, are a part of the Deuteronomic understanding of the sovereignty of the God of Israel. The latter is specifically attested in 32:34, where the eventual disclosure is not only revelatory but salvific for Israel, as those who have destroyed the nation are set back and the Lord looks with compassion upon the people.

The theme of this long concluding section, which is mostly divine speech either direct or quoted (vv. 37–38), is the vengeance of God. It is one of the Old Testament texts that speaks most about that topic and reflects the various dimensions of that difficult notion. One can not miss the bloodiness of the language, particularly in verses 41–43. There the imagery of the divine warrior with sword and bow and arrows in hand is vivid. It is neither to be ignored nor exaggerated. That imagery is one of the ways in which the Old Testament speaks in the vernacular of its time and milieu and with the linguistic currency of most value. It is also an important image for conveying the power of God to carry out the divine purposes and God's just rule (Miller, "The Sovereignty of God"). One must be careful about giving the image, one of many divine images in Scripture, a greater potency than the purpose. The purpose is expressed in the word "vengeance," but that English word only partially expresses what the text here and elsewhere is talking about. It is consistent with the martial imagery but incomplete. The notion of *vindication* better embodies the whole of what the biblical language of vengeance is meant to express. It is the exercise of God's power for the protection of God's people and the accomplishment of God's purpose, the executive action of the deity to effect moral order and just rule in the universe. Its possibility belongs to the sovereign Lord (v. 35), who alone is the final power at work for good and ill, life and death (v. 39). The manifestation of that vindication may be the undoing of the corrupt and wicked, even those who have been agents of the Lord's rule—or, better, *especially* such ones, when their agency has been corrupt (vv. 32–33) and presumptuous (v. 27b). It may also be the lifting up of the weak and the powerless, the hurt and the suffering, even those who have been rendered that way by the Lord's vindicating (in this case, judging) power—or, more precisely, especially when they are powerless and aware of their helplessness and the impotence of any helper but the Lord (vv. 36–38). Indeed, the Lord's vindication may be an act of both lifting up for some and putting down for others. The fact that the positive or negative character of the divine vengeance is shaped by the circumstances is well seen in verse 36. The Hebrew uses a verb there more often translated "judge" (*dîn*),

233

not the usual root for vengeance (*nqm;* see vv. 35, 41, and 43 [twice]), but the Revised Standard Version properly translates "vindicate." Often the Lord's righteous judgment is an act of punishment. But sometimes it is an act of deliverance, as indicated here by the parallel statement, "He will have compassion on his servants," as well as by Psalm 54:3, where the plea for God to judge the petitioner is paralleled by the cry, "Save me!" In the case of the Song of Moses, the vindication and compassion registered toward the people are manifest in an overthrow of their former conquerors. The purpose of God to discipline the Lord's own people to keep the way of righteousness and justice and blessing going in the world is vindicated in the complex events hinted at in the song.

It should be recognized that while the vindication alluded to in verse 35 is a manifestation of divine justice, the nature of that justice is seen here as a power at work to deliver and protect the weak and helpless, the little and powerless. Most often it is a call for justice for the widow, the poor, and the orphan. But in the visions of Amos 7, the plea is for divine compassion for a sinful Israel simply on the grounds, "He is so small." It is a people who have now lost their power (v. 36*b*). The expression "there is none remaining," or "neither bond nor free remaining," belongs entirely to experiences of harsh judgment upon Israel and is illumined here by its use in II Kings 14:26–27:

> For the LORD saw that the affliction of Israel was very bitter, for there was none left, bond or free, *and there was none to help Israel.* But the LORD had not said that he would blot out the name of Israel from under heaven, so he saved them by the hand of Jeroboam the son of Joash (emphasis added).

It is just such an occasion as this, when a haughty and disobedient people have been rendered powerless and helpless but are still the Lord's people, that divine justice and vindication come in deliverance and help.

The expression "Vengeance is mine, and recompense" (v. 35) is quoted by Paul in Romans 12:19. It takes the important theological claim of Deuteronomy 32 that the Lord will have vindication over all those who resist the Lord's way of righteousness and obedience and sees in it an ethical or moral claim: that the vindication God will bring about is not something others can claim. Here Paul has understood this vindication specifically as requital for a wrong deed, and in this case a wrong deed on the human plane, within the human community. If it is the case that a gracious, merciful, and just God will vindicate the divine purposes and overcome evil in that process, it is equally true that that right or responsibility of vindication does not belong to human beings. "Vengeance [or vindication] is mine" means not only that the Lord will have it but that we may *not* have it. The human response to evil is found in the way of forgiveness and reconciliation. For Paul, that response has its own part in the vindication of God's good purposes, as evil is thereby overcome with good.

So the song concludes with the promise of forgiveness and the cleansing of guilt (v. 43). That promise does not vitiate the force of the testimony or judgment against a faithless people. It does make clear that new possibilities are created by God's own intention and faithfulness. The bracketing prose conclusion (32:44–47), matching the long introduction in 31:16–29, reinforces the Deuteronomic claim that in this song and in this torah, both of which have been set before the people, they will find their life. It is indeed no trivial concern. It is a matter of life and death. (For discussion of 32:48–52 see commentary on chapter 34.)

PART FOUR

The Death of Moses

DEUTERONOMY 33—34

The final section of the Book of Deuteronomy is identified by its superscription at 33:1. This is the blessing with which Moses the man of God blessed the children of Israel before his death. The heading reveals that this section is about Moses' testamentary blessing upon the tribes of Israel and his death. It is already clear from what has preceded that Moses' death is not dealt with simply to close off accounts. His departure was a momentous event for the people. It posed two questions: Why does the leader of the people not get to go into the land? and What will happen to us? Both questions have already been addressed. But it is not possible for the people to move on until the matter of Moses—or, more precisely, Moses himself—is laid to rest. That now takes place at the end of the book.

Deuteronomy 33
A Final Blessing

Before Moses' death, however, he has a final word. Because of its poetic character and its position immediately after the Song of Moses (Deut. 32), it is often linked with that chapter. And indeed proximity does call attention to the two poems as the last of Moses' words to the people. There is an important distinction between the two chapters, however, reflected implicitly in the separation of chapter 33 from 32 by the new heading at verse 1. The previous chapter, while delivered by

Moses, is explicitly identified, like nearly all of Moses' instruction (cf. 4:5; 6:1; 29:1), as words that the Lord has instructed Moses to give to the people. Chapter 33, however, is Moses' own final word to the people; it is a word of blessing, one that is reminiscent of the blessing of Jacob upon his sons just before his death (Gen. 49). It is, therefore, a kind of last will and testament, Moses' final provision for the people as they go into the land and the future without him.

The blessings per se are framed by an introduction and conclusion through which this final Mosaic word is placed, like the rest of the book, on the boundary. In the introduction, the past theophany and direction of the Lord are recalled as well as the giving of the law. The whole experience of the people and the story that Deuteronomy recounts are recapitulated in verses 2–5. The deliverance of the people and the provision of a structure and polity for their life under God are succinctly remembered and celebrated.

The recollection of God's deliverance is couched in the imagery of the divine warrior who comes at the head of the armies of heaven, the heavenly host, and the armies of earth, the Israelite militia (on this imagery and its relation to the purpose and power of God, see the commentary on Deut. 32:34–43). The ancient tradition of the Lord's dwelling in the south and marching in battle from that region, sometimes identified specifically as Sinai and sometimes Seir, is articulated here (see Judg. 5:4–5; Ps. 68:7–8; cf. Hab. 3:3–4). The giving of the law to the people as a guide for their life in the land is then specifically recalled.

Verse 5 is ambiguous. Its first line simply says, "There was a king in Jeshurun," Jeshurun being another name for Israel, or "He became king in Jeshurun." The latter meaning is usually understood to be a reference to the kingship of the Lord over Israel, which is seen to be claimed and validated by the Lord's defeat of Israel's enemies and bringing them into the land. The acknowledgment of the Lord's rule over Israel is typical of other early Hebrew poems: for example, Exodus 15:18; Numbers 23:21; and Psalms 29:10; 68:24. The picture of divine victory over enemies that serves to establish the right of rule is familiar from both ancient Near Eastern texts and the Bible.

It is also possible, however, that the reference is to the rise of kingship in Israel, "which suggests, if the verse itself is not secondary, that the framework was added in the monarchic period, or that the poem as a whole reflects the transition period from tribal confederacy to monarchy, i.e., the time of Saul" (Freedman, p. 69).

The anachronistic reference to kingship in Israel, if that is what we have in Moses' blessing, serves to place the future well-being of the tribes in the context of three realities: the divine deliverance and protection, the provision of a manual of direction and instruction for their life together, and the institution of a structure of government centered in kingship. The recapitulation of the past, therefore, offers a fundamental clue about the context in which blessing is possible under God's provision. It is dependent on the power of God to protect a people who have not and cannot make it simply by their own power (see Deut. 8:17–18). Adherence to the directions provided in all the commandments, statutes, and ordinances makes it possible to create and maintain community under the rule of God. Family structures joined together under the leadership of one who rules in the name of the Lord and according to the Lord's instruction (see the law of the king in Deut. 17:14–20) give a shape for administering the life of a people in which the parts are not dissolved in the whole and the whole is not shattered by the parts. The record will show that this threefold context was difficult to maintain in Israel's history, but it was never relinquished as the assumed context in which the Lord's provision for life could become actualized.

The poem then anticipates (or, more accurately, reflects) the life of the tribes in the land as it goes on to describe the blessing that Moses places upon each of them. The poem is enigmatic and difficult to translate, but the themes that predominate within the series of blessings are clear. They are God's provision of material abundance for the well-being and prosperity of the tribes and God's protection of them in the face of their enemies. The former note is sounded in the extravagant picture of the bounteous fruits and crops that the tribe of Joseph will enjoy in the hill country (vv. 13–17), the affluence of the seas (which may have to do with maritime activity or caravan trades) that will come to Zebulun and Issachar (vv. 18–19), and the abundant oil that will be available to Asher (v. 24). The power of the tribes to withstand their enemies under the protection of the Lord is signaled several times in these blessings: the Lord's help and strength provided to Judah (v. 7), the smiting of the enemies of Levi (v. 11—though this may have been originally a part of the blessing of Judah), and Joseph's power like a bull to go against other peoples (v. 17). So throughout the individual blessings Moses invokes the providence of God as the context for the life of the tribes. That providence is especially manifest in the daily, ongoing provision of the means for life and in the sheltering protection from harm. The blessing of Moses makes concrete and specific what is prayed for regularly in the Aaronic benediction (Num. 6:22–27). The care of God that provides for life and protects life is embodied in the particularities of these blessings.

Special note should be made of the blessing of Levi, for it sets forth a kind of charter for the Levites as the teachers and priests of Israel. Their faithfulness to the Lord's covenant (see Exod. 32:25–29) shall have as its blessed outcome their capacity and right to instruct the people in the way of the Lord and to represent the people before the Lord in the offering of sacrifices. Precisely here one finds the roots of the creation of a continuing group of persons in the midst of God's people who shall be responsible for their instruction, for the communication of the Lord's word, and for standing before the Lord in behalf of the people to seek God's favor and forgiveness and continuing care. The blessing upon the Levites here is essentially consistent with the significant role they play elsewhere in Deuteronomy (e.g., 18:1–8; 27:9–26; 31:24–25). Not to be missed is the fact that the right and responsibility of priesthood is granted to those who have been faithful to the covenant demands when others have abandoned them. In Exodus 32:25–29 and Numbers 25, the Levites are assigned their role because of their passionate zeal for the Lord and their adherence to the basic commandment to love only the Lord. The manifestation of their zeal in these incidents takes place in actions that seem to us extreme, but we must not miss the force of the stories in their clear indication that those who are ordained to the Lord's service and have the right to instruct the people and represent them are those who have refused to waffle on the basic requirement of the covenant, the full devotion of one's whole being to the Lord and the refusal to be tempted to spread that devotion around among other attractive offers.

The Mosaic blessing concludes in verses 26–29 as it began, in praise and celebration of the Lord and the Lord's protecting power over Israel. While this section is a part of the bracketing framework around the particular blessings, one reads the blessings into the apostrophic conclusion. That is, the picture of divine blessing, prosperity, and protection against enemies that is the future prospect of the tribes is so clearly a manifestation of the powerful and benevolent work of the Lord that its conclusion evokes a burst of exultant praise and confession; there is none like this God, the one who so cares for and provides for these tribes. The imagery of the divine warrior provides an important theological vehicle in chapter 32 and continues at the beginning of this poem. It appears again here at the end to speak once more of the power of this God to protect the people, overcome the real threat of enemies, and give them security and well-being in the land. At the boundary, the Mosaic blessing takes seriously the dangers that lie ahead, the genuine threats to survival, and the uncertainty of the unknown. But the assurance it offers in the face of those risks is set entirely in the hands of the everlasting God, whose might against the enemy and protecting care of the people are not contradictions but two facets of a single reality. Deuteronomy has from beginning to end faced the question of how the people shall live when they cross over the boundary. Frequently and consistently, it has argued that God's people live by the Lord's blessing and according to the Lord's ways. This is assuredly where and how life is possible. Here at the end, Moses repeats the argument once more. The large theme of the poem, in its framework (vv. 2–5 and 26–29) and in the particular blessings, is the providential care and help of the Lord. In both framework and blessings, however, the torah of the Lord as the guide for the people's life is once more and finally set before them. It is their inheritance from Moses as he goes from their midst (v. 4), and its continued effect in their corporate and individual life is secured and emphasized in the blessing of Levi. Under the blessing and protection of the Lord and with the torah in their midst, they are ready to cross over into a new land.

Deuteronomy 32:48–52; 34:1–12
Farewell to Moses

The Book of Deuteronomy, the Torah—Genesis through Deuteronomy—and the era of Israel's foundations all come to an end with the death of Moses. He has led them out of Egyptian slavery and has guided them through the wilderness and the various difficulties and vicissitudes of their life together in those difficult circumstances. He has taught them all the instruction or law that the Lord gives them as the means of life. He has interceded for them when they did not keep the commandments; he has reprimanded them when they complained to him and to the Lord about their condition. He is truly the servant of the Lord, as he is designated here (34:5). There is nothing more for him to do except to lead the people into the land. But that is the one thing not given to Moses to do.

When we are told at the beginning of the book the extraordinary fact that Moses will not be allowed to go into the land to which he has led the people, we are given a clue to the reason in the Lord's words to Moses (1:37; 3:23–29). He will not be permitted to enter the promised land because the Lord was angry with Moses on account of the people (see commentary on 3:12–29). We are also given a human glimpse into Moses' own feelings as he pleads with the Lord to see the beautiful land that the Lord is giving (3:23–25). He even seeks to motivate God by appealing to the Lord's power and greatness. But a second time the book records the divine no to Moses. Then a third time Moses is kept from going in, this time near the end of the book at the conclusion of the Song of Moses (32:48–52). On this occasion, the text gives a quite different reason for the denial of Moses, his presumption or unfaithfulness at Meribat-kadesh (see Num. 20:10–13—the precise character of Moses' unfaithfulness in that event is not clear from the text). A serious tension thus arises between the reason given here and the earlier accounts of Moses' denial in chapters 1 and 3. Finally, in chapter 34, as he is about to die, Moses is told that he may not go in, but this time no reason is given. The fact is simply stated. Furthermore, in chapter 31, Moses' death is alluded to several more times (vv. 2, 14, 16, and 27–29), and in the first instance there is an allusion to his denial, which, like chapter 34, is not given a reason.

The tension or conflict that seems to exist between these accounts as to whether Moses' denial was because of his sin or that of the people may be resolved by recognizing that Deuteronomy 32:48–52 stems from another source than the Deuteronomic school. Indeed, most literary analysis has viewed these verses as being the work of the Priestly circle, an interpretation that may be correct. The reason for Moses' denial given there

242

is similar to the earlier Priestly reports in Numbers 20:10–13 and 27:12–14. If such an analysis is correct, it accounts for the conflict in the growth of the tradition and the text.

What it does not account for, however, is the *effect* of that activity, which is the same as it would be if all these reports of the denial of Moses came from the same source. Seven or eight times in the book, allusion is made to Moses' impending death, and then at the end it is finally reported. In every case (if one sees the reference in 31:2 as covering the other allusions in this chapter) explicit reference is made to the fact that he is not being allowed to enter the land, with conflicting reasons being given (1:37 and 2:26 versus 32:51). What is clear, therefore, is the strong interest in Moses' death. Furthermore, like many deaths, it raises the question of why, a question that is seen to have to do both with the person and with God. Moses' death outside the land is inexplicable. If anybody went into the land, it should have been Moses. Whether or not Moses is viewed as a tragic figure, certainly the tradition seems to see in his death an unfulfillment of the highest order, in that a life is cut short of the goal toward which it has always been directed. Such failure is often what seems to make death a tragic part of human existence.

At one level, the tradition seems not to leave Moses' death without meaning. That is, reasons are given to explain the otherwise inexplicable and terribly unjust fact that Moses does not receive the land, is even allowed to set foot in it. These reasons are not unlike other reasons given in Scripture to account for suffering. It is characteristic of the Deuteronomic perspective to account for what happens to individuals and the community by their actions in life. So here Moses' death is rooted in God's judgment. Even that, however, is not a simple resolution, for the tradition sets forth in this one book conflicting understandings of whose sin precipitated God's judgment on Moses, his or the people's.

All these facts—the frequent references to his death coupled with the equally numerous indications of his denied access to the land, the obvious lack of fairness in Moses' being deprived of that opportunity toward which his whole life had been set by God, and the varying and indeed conflicting reasons put forth to give justice to the reality—seem to suggest an inability finally to account adequately for what has happened, an inability indicated at the end in a literary fashion when the text no longer

243

seeks to explain but simply reports the fact and sees it as a part of the (mysterious) will of God, a mystery accentuated by the laconic note that "he" (Yahweh? someone?) buried him and the burial place of Israel's greatest leader is no longer known. So the Book of Deuteronomy, which seems to reflect that perspective against which the Book of Job struggles—the rational justification of apparently undeserved suffering—in the end subtly but clearly joins Job in undercutting that effort and confronts us with a familiar human truth about tragedy and suffering. Possible and sometimes meaningful reasons may be given, but they are not finally adequate. Even the efforts of the best theological enterprises (e.g., Deuteronomy) are not finally sufficient to explain the tragedies of human existence. Deuteronomy thus ends on a subversive note, but at least it is one that may make more sense to us than all the sensible explanations.

The emphasis on Moses' death in this book is, of course, not simply because of its seemingly unfair timing by God but also because the death of Israel's first great leader marks a major turning point. Indeed, along with the explicit and not totally satisfying reasons given, there is an implicit reason for his death outside the land. Moses' work is truly done. The people have the word of the Lord that Moses taught, which will be their guide in the land God has promised. Israel is to live from now on by the torah that Moses has taught and thus truly does not need Moses. The "closing" of the Torah is coincidental with the death of Moses in a real sense. He now moves off the scene, and Israel henceforth will not be led by a great authority figure but by the living word of the torah that Moses taught and that goes always with the people in the ark (10:1–5), God's word in the midst of the people. Note is made here at the end that Joshua takes over as leader and does so with the spirit of wisdom that came with the laying on of Moses' hands in his commissioning. He is now the leader. But he is not Moses. Moses is the "servant of God"; Joshua is Moses' minister (Josh. 1:1) and is not called "servant of God," although Moses will be so designated throughout the Book of Joshua. At the commissioning of Joshua it is made clear (and indeed emphatically so in the Hebrew text) that it is the *Lord* who goes over before Israel and will be with Israel (31:3, 7–8). Joshua will be the human leader of the people in battle and will allot the land, but he is not the authority figure who spoke face to face with God and received the teaching of the Lord for the people. (He does, of course, speak with God in the Book of

244

Joshua, but this is not emphasized in the same way as is the case with Moses.) If such a figure moved onto the scene, then the whole weight and purpose of the instruction Moses gave, as charged by the Lord, would be undermined (on verses 10–12 see the commentary on 18:9–22).

So the first stage of Israel's story as the people of the Lord comes to an end. They have been delivered from slavery, led and directed by the Lord to the boundary of the promised land. Deuteronomy concludes the Torah, or Pentateuch, by leaving Israel poised before the promise, the land. Torah is complete now. The promise is real and there, but it is not guaranteed by the Torah. Indeed, the primary generation that experienced this story will not receive the land. Theologically, it is not unimportant that Torah is complete without land. Torah opens up the promises of God, explains the intention of God, lays out the way for God's people, says what is necessary to realize the promise and the land, even looks *beyond* land and disobedience to the future and speaks about the continuing possibility of the promise and land. But Torah does not guarantee land and security and blessing. It offers it and describes the way to it.

That is the theological significance of the break after Deuteronomy, the theological meaning of the Pentateuch. Joshua and the books that follow will tell what happened with this people who have Torah: that is, promise and instruction. It is a complex, mixed, continuing story, the character of which is already anticipated by Deuteronomy and other voices in the Pentateuch.

Deuteronomy, however, not only stands at the end of an era. It opens up the next one, for by its canons, the instruction God gave to Moses, the people are to live and will be judged. That story is still going on.

BIBLIOGRAPHY

For further study

ACHTEMEIER, ELIZABETH. *Deuteronomy, Jeremiah.* PROC-LAMATION COMMENTARIES (Philadelphia: Fortress Press, 1978).

CLEMENTS, RONALD. *God's Chosen People: A Theological Interpretation of the Book of Deuteronomy* (London: SCM Press, 1968).

CRAIGIE, PETER. *The Book of Deuteronomy.* THE NEW INTERNATIONAL COMMENTARY ON THE OLD TESTAMENT (Grand Rapids: Wm. B. Eerdmans Publishing Co., 1976).

DRIVER, S. R. *Deuteronomy.* INTERNATIONAL CRITICAL COMMENTARY (Edinburgh: T. & T. Clark, 1902).

HARRELSON, WALTER. *The Ten Commandments and Human Rights.* OVERTURES TO BIBLICAL THEOLOGY (Philadelphia: Fortress Press, 1980).

LOHFINK, NORBERT. *Great Themes from the Old Testament* (Edinburgh: T. & T. Clark, 1982).

McBRIDE, S. DEAN. "Polity of the Covenant People: The Book of Deuteronomy," *Interpretation: A Journal of Bible and Theology* 41:229–244 (1987).

McCONVILLE, J. G. *Law and Theology in Deuteronomy.* JOURNAL FOR THE STUDY OF THE OLD TESTAMENT SUPPLEMENT SERIES (Sheffield: JSOT Press, 1984).

MAYES, A. D. H. *Deuteronomy.* THE NEW CENTURY BIBLE (Grand Rapids: Wm. B. Eerdmans Publishing Co., 1981).

NICHOLSON, E. W. *Deuteronomy and Tradition: Literary and Historical Problems in the Book of Deuteronomy* (Philadelphia: Fortress Press, 1967).

POLZIN, ROBERT. *Moses and the Deuteronomist: A Literary Study of the Deuteronomistic History* (New York: Seabury Press, 1980).

RAD, GERHARD VON. *Deuteronomy.* THE OLD TESTAMENT LIBRARY (Philadelphia: Westminster Press, 1966).

STAMM, J. S., and M. E. ANDREWS. *The Ten Commandments in Recent Research* (London: SCM Press, 1967).

WEINFELD, MOSHE. *Deuteronomy and the Deuteronomic School* (Oxford: Clarendon Press, 1972).

WILLIAMS, JAY. *Ten Words of Freedom: An Introduction to the Faith of Israel* (Philadelphia: Fortress Press, 1971).

Literature cited

ACHTEMEIER, ELIZABETH. *Deuteronomy, Jeremiah.* PROCLAMATION COMMENTARIES (Philadelphia: Fortress Press, 1978).

ACHTEMEIER, PAUL. *Romans.* INTERPRETATION: A BIBLE COMMENTARY FOR TEACHING AND PREACHING (Atlanta: John Knox Press, 1985).

BALTZER, KLAUS. *The Covenant Formulary* (Philadelphia: Fortress Press, 1971).

BARTH, KARL. *Church Dogmatics* (Edinburgh: T. & T. Clark, 1936–1977).

BELLEFONTAINE, ELIZABETH. "The Curses of Deuteronomy 27: Their Relationship to the Prohibitives," in J. Flanagan and J. M. Robinson, eds., *No Famine in the Land* (Missoula, Mont.: Scholars Press, 1975), pp. 49–61.

BIRD, PHYLLIS. "The Place of Women in the Israelite Cultus," in Patrick D. Miller, Jr., Paul D. Hanson, and S. Dean McBride, eds., *Ancient Israelite Religion: Essays in Honor of Frank Moore Cross* (Philadelphia: Fortress Press, 1987), pp. 397–419.

BOK, SISSELA. *Lying: Moral Choice in Public and Private Life* (New York: Pantheon Books, 1978).

BRAULIK, GEORG. "Law as Gospel: Justification and Pardon According to the Deuteronomic Torah," *Interpretation: A Journal of Bible and Theology* 38:5–14 (1984).

―――. "Weisheit, Gottesnähe, and Gesetz—Zum Kerygma von Deuteronomium 4, 5–8," in Georg Braulik, ed., *Studien zum Pentateuch: Walter Kornfeld zum 60. Geburtstag* (Wien: Herder & Herder, 1977), pp. 165–195.

BREKELMANS, C. H. W. *De Herem in het Oude Testament* (Nijmegen: Centrale Drukkerij, 1959).

CALVIN, JOHN. *Commentaries on the Four Last Books of Moses, arranged in the Form of a Harmony,* 5 vols. (Edinburgh: Calvin Translation Society, 1852).

―――. *The Sermons of John Calvin Upon the Fifth Book of Moses Called Deuteronomy* (London: Henry Middleton, 1583).

CHILDS, BREVARD S. *The Book of Exodus.* THE OLD TESTA-
MENT LIBRARY (Philadelphia: Westminster Press, 1974).

CRAIGIE, PETER. *The Book of Deuteronomy.* THE NEW IN-
TERNATIONAL COMMENTARY ON THE OLD TESTAMENT
(Grand Rapids: Wm. B. Eerdmans Publishing Co., 1976).

CROSS, FRANK MOORE. "Epigraphic Notes on Hebrew Doc-
uments of the Eighth–Sixth Centuries B.C.: 2. The *Murab-
ba'ât* Papyrus and the Letter Found Near Yabneh-yam,"
Bulletin of the American Schools of American Research
165:34–46 (1962).

ELLUL, JACQUES. *The Theological Foundation of Law* (Garden City, N.Y.: Doubleday & Co., 1960).

FISCH, HAROLD. *Poetry with a Purpose: Biblical Poetics and
Interpretation.* INDIANA STUDIES IN BIBLICAL LITERA-
TURE (Bloomington, Ind.: Indiana University Press, 1988).

FITZMYER, JOSEPH. *The Gospel According to Luke X–XXIV.*
THE ANCHOR BIBLE (Garden City, N.Y.: Doubleday & Co.,
1985).

FREEDMAN, DAVID N. "Divine Names and Titles in Early
Hebrew Poetry," in Frank Moore Cross, Werner E. Lemke,
and Patrick D. Miller, Jr., eds., *Magnalia Dei: The Mighty
Acts of God. Essays on the Bible and Archaeology in Mem-
ory of G. Ernest Wright* (Garden City, N.Y.: Doubleday &
Co., 1976), pp. 55–107.

GERHARDSSON, BIRGER. *The Testing of God's Son: An
Analysis of an Early Christian Midrash* (Lund: Gleerup,
1966).

HARRELSON, WALTER. *The Ten Commandments and
Human Rights.* OVERTURES TO BIBLICAL THEOLOGY (Philadelphia: Fortress Press, 1980).

HESCHEL, ABRAHAM J. *The Sabbath: Its Meaning for Modern Man* (New York: Farrar, Straus & Young, 1951).

HILLERS, DELBERT. *Treaty Curses and the Old Testament
Prophets.* BIBLICA ET ORIENTALIA (Rome: Pontifical Biblical Institute, 1964).

JANZEN, J. G. "On the Most Important Word in the Shema,"
Vetus Testamentum 37:280–300 (1987).

––––––. "Yahweh Our God, Yahweh Is One," *Encounter* 48:
53–60 (1987).

KAUFMAN, STEPHEN. "The Structure of the Deuteronomic
Law," *MAARAV* 1:105–158 (1979).

LEHMAN, PAUL. *Ethics in a Christian Context* (New York: Harper & Row, 1963).

LEITH, JOHN H. "John Calvin's Polemic Against Idolatry," *Soli Deo Gloria: New Testament Studies in Honor of William Childs Robinson* (Richmond: John Knox Press, 1968), pp. 111–124.

LEVENSON, JON. "Is There a Counterpart in the Hebrew Bible to New Testament Antisemitism?" *Journal of Ecumenical Studies* 22:242–260 (1985).

———. "Who Inserted the Book of the Torah?" *Harvard Theological Review* 68:203–233 (1975).

LEWIS, ANTHONY. *Gideon's Trumpet* (New York: Random House, 1964).

LITTLE, DAVID. "Exodus 20:15—'Thou shalt not steal,' " *Interpretation: A Journal of Bible and Theology* 34:399–405 (1980).

LOHFINK, NORBERT. "The Deuteronomist and the Idea of Separation of Powers," paper read at the Los Angeles International Congress of Learned Societies in the Field of Religion (1972).

———. *Great Themes from the Old Testament* (Edinburgh: T. & T. Clark, 1982).

———. *Das Hauptgebot: Eine Untersuchung literarischer Einleitungsfragen zu Dtn 5–11.* ANALECTA BIBLICA (Rome: Pontifical Biblical Institute, 1963).

———. *Höre, Israel: Auslegung von Texten aus dem Buch Deuteronomium* (Düsseldorf: Patmos Verlag, 1965).

LONG, BURKE. "Two Question and Answer Schemata in the Prophets," *Journal of Biblical Literature* 90:129–139 (1971).

LUTHER, MARTIN. *Lectures on Deuteronomy.* LUTHER'S WORKS (St. Louis: Concordia Publishing House, 1960).

McBRIDE, S. DEAN. "Deuteronomium," *Theologische Realenzyklopädie 8* (Berlin: Walter de Gruyter, n.d.), pp. 530–543).

———. "Polity of the Covenant People: The Book of Deuteronomy," *Interpretation: A Journal of Bible and Theology* 41: 229–244 (1987).

———. "The Yoke of the Kingdom: An Exposition of Deuteronomy 6:4–5," *Interpretation: A Journal of Bible and Theology* 27:273–306 (1973).

McCARTHY, DENNIS J. "An Installation Genre," *Journal of Biblical Literature* 90:31–41 (1971).

———. *Treaty and Covenant*, 2nd ed. ANALECTA BIBLICA (Rome: Pontifical Biblical Institute, 1978).

McCONVILLE, J. G. *Law and Theology in Deuteronomy.* JOURNAL FOR THE STUDY OF THE OLD TESTAMENT SUPPLEMENT SERIES (Sheffield: JSOT Press, 1984).

MAYES, A. D. H. *Deuteronomy.* THE NEW CENTURY BIBLE (Grand Rapids: Wm. B. Eerdmans Publishing Co., 1981).

MERENDINO, R. P. *Das deuteronomische Gesetz: Eine literarkritische, gattungs- und überlieferungsgeschichtliche Untersuchung zu Deuteronomium 12–26.* BONNER BIBLISCHE BEITRÄGE (Bonn: P. Hanstein, 1969).

MILGROM, JACOB. "The Biblical Diet Laws as an Ethical System: Food and Faith," *Interpretation: A Journal of Bible and Theology* 17:288–301 (1963).

MILLER, PATRICK D. "Apotropaic Imagery in Proverbs 6:30–32," *Journal of Near Eastern Studies* 29:129–130 (1970).

———. "Faith and Ideology in the Old Testament," in Frank Moore Cross, Werner E. Lemke, and Patrick D. Miller, Jr., eds., *Magnalia Dei: The Mighty Acts of God. Essays on the Bible and Archaeology in Memory of G. Ernest Wright* (Garden City, N.Y.: Doubleday & Co., 1976), pp. 464–479).

———. "Fire in the Mythology of Canaan and Israel," *Catholic Biblical Quarterly* 27:256–261 (1965).

———. "The Gift of God: The Deuteronomic Theology of the Land," *Interpretation* 23:451–465 (1969).

———. "The Human Sabbath: A Study in Deuteronomic Theology," *Princeton Theological Seminary Bulletin* 6:81–97 (1985).

———. "Luke 4:16–21," *Interpretation* 29:417–421 (1975).

———. "Moses, My Servant: A Deuteronomic Portrait of Moses," *Interpretation* 41: 245–255 (1987).

———. "The Most Important Word: The Yoke of the Kingdom," *Iliff Review* 41:17–30 (1984).

———. "The Place of the Decalogue in the Old Testament and Its Law," *Interpretation* 43:229–242 (1989).

———. *Sin and Judgment in the Prophets.* SOCIETY OF BIBLICAL LITERATURE MONOGRAPH SERIES (Chico, Calif.: Scholars Press, 1982).

———. "The Sovereignty of God," *The Hermeneutical Quest:*

Essays in Honor of James Luther Mays on His Sixty-fifth Birthday (Pittsburgh: Pickwick Publications, 1987), pp. 129–144.

———. "Syntax and Theology in Genesis 12:3a," *Vetus Testamentum* 34:472–476 (1984).

———. "The Way of Torah," *Princeton Theological Seminary Bulletin* 8:17–27 (1987).

——— and J. J. M. Roberts. *The Hand of the Lord: A Reassessment of the "Ark Narrative" of I Samuel* (Baltimore: Johns Hopkins University Press, 1977).

"The Nature and Value of Human Life" (Atlanta: Stated Clerk, General Assembly of the Presbyterian Church in the United States, 1981).

NICHOLSON, E. W. *Deuteronomy and Tradition: Literary and Historical Problems in the Book of Deuteronomy* (Philadelphia: Fortress Press, 1967).

NOTH, MARTIN. *The Deuteronomistic History.* JOURNAL FOR THE STUDY OF THE OLD TESTAMENT SUPPLEMENT SERIES (Sheffield: JSOT Press, 1981).

PHILLIPS, ANTHONY. *Ancient Israel's Criminal Law: A New Approach to the Decalogue* (Oxford: Basil Blackwell, 1970).

PRITCHARD, JAMES B., ed. *Ancient Near Eastern Texts Relating to the Old Testament* (Princeton, N.J.: Princeton University Press, 1969).

RAD, GERHARD VON. *Deuteronomy.* THE OLD TESTAMENT LIBRARY (Philadelphia: Westminster Press, 1966).

———. "The Form-Critical Problem of the Hexateuch," in *The Problem of the Hexateuch and Other Essays* (New York: McGraw-Hill Book Co., 1966), pp. 1–78.

———. *Old Testament Theology* (New York: Harper & Row, 1962).

———. *Studies in Deuteronomy.* STUDIES IN BIBLICAL THEOLOGY (Chicago: Henry Regnery Co., 1953).

———. "There Remains Still a Rest for the People of God: An Investigation of a Biblical Concept," in *The Problem of the Hexateuch and Other Essays* (New York: McGraw-Hill Book Co., 1966), pp. 94–102.

ROBINSON, ROBERT. *Roman Catholic Exegesis Since Divino Afflante Spiritu: Hermeneutical Implications.* SOCIETY OF BIBLICAL LITERATURE DISSERTATION SERIES (Atlanta: Scholars Press, 1988).

SWEZEY, CHARLES M. "Exodus 20:16—'Thou shalt not bear

false witness against thy neighbor,' " *Interpretation: A Journal of Bible and Theology* 34:405–410 (1980).

WEINFELD, MOSHE. *Deuteronomy and the Deuteronomic School* (Oxford: Clarendon Press, 1972).

WELLHAUSEN, JULIUS. *Prolegomena to the History of Ancient Israel* (New York: Meridian Books, 1957).

WENHAM, G. J. "The Restoration of Marriage Reconsidered," *Journal of Jewish Studies* 30:36–40 (1979).

WESTERMANN, CLAUS. *Isaiah 40–66.* THE OLD TESTAMENT LIBRARY (Philadelphia: Westminster Press, 1969).

WIESELTIER, LEON. "Leviticus," in David Rosenberg, ed., *Congregation* (New York: Harcourt Brace Jovanovich, 1987), pp. 27–38.

WINN, ALBERT C. "Whatever Happened to the Fourth Commandment?" Unpublished sermon preached at Second Presbyterian Church, Richmond, Va., September 5, 1976.

WOLFF, HANS WALTER. "The Kerygma of the Yahwist," in Walter Brueggemann and Hans Walter Wolff, *The Vitality of Old Testament Traditions* (Richmond: John Knox Press, 1975), pp. 41–66.

WRIGHT, G. ERNEST. "The Lawsuit of God: A Form-Critical Study of Deuteronomy 32," in Bernhard W. Anderson and Walter Harrelson, eds., *Israel's Prophetic Heritage: Essays in Honor of James Muilenburg* (New York: Harper & Brothers, 1962).

YODER, JOHN H. "Exodus 20:13—'Thou shalt not kill,' " *Interpretation: A Journal of Bible and Theology* 34:394–399 (1980).

CPSIA information can be obtained at www.ICGtesting.com
Printed in the USA
BVOW011156290712

296469BV00005B/35/P

9 780664 238605